Reading Graphic Design History

Reading Graphic Design History

Image, Text, and Context

David Raizman

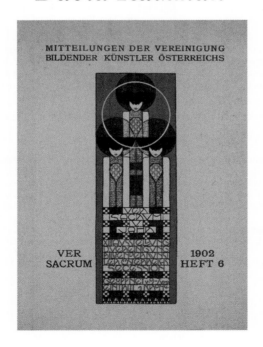

BLOOMSBURY VISUAL ARTS
LONDON • NEW YORK • OXFORD • NEW DELHI • SYDNEY

BLOOMSBURY VISUAL ARTS
Bloomsbury Publishing Plc
50 Bedford Square, London, WC1B 3DP, UK
1385 Broadway, New York, NY 10018, USA

BLOOMSBURY, BLOOMSBURY VISUAL ARTS and the Diana logo are trademarks of
Bloomsbury Publishing Plc

First published in Great Britain 2021

Cover design by Louise Dugdale
Cover image: Moser, Koloman (1868–1918) Poster for the 13th exhibition of
the Viennese Secession. Vienna, 1902. Printed by Albert Berger © 2020.
Photo Austrian Archives / Scala Florence.

A catalogue record for this book is available from the British Library.

Library of Congress Cataloging-in-Publication Data
Names: Raizman, David Seth, author.
Title: Reading graphic design history : image, text and context / David Raizman.
Description: London ; New York : Bloomsbury Visual Arts, 2020. |
Series: Cultural histories of design | Includes bibliographical references and index.
Identifiers: LCCN 2020011223 (print) | LCCN 2020011224 (ebook) |
ISBN 9781474299411 (pb) | ISBN 9781474299398 (hb) | ISBN 9781474299381 (epub) |
ISBN 9781474299374 (epdf)
Subjects: LCSH: Graphic arts–Social aspects. | Graphic arts–Political aspects. | Graphic arts–History.
Classification: LCC NC998 .R35 2020 (print) | LCC NC998 (ebook) | DDC 741.609–dc23
LC record available at https://lccn.loc.gov/2020011223
LC ebook record available at https://lccn.loc.gov/2020011224

ISBN: HB: 978-1-4742-9939-8
        PB: 978-1-4742-9941-1
        ePDF: 978-1-4742-9937-4
        eBook: 978-1-4742-9938-1

Typeset by Integra Software Services Pvt. Ltd.
Printed and bound in India

To find out more about our authors and books visit www.bloomsbury.com
and sign up for our newsletters.

CONTENTS

ILLUSTRATIONS

Figures

Color Plates

1.1 Josef Müller-Brockmann, © ARS, NY. Poster, schützt das Kind! [Protect the Child!], 1953. Offset lithograph on wove paper, lined, 1275 × 905 mm (50 3/16 × 35 5/8 in.) Museum purchase from General Acquisitions Endowment Fund. 1999-46- Photo Credit: Cooper Hewitt, Smithsonian Design Museum/Art Resource, NY. Photo: Matt Flynn © Smithsonian Institution, Cooper Hewitt, Smithsonian Design Museum, New York, NY, USA Artists Rights Society

1.7 Hans Thöni, "Vorsicht—Kinder!" (Watch out—Children!), poster, chromolithography, 1955, 128 × 90.5 cm, Plakatsammlung SfG Basel

1.11 Herbert Matter, © Copyright. Poster: Engelberg, Trübsee/Switzerland. Switzerland, 1936. Offset lithograph on white wove paper. 1019 × 637 mm (40 1/8 × 25 1/16 in.). Museum purchase from General Acquisitions Endowment Fund, 2006-15-1. Photo: Matt Flynn, Cooper Hewitt, Smithsonian Design Museum. Photo Credit: Cooper Hewitt, Smithsonian Design Museum/Art Resource, NY; Artists Rights Society

2.1 Ettore Sottsass, "Yellow Cabinet" (Mobile Giallo), Burled maple, briar, ebonized oak veneer, gilded wood knobs, 57 ½ × 51 7/8 × 18 1/8 in., 1988–9, Bridgeman, Artists Rights Society

2.3 Moser, Koloman (Kolo) (1868–1918). Ver Sacrum, XIII, Poster for the 13th Secession exhibition. 1902. Lithograph, 73 3/16 × 25 3/16 in. (185.9 × 64 cm). Printer: Lith. Anst. A. Berger, Wien. Gift of Joseph H. Heil, by exchange. The Museum of Modern Art. Digital Image © The Museum of Modern Art/Licensed by SCALA/Art Resource, NY

2.4 Koloman Moser, Fifth Secession Exhibition Poster, 98.4 × 66.7 cm, chromolithography, 1899, MAK–Österreichisches Museum für angewandte Kunst/Gegenwartskunst

FOREWORD

For those who believe that the history of graphic design does not make for page-turner reading, think again; in fact, read again—especially if you are a graphic designer or designer of any kind. You will, after reading David Raizman's anthology of historical essays, find critical commentaries on this essential popular art and craft as inspiring as they are edifying. I believe this book is both a pleasure and requisite for all design teachers and students.

Raizman's book is not the first or last "reader" on graphic design history or practice, but more is better for all concerned. For decades, Raizman has been laying the foundation(s) and building the structure(s) that continue to legitimize the heritage of all design. Through books and essays he has provided detailed overviews and in-depth analyses of the iconic objects from industrial, product, and communication design that individually and together define design's and designers' achievements since the mid-nineteenth century. In this volume he discusses makers and their outputs covering a wide range of material.

From classics to relics, this anthology covers the masterworks from Austrian Koloman Moser's landmark Austrian Secession poster to A. M. Cassandre's style-defining French Dubonnet poster. He takes on the social impact of design and advertising through his work on the 1960s' incomparable Levy's Jewish Rye ad campaign and at the opposite pole of the design spectrum he covers "Politics of Learning" about John Fell's types for Oxford University. Speaking of politics, Raizman addresses a subject unknown to many old and young designers, cartoonist Thomas Nast's visual critique of New York's nineteenth-century corrupt political machine: his design of the Tammany Tiger (Nast also made the first drawings of the Democratic Donkey, Republican Elephant, and the American version of Santa Claus).

Students routinely ask me, "Is it necessary to take a design history class?" My answer is simple: Yes. They rightly respond, "Please explain." Not all universities even offer design history, which they should since a general art history is not an umbrella for the design legacy. This is where books like Raizman's are essential. It is unacceptable *NOT* to have a knowledge of and indeed fluency in the history of the form in all its various disciplines—from advertising to publication design, from information (data-viz) to propaganda design. Just think what is lost without historical underpinning. Then think about how design works in the world (in fact, how the world works) and how this can be told without a historical perspective.

Is this a page turner? Well, it is more … it is an important companion to any design education.

Steven Heller

ACKNOWLEDGMENTS

Reading Graphic Design History: Image, Text, and Context took shape over many years of teaching, travel, and ongoing research. At the outset I was motivated by curiosity as I prepared for the classes I was teaching in design history from one year to the next and the questions the material was bringing to mind, followed by active archival research, reading, endless correspondence with scholars, curators, and librarians, the presentation of individual case studies at conferences, and finally to the writing and lengthy editing process.

I want to thank Rebecca Barden and assistant editors Claire Collins and Olivia Davies at Bloomsbury Publishing in London for their initial and ongoing interest in and encouragement of this project, and for their patience and cooperation through delays, changes to content, format, and extensions. I also want to acknowledge the copy-editing and production team at Bloomsbury for their assistance throughout the later stages of the project. Research could not have progressed without the assistance of Shannon Robinson, liaison librarian to the Westphal College of Media Arts & Design at Drexel University. Shannon was always willing to investigate various leads for information, was ready to share ideas for where to find both print and online information, and her helpfulness continued after I retired from the university in the fall of 2017 and my status shifted to emeritus. I suppose it also helps that Drexel University is but a block or two away from the vast resources at the University of Pennsylvania. There John Pollack at the Kislak Center for Special Collections in the Van Pelt Library permitted access to rare books and archival materials that figure in the chapters on John Fell and *Holiday* magazine.

The increasing amount of archival material that has come online in the past decade immeasurably aided my ability to complete this book. While I made an effort to see both featured and related work for each chapter in person, the availability of newspapers and trade journals online was of tremendous benefit to my research along with robust online resources offered by museums and collections. In that effort I should add my thanks to those libraries who participate in interlibrary loan, and to the librarians who facilitate requests, for that resource also proved to be an essential part of my research.

Room 300 at the New York Public Library on 5th Avenue was a preferred venue for work. Their extensive collection of relevant materials, the ease of requesting local and offsite books and journals, the peace and quiet of the room, and general helpfulness of their staff, all contributed to making my research both rewarding and enjoyable. I was also aided by timely responses and invitations to view materials at the New York Historical Society, The Cooper Hewitt National Design Museum, and the Museum of Modern Art, both on site and at their respective offsite locations. In particular I'd like to mention Caroline O'Connell (Cooper Hewitt), Mariam Touba (New York Historical Society), and Paul Galloway and Pamela Popeson (MoMA).

Over the course of preparing *Reading Graphic Design History*, I communicated with a number of scholars and graphic designers, sometimes for information, other times as a sounding board for ideas, and also as readers of early drafts to solicit reactions and comments on specific chapters. In addition to the anonymous readers of the *Reading Graphic Design History* manuscript I want to thank Karen Carter of Ferris University, Michigan, Gunnar Swanson of East Carolina University, both members of the network of friends who participated in the NEH Summer Institute I directed in the summer 2015 with Carma Gorman; Craig Eliason at St. Thomas University in St. Paul, Minnesota; Richard Holllis; Steven Heller; Jeremy Aynsley at the University of Brighton; Ethan Robey (Penn State University); Baird Jarman (Carleton College); Kerri Steinberg (Otis College of Art, Los Angeles); Michael Golec of the School of the Art Institute Chicago, George Lois, and my Drexel colleagues Linda Kim (art and art history), Mark Willie, and Eric Karnes, both faculty in the college's graphic design program.

The latter stages of *Reading Graphic Design History* coincided with my retirement from the university before the start of the 2017–18 academic year. I want to thank my department head LiLy Milroy and Dean Allen Sabinson for supporting a sabbatical leave for two-thirds of my final year of employment to conduct research. Retirement only intensified my interest in the material for *Reading Graphic Design History*, and proved anything but "retiring" once my teaching responsibilities ceased—it was more like an extended sabbatical without an end date. As research and writing for *Reading Graphic Design History* progressed, it became clear that a major emphasis of the project would be upon providing ample illustrations and comparisons from a wide variety of print and other media sources. External readers remarked that the illustration program contributed to the overall strength of the project, but also required a good deal of time in locating sources for images and rights. Procuring images and rights for more than 200 illustrations was a time-consuming task. Almost all image and permission providers were generous and timely in helping with this process, though one might wish the process was less complicated and expensive. The final stages of this process coincided with my service as interim executive director of the College Art Association in New York adding yet more complications to an already drawn-out process. I also want to thank my wife, Lucy Salem Raizman, for her patience and support, and for being such a willing companion to countless museum exhibitions and collections and a partner on trips that were falsely promised as "vacations."

The most substantial debt I owe is to the undergraduate graphic design students in the Westphal College, both in Philadelphia and during Study Abroad in London, who listened to the presentation of the book's material over many years. Their questions and insights kept my level of interest in the material for this book always at a high level, and encouraged my efforts, and it's my hope that future students in the program (and others!) will find the chapters both thought-provoking and useful.

Introduction

Introduction

Reading Graphic Design History comprises seven well-illustrated studies of examples of graphic design, in-depth examinations focusing upon a single work or closely related body of work associated with particular designers and art directors. It is intended for instructors of courses in graphic design history and their students, for whom such courses are often required or recommended whether in place of or in addition to the history of art in most graphic design curricula. While the subject of graphic design history has expanded considerably since the publication of Philip Meggs' *History of Graphic Design* survey in 1983, much of the published work in the field focuses upon national histories (e.g., "Swiss graphic Design," "Dutch Graphic Design,") styles (e.g., "psychedelic posters," "art nouveau posters," "World War I propaganda"), or monographs on the oeuvres and careers of individual designers, partnerships, and consultancies. By working outward from individual works, *Reading Graphic Design History* complements as well as challenges existing treatments or interpretations of each of its subjects.

Case Studies, Method, Teaching

The case study seems to me an appropriate point of entry and certainly navigates less charted territory in the field: not only would each chapter permit a detailed investigation of an individual work, but the studies also would afford the opportunity to explore a broader historical and cultural framework to consider the meaning of a poster, advertisement, journal, or newspaper. My objective has been to stimulate an appreciation of the complex, collaborative, and interdependent nature of the graphic design enterprise, not simply in terms of the division of labor involved in the preparation and execution of work and its reproduction, but also exploring the role of clients, publishers, editors, market researchers, and their audiences in the decision-making process that leads to the final work. They would attempt to describe the specific rather than general social dimensions of graphic design, whether in relation to the representation of race, gender, or class, and its political dimensions in representing the public interest. Case studies of graphic design that I've read over the years suggested to me the value of this approach, for instance, Ruth Iskin's study of Toulouse-Lautrec's 1892 chromolithographic book cover for *La Reine de Joie* (*Nineteenth-Century Art Worldwide*, 2009) Michael Golec's article on Lester Beall's 1937 REA posters (*JoDH*, 26, 4, 2013), essays in Aynsley & Forde's (eds.) *Design and the Modern Magazine* (2007), and Richard Ohmann's study of the later nineteenth-century Quaker Oats brand (*Modernity and Mass Culture*, Bloomington, 1991). I've assigned some of these articles and chapters to my students, along with shorter studies such as Philip Meggs' analyses of Piet Zwart's *NKF Catalog* or El Lissitzky's *For the Voice* (both found in *Graphic Design History*, eds. Steven Heller and Georgette Ballance, NY, Allworth, 2001), as examples of the benefits of the detailed analysis of specific works of graphic design.

At a basic level I found that paying attention to the size and format of my examples, along with the specific, "physical" context that mediated their meaning, whether a magazine ad, full page or quarter page, the side of a building or the wall of a subway station, deserved more careful attention than sometimes provided in surveys and monographs. These considerations were significant in the overall design process and conditioned in one way or another the design decisions that resulted in the finished work. I've tried to introduce this kind of "typology" of graphic design in each chapter, in part as a reminder for students to be aware of original format, size, scale, and the technologies of reproduction, whether wood-engraving, chromolithography, rotogravure, or color offset lithography.

Each chapter begins with or incorporates early on a detailed, thorough visual examination of the chosen work. I once had a professor in graduate school who would listen patiently to students' seminar presentations of a painting or illumination and then proceed to query them on elements in the image that he had observed but that they had neglected to mention in their reports. Students were generally looking for things that pertained to or reinforced the thesis they wanted to develop rather than remembering to leave no stone unturned, and were reminded, at their peril, of what they'd omitted. And so I've tried to learn from witnessing those uncomfortable experiences, along with considering each work's place in the historiography of graphic design history, thinking about the audience for whom a work was intended, and its broader cultural context, that is, the values and beliefs it communicates through its form and content, and that touches, directly or indirectly, upon broader issues of politics, gender, race, and social relations.

The study of individual examples of graphic design inevitably led to questions and details that helped to dictate my working method; for example, Thomas Nast's use of the Roman amphitheater as the setting for "THE TAMMANY TIGER LOOSE" for *Harpers Weekly* (chapter 6), the "disconnect" between Josef Müller-Brockmann's alarmist "schutzt das kind!" poster and the general restraint associated with post-World War II Swiss graphic design (chapter 1), the iconography of the three women who appear in Koloman Moser's poster for the Thirteenth Vienna Secession Exhibition in 1902 (chapter 2), or associations that have been made in survey texts linking the "New Advertising" with the 1960s counterculture in chapter 5 on the Levy's "You don't have to be Jewish" rye bread campaign.

After teaching the history of graphic design for several years and occasionally being asked for advice by students as they prepared for their various graphic design projects and assignments, I began to be invited by my graphic design colleagues to attend undergraduate senior thesis presentations to observe and to offer comments along with the graphic design studio faculty. I also participated in faculty deliberations following each day's presentations and enjoyed listening to my colleagues as they shared their reactions to each student's project. When students choose their topic with their advisors, they are expected to do "research" on their subject, whether a restaurant or other company identity, a product launch, an illustrated book, an information graphic project, a propaganda or marketing campaign, or a web application. Student research often consists of acquiring background information (which sometimes involves history, for instance, a traveler's guide to a city) and then using that information to create an effective and original solution to a complex graphic design problem. The essays in *Reading Graphic Design History* offer extended examples of this approach to research, carefully examining all aspects of a particular work, using comparison and contrast as a tool of analysis and comprehension, and exploring the physical and cultural context in which a work was designed, produced, and experienced. One example is the comparison between Koloman Moser's Thirteenth Vienna Secession Exhibition poster from 1902 (chapter 2) and book-size versions of the poster as exhibition announcements that were reproduced in the Secession's journal *Ver Sacrum*, considering how differences in size convey the purpose and meaning in each work, their relationship to the viewer, and to the works' audience in *fin del siècle* Vienna. Of course I've had considerably more time (as well as experience) than our students to work on the essays for this book, drawing upon the works themselves, a variety of primary sources, and secondary sources not just in graphic design and graphic design history but in history, literature, material culture, and media studies, while students are often under considerable time pressures as they pursue their own investigations.

Another methodological issue that informs the case studies in *Reading Graphic Design History* is the degree to which the treatment of works of graphic design draws upon the writings of their designers. That many statements by twentieth-century designers about their own work is self-serving is perhaps self-evident. But the fact that the study of Josef Müller-Brockmann's oeuvre draws heavily upon his own observations in print seems to merit further scrutiny (chapter 1), along with acknowledging the many, and occasionally contradictory, statements of A. M. Cassandre (chapter 3) on his posters. After all, designers were also astute businessmen, and placing themselves in a historical context, or being the subject of museum exhibitions or articles in professional journals or essays in books, lent a degree of prestige and a promotional boost to their design practices. The same might apply to William Bernbach, one of the founders of the advertising firm Doyle Dane Bernbach, who also created his own "narrative" (really a legend) surrounding the success of his agency in countless interviews and speeches (chapter 5). Artists' (or art directors') statements are evidence, but might be balanced by a harder look at the works themselves and their relation to other texts and contexts.

Subjects

The choice of subjects for *Reading Graphic Design* is in one sense arbitrary; each chapter stemmed initially from my own curiosity over the years in teaching courses in graphic design and type history to graphic design juniors and seniors, looking at a poster, magazine layout, or print advertisement, soliciting student reactions and observations, asking them to think about the motivations for the design decisions that resulted in the finished work, and the specific circumstances of the work's commission, its audience, and its relation to culture. This process led me to question the often cursory, even misleading statements that appear in the existing introductory literature, and to propose to Bloomsbury a book that would address some of the discrepancies between my own analyses and the existing literature in the field. Suggestions from the anonymous readers of my initial book proposal helped to determine the final choice of subjects: readers felt that focusing upon more familiar examples of graphic design would provide some connection among the individual chapters, revealing how much is left unsaid even among reasonably well-known works, and how an individual work may not always align with general assumptions about a designer's oeuvre or a graphic design "style." The objects for investigation in each chapter may be found in the standard graphic design history surveys and monographs. Most can be found in major museum collections or academic libraries—some might be aptly called "icons" of graphic design, often reproduced and connected with well-known designers who occupy a prominent place in the canon of graphic design history.

The inclusion of two of the chapters may require some further explanation: political cartoons are less frequently found in survey texts, and the choice of Thomas Nast may be less familiar to students living outside of the United States. That said, Nast's oeuvre is part of the history of nineteenth-century illustration, and the broader history of Western narrative art. As to the chapter on the Fell Types, it is admittedly an outlier. A visit to the Oxford University Press museum some years ago kindled my interest the early years of Bishop Fell's efforts to create a learned press at Oxford, and led me to wonder about his motivations. It also seemed important to me to include something about body type, because in my teaching I found that students take little interest generally in typefaces for books, ignoring the rich history of the letterpress. It seemed to me that that there might be more to choosing a typeface than clicking on the myriad options on a drop-down word-processing menu, and so I proceeded to reflect upon and include the Fell Types as a case study, a story I hope is worth telling, and one that credits the contributions of a series of dedicated type scholars and practitioners who devoted their careers to preserving and interpreting that history.

In writing each chapter several connections among them have emerged, not intentionally but simply as a by-product of my investigations. These include the use of stereotypes, echoes of Cassandre's 1932 Dubonnet posters in a 1952 print advertisement for Levy's real Jewish rye bread to name but two examples. While reading about Edward Steichen's 1955 "Family of Man" photographic exhibition at the Museum of Modern art in New York in relation to the Levy's Rye Bread advertising campaign (chapter 5), I learned how American attitudes and government policies toward postwar Western Europe that emerge in that exhibition also relate to the feature article in *Holiday* magazine and tourism (chapter 4). It's been my hope that parts of each chapter would not only awaken interest in the past, but demonstrate the awareness and relevance of a broader history at any given moment in graphic design's own history. Thomas Nast's familiarity with the "lingua franca" of Western history painting, or Kolo Moser's use of Greco-Roman symbols in forging a "modern" visual language of print communication in Vienna are but two examples of motifs and visual as well as verbal strategies that the designers knew their local audiences would recognize. The chapters also treat themes that remain relevant to graphic designers working today. These include promoting the use of leisure time (chapter 4), food (chapter 5), and exposing the tension between individual freedom and the public welfare (chapters 1 and 6).

My selection of subjects for the chapters of *Reading Graphic Design History* also demonstrates the limitations of perhaps any single-author book. While my own teaching, speaking, reading and travels have expanded the scope of my knowledge over the years, they have not provided sufficient familiarity with non-Western material, for instance, the graphic design of Japan and other Asian nations, or for that matter Africa or the rich graphic design heritage of Latin America. I can only hope that future studies, perhaps an edited volume with contributions from a wide range of author/experts, may bring together for investigation a more global selection of materials.

Graphic Design, Advertising, and Business Histories

During the course of my investigations I've become more keenly aware of how little attention is paid to business and advertising history in the history of graphic design. While the title and text of Steven Heller's 1995 essay "Advertising: The Mother of Graphic Design" (Heller, 1995; Heller and Balance, 2004) confronted this caveat quite directly, design historians have generally continued to ignore or downplay the profession's roots in advertising. As Michael Golec observed in 2004, the field "has maintained something of an historical false consciousness when it views advertising as an entity apart from the more loftier concerns of graphic design" (Golec, 2004). And as Heller wrote: "Graphic design history is an integral part of advertising history, yet in most accounts of graphic design's origins advertising is virtually denied, or hidden behind more benign words such as 'publicity' and 'promotion.'" My own research confirmed Heller's and Golec's views, and several of the chapters in *Reading Graphic Design History* attempt to introduce advertising history into graphic design history. These include chapter 3 on Cassandre's 1932 posters for Dubonnet that considers the distinction between publicity and advertising and its relationship to the trajectory of the designer's own career and the changing reception of his poster work. Advertising history also plays a role in Moser's Thirteenth Vienna Secession Poster (chapter 2), and is a consideration in thinking about magazine content in the chapter on *Holiday* magazine (chapter 4) and the Levy's Rye Bread campaign (chapter 5).

I might add that business and advertising historians tend to concentrate upon words rather than images, and the chapters of *Reading Graphic Design History* seek to provide ample comparative illustrations to explore advertising history more *visually* while considering the interaction of words and images in each case study. I suppose the "literary" nature of the history of advertising has its roots in the business of advertising itself; originating in the mid-nineteenth century with the first advertising agencies, the field was first and foremost about copy, based upon a consideration of the attention span of readers or pedestrians and the use of market research as a gauge of effectiveness. In the effort to be more inclusive of advertising in the chapters of *Reading Graphic Design History*, I utilized material in advertising trade journals such as *Printers Ink* and *Advertising Age*, along with the classic texts of Daniel Starch (1923), Claude Hopkins (1936), and Harry D. Kitson (1926).

To return to the Fell Types, interdependence between business and graphic design extends to type history as well. In the introduction to his classic two-volume *Printing Types* published in 1923, the printer and type historian Daniel Berkeley Updike writes that his study grew out of a series of lectures he'd been invited to present for faculty and students at the Harvard Business School. Years ago when I first read this introduction it struck me as odd that a business school would have an interest in the history of typography, until I realized that the faculty of the business school in the 1920s who would have attended Updike's lecture series were the same faculty who were developing the theory and practice of scientific advertising, studying both language and its *visual presentation* in advertisements that would attract consumer interest and convert readers into buyers; they surely sensed connections, both practical as well as aesthetic, between typography and advertising, and the role typography played in promoting the interests of American business.

Graphic Design and Fine Art

More than one of the essays in *Reading Graphic Design* considers the question of graphic design's relation to fine art. That relationship has been a hierarchical one, a spin-off from art history with fine art viewed as a pure form of individual expression and graphic design as constrained, tainted by commercial and management considerations (and often viewed as interference). In an essay entitled "Design Is Good Will" (1987) Paul Rand wrote:

> The relationship that exists between the designer and management is dichotomous. On the one hand, the designer is fiercely independent: on the other, he or she is dependent on management for support against bureaucracy and the caprice of the marketplace. ... Design quality is proportionately related to the distance that exists between the designer and the management at the top. The closer this relationship, the more likely chances are for a meaningful design. (Rand, 1987)

The statement expresses a desire for the kind of independence and autonomy associated with the modern fine arts. This relationship between fine art and graphic design also surfaces in succinct form in Susan Sontag's seminal 1970 essay on the poster ("Posters: Advertisement, Art, Political Artifact, Commodity"), where the author asserts what must have appeared at the time obvious from a fine art-historical perspective:

> Aesthetically, the poster has always been parasitic on the respectable arts of painting, sculpture, even architecture. In the numerous posters they did, Toulouse-Lautrec, Mucha, and Beardsley only transposed a style already articulated in their paintings and drawings. The work of those painters ... is not only not innovative but mainly casts into a more accessible form their most distinctive and familiar stylistic mannerisms. (Sontag, 1970)

Surely this issue is more nuanced than Sontag suggests. As Lorenz Eitner and others have demonstrated, whether through direct borrowing or general awareness, modern painters, and writers, acknowledged the vitality and originality of popular prints in their subject matter, execution, and their connection with the experience of contemporary life (Eitner, 1990). The primacy of fine art in the history of Modernism appears based upon the premise of the freedom of original unfettered creation, lending autonomy and prestige to artists; yet such a view conflicts at times with artists' desire for a broader cultural renewal and relevance for their work beyond a narrow circle of like-minded collectors, museums, and gallery walls. In that conflict lies a connection between the worlds of fine art and graphic design that goes beyond the "parasitic." A case in point is the poster artist A. M. Cassandre, whose own oeuvre and writings reveal an ambivalence about the relationship between art and advertising (chapter 3). Along these lines perhaps case studies provide a means to examine this relationship with care as well as an open mind. The whole question of "influence" suggests a kind of "one way" communication that rarely takes into account particular contexts and relationships among objects. In a similar vein, some of the issues addressed in the essays are merely "fact-checking": is "schutzt das Kind!" "objective"? How, precisely, is Cassandre's "Dubo-Dubon-Dubonnet" "cinematic"? *What* exactly is it that makes graphic design effective as propaganda in the cartoons of Thomas Nast? How does Moser's Thirteenth Secession Exhibition Poster fare as an example of advertising? And in what sense is the series of Levy's Rye Bread subway station posters "rebellious"?

The Chapters

Reading Graphic Design begins with a study of Josef Müller-Brockmann's 1952/3 "schutzt das Kind!" poster for the Automobile Club (ACS) of Switzerland. After a description of the poster's subject and composition, the chapter examines some general statements made about the poster and about Swiss graphic design, in particular the use of "objectivity" and "factual" to describe the movement, and questioning the applicability of these terms to the "shutzt das Kind!" poster in comparison with other approaches along with the automobile club's campaign to promote traffic safety in Zurich. In the process we consider statistical information on traffic accidents in the city, the ambiguous role of the ACS in promoting traffic safety while at the same time encouraging automobile use, and a rich but generally underrepresented illustrative tradition of social awareness in Swiss poster design that encouraged empathy for its neediest, most vulnerable citizens.

Chapter 2 explores Koloman Moser's 1902 poster for the Thirteenth Exhibition of the Vienna Secession. Long a mainstay in the literature on Viennese graphic design at the turn of the twentieth century, the poster invites a consideration of the function of posters as advertising and as "art," and describes in detail the graphic vocabulary that Moser developed in this severely geometric example from his wide-ranging oeuvre. Appreciating the poster involves looking in particular at Moser's extensive work in book illustration and magazine art direction for the Secession's journal *Ver Sacrum*, the critical reception of the Secession posters, the organization's exhibitions in Vienna, and the culture of Vienna's celebrated "café society."

Chapter 3 examines another well-known poster by a celebrated designer, A. M. Cassandre's mural-sized "Dubo-Dubon-Dubonnet" of 1932. The essay considers the ways in which critics wrote about the poster in the interwar period in France, in particular its connection to the "spectacle of the street," to "publicité," and to fine art. The chapter also examines Cassandre's own conflicting statements about the advertising enterprise, and considers the role the emerging "science" of advertising played at the time, in which "persuasion" competed with information, entertainment, or edification as objectives of advertising investment.

The fourth chapter is a study of the American travel magazine *Holiday* under the art direction of Frank Zachary and editorship of Ted Patrick for the Philadelphia-based Curtis Publishing Company in the 1950s and early 1960s. Zachary and *Holiday* are part of the canon of graphic design history, though perhaps less celebrated generally than the fashion magazines *Harper's Bazaar* or *Vogue*. Yet the subject of leisure and tourism in post-World War II America beckon more thorough treatment, and the chapter places the magazine in the context of contemporary debates surrounding the pursuit of happiness, the so-called "Third Right" guaranteed in the Declaration of Independence as the broader context for *Holiday* that relates to photography, to fashion, advertising, taste, and America's postwar national identity and increasing economic and political role internationally.

Chapter 5 is a fairly lengthy study of the 1960s Levy's rye bread advertising campaign that introduced the popular tagline "You Don't Have to be Jewish to love Levy's *real* Jewish rye" designed by the Doyle Dane Bernbach advertising agency in New York. Ubiquitous on the tiled walls of New York City subway stations throughout the 1960s, the representation of diverse races and ethnicities in this series of ads was unique, even striking at the time in advertising, and is often illustrated in surveys of graphic design. The campaign illustrates many of the strategies associated with the "New Advertising," but also raises broader questions about the advertising industry after World War II, and its response to public and governmental concerns with "honesty" in advertising that appeared at the time in advertising trade journals such as *Printers Ink* and *Advertising Age*. It also considers the use of stereotypes in advertising and takes up the issue of race relations in the United States, as well as globalism and diversity. I examine the development of the agency's promotion for the Levy's Baking Company from its beginnings in 1950 to the poster campaign initiated in 1963. In its inclusive treatment of race the Levy's advertising campaign invites comparison with several contemporary publications and exhibitions, including the Museum of Modern Art's "Family of Man" exhibition (1955 ff.) and James Baldwin and Richard Avedon's *Nothing Personal* book (1964). These and other comparisons reveal similarities and differences in point of view in the treatment of controversial subjects by writers, curators, and advertisers.

Chapter 6 considers one of the nineteenth-century illustrator Thomas Nast's best-known political cartoon for *Harper's Weekly*, titled "THE TAMMANY TIGER LOOSE: What Are You Going To Do About It?" The chapter examines in some detail the iconography of the often-reproduced double-page cartoon, the meaning of ancient Roman history to the readership of *Harper's Weekly*, and the tradition of academic painting that informed Nast's compositional choices for the cartoon. It also considers the issue of political activism and the role of graphic design in bringing about political change.

As noted above the final chapter is a bit of an anomaly—its subject is known to most typophiles (especially those in the United Kingdom), but more strictly belongs to the history of the printed book rather than to the history of graphic design as students generally understand and practice it professionally. Its subject is later seventeenth-century typography, in particular the types assembled at the Oxford University Press established by Bishop John Fell (1625– 86) and known as the "Fell Types." The Fell Types interested me because of the meaning they held for Bishop Fell and for English type historians, and my desire to better understand and appreciate the reasons behind his obsessive pursuit and assembly of types for the "learned" press at Oxford University. In the course of my research I realized that the history of typography is almost exclusively the history of the tradition of "fine printing," a way of thinking about how institutions communicate authority and exclusivity.

Hopefully, the value of these essays accrues from the thoroughness with which the individual works are examined and in the consideration given to the history of advertising as an important and undervalued point of view in the study of graphic design history. In each case the approach has been to look carefully at my examples, question some of the assumptions made about them in the existing literature, and consider them as the "center" of an investigation of graphic design history rather than as peripheral or incorporated as part of a general and not always accurate treatment of a period or movement. The chapters include, and in some cases expand upon, information that is readily available in print or even online. With the help of librarians and colleagues I've investigated as many leads and suggestions as possible and examined primary source material wherever possible. Sometimes these efforts have been successful, particularly in the case of newspapers and trade journals that are accessible in libraries and online, while at other times I've encountered dead ends, for instance in locating early records from the Doyle Dane Bernbach advertising agency (now DDB Worldwide, chapter 5), or records from the Automobile Club of Switzerland which were destroyed due to flooding at their headquarters. And yet, the essays go beyond the usual reliance upon the designer's own recollections or writings, attempting to introduce a wide range of primary sources and secondary material from a range of disciplines that expands our understanding of the context for the work of graphic designers, in particular its complexity both in terms of process and in its broader cultural meaning.

Finally, as an art and design historian in addressing an audience of designers, both students and faculty as *well* as other historians, *Reading Graphic Design History* is avowedly an "instrumental" book, that is, it attempts to demonstrate the relevance and value of graphic design history to the graphic design profession. During the many years I taught graphic design history, my office during most of that time was housed in the graphic design program area. Moreover, a good number of graphic designers, graphic design students, and graphic design historians all share the space of the academy, along with historians of business, media, and material culture. It's been my goal to contribute in some way to the education of future designers in addition to suggesting avenues of investigation that add to design history as a discipline in its own right. Some writers and critics see "instrumentalism" as a constraint that prevents design history from establishing its own identity (Fallan, 2013). While the separation of design history from art history in the United Kingdom (and perhaps elsewhere) provides design history with a more independent disciplinary identity, the situation in the United States is somewhat different—designers often teach courses in design history, and the two US-based journals, *Design and Culture* and *Design Issues*, also try to combine design practice, theory, and history. It's been my hope that *Reading Graphic Design History* would demonstrate that it can be as rewarding to analyse and investigate historically an example of advertising as a painting by an old master, and that such investigations would also be "useful" to the graphic design profession.

Chapter 1

Josef Müller-Brockmann: "schutzt das Kind!" and the Mythology of Swiss Design

Josef-Müller-Brockmann (1914–96) was one of a group of graphic designers who defined a "Swiss" or "International Typographic Style" after World War II. With a successful professional practice based in Zurich and a wide range of corporate and non-profit clients, as a teacher at the city's Kunstgewerbeschule (1957–60), through exhibitions he helped to organize, as founding editor of the trilingual journal *Neue Grafik* together with Richard Lohse, Carlo Vivarelli, and Hans Neuberg (1958–65), and as an author through his own extensive publications (e.g., *The Graphic Designer and his Design Problems* [1961]; *A History of Visual Communication* [1971]; *Grid Systems in Graphic Design* [1981]), Müller-Brockmann occupies a privileged place in twentieth-century graphic design history, a position he played no small part in establishing himself through his own writings.

Among the designer's best-known and frequently reproduced works is the offset poster "schutzt das Kind!" (mind the Child! or, protect the Child!) dating to 1952 and 1953, the winning design in a competition sponsored by the Automobile Club of Switzerland (ACS). The poster measures 127.5 × 90.5 cm (50 3/16 × 35 5/8 in., Figure 1.1), and a photo (Figure 1.2) shows how it was mounted on sidewalk stands (rather than a wall or kiosk) for viewing in Zurich by passing motorists.

The competition brief asked designers to illustrate the tagline "schutzt das Kind!" and was part of an ACS initiative to promote automobile safety that included a changing display of statistics and photographs reporting traffic accidents and deaths (Unfallbarometer—Accident Barometer) located in a prominent Zurich public square (Figure 1.3), also designed by Müller-Brockmann. Müller-Brockmann created a series of posters for the campaign in the early 1950s, and in subsequent years the designer and his office produced brochures and related print materials for the ACS (Purcell, 2006).

Survey texts that mention or illustrate the poster focus heavily upon the technical refinement of its printing, due in no small measure to the perfection of the offset lithographic process after World War II in Switzerland, using finer half-tone screens to produce the rich, even tones of each print, most evident in the deep, almost soft, tactile black and deep gray areas on the matte paper surface in our example. The Swiss reputation for quality, dependability, and precision, in the manufacture of watches no less than in printing, was in turn part of the small nation's identity

FIGURE 1.1 (and color plate) *Josef Müller-Brockmann, © ARS, NY. Poster, schützt das Kind!*
[Protect the Child!], 1953. Offset lithograph on wove paper, lined, 1275 × 905 mm (50 3/16 × 35 5/8 in.)
Museum purchase from General Acquisitions Endowment Fund. 1999-46. Photo Credit: Cooper Hewitt,
Smithsonian Design Museum/Art Resource, NY. Photo: Matt Flynn © Smithsonian Institution, Cooper
Hewitt, Smithsonian Design Museum, New York, NY, USA. Artists Rights Society

FIGURE 1.2 *Josef Müller-Brockmann, "schutzt das Kind!" (Protect the Child!), poster displayed on sidewalk, Zurich, 1953, Museum for Design, Zurich*

FIGURE 1.3 *Josef Müller-Brockmann, "Accident Barometer," 1952, Paradeplatz, Zurich, commissioned by the Automobile Club of Switzerland (ACS), Zurcher Hochschule der Kunste ZhdK*

and reputation internationally that persists to the present day. Through recent publications and conferences, Swiss scholars are lobbying to include Swiss graphic design on the "List of Intangible Cultural Heritage" through the United Nations Educational, Scientific and Cultural Organization (UNESCO; Lizcar et al., 2018).

Authors also note the design's reductive arrangement of simple compositional units. This approach rejects drawing or illustration in favor of photography and employs a limited color palette, here including a horizontal yellow band at the bottom of the poster that draws attention to that area, the unprinted white space to the right of the motorcycle wheel that contrasts with and isolates the running child and emphasizes the disparity between him and the speeding wheel, and the use of the crisp sans serif Akzidenz Grotesk font in the upper left corner silhouetted against the cycle's motor housing. The tension created by the unequal formal arrangement of asymmetrical abstract shapes, dominated by the aggressive dark triangle of the wheel at the left and its lighter, smaller counterpart to the right, the repetition of parallel diagonal lines that includes the outer edge of the wheel and shock absorber and the left contour of the running child, and overall simplicity of the composition produce a unified image with a striking and immediate impact upon the viewer. The canonical status of "schutzt das Kind!" results from its frequent reproduction not only in survey books but also its inclusion in exhibitions, for instance the "Meister der Plakatkunst" exhibition in Zurich in 1959, and in journals, including the very first issue of *Neue Grafik* in September, 1958 (Lizcar and Fornari, 2016).

A similar design strategy applies to other posters designed by Müller-Brockmann for the ACS series, though with less dramatic effect, for instance, "Überholen …? Im Zweifel nie!" (Overtake? If in doubt, never! Figure 1.4).

FIGURE 1.4 *Josef Müller-Brockmann © ARS, NY. Überholen…? Im Zweifel nie! 1957. Offset lithograph, 50 1/2 × 35 1/2" (128 × 90 cm). Printer: Lithographie & Cartonnage A.G., Zürich. Purchase and partial gift of Leslie J. Schreyer. The Museum of Modern Art, New York, NY, USA. Digital Image © The Museum of Modern Art/Licensed by SCALA/Art Resource, NY*

Here the negative white space positions a smaller motorcyclist *between* as well as *behind* two automobiles, collapsing space and suggesting a tight squeeze. In addition to eliminating background distractions, the repetition of the circular shapes of rear-view mirrors, helmet, and headlights creates visual unity and concentration, but the rectangular rather than slanted shapes of the cars and cyclist are less dynamic than the raking diagonals of "schutzt das Kind!" and the situation "Überholen ..." describes appears less immanently threatening.

What IS "Swiss Style"?

The technical perfection of "schutzt das Kind!," its clean, reductive approach to design, and the active use of negative space are characteristics that inform our general understanding of Swiss design or a Swiss style after World War II. Survey texts and monographs have made this style or Swiss School a standard, even dominant, part of the history of modern twentieth-century graphic design. Here, for instance, is a passage from the introduction to post-World War II Swiss graphic design in Philip Meggs and Allston Purvis's *History of Graphic Design*, now in its sixth edition:

> During the 1950s a design movement emerged from Switzerland and Germany that has been called Swiss design, or, more appropriately, the International Typographic Style. The objective clarity of this design movement won converts throughout the world. It remained a major force for over two decades, and its influence continues today.
>
> The visual characteristics of this style include a unity of design achieved by asymmetrical organization of the design elements on a mathematically constructed grid; objective photography and copy that present visual and verbal information in a clear and factual manner, free from the exaggerated claims of propaganda and commercial advertising; and use of sans-serif typography set in a flush-left and ragged-right margin configuration. The initiators of this movement believed sans-serif typography expressed the spirit of a more progressive age and that mathematical grids are the most legible and harmonious means for structuring information. (Meggs/Purvis, 2016)

In *Graphic Design: A Critical Guide*, authors Johanna Drucker and Emily McVarish restate the basic elements of Swiss design, preferring "International Style" in order to emphasize its near-universal adoption as the accepted visual language for corporate communications, serving the expanding post-World War II national and multinational chemical, travel, communications, entertainment, pharmaceutical, and oil industries: "Visually, the International style was characterized by underlying grid structures, asymmetrical layouts, and sans serif type. It also favored straightforward, "objective" photography, geometric forms, and an almost total absence of decoration or illustration. ... Clean, unfussy directness was the primary aim of this approach" (Drucker and McVarish, 2013).

But these and other sources do not present Swiss design, Swiss School, or International Typographic Style only as a set of formal choices and technical achievement: authors almost invariably point to the way in which the style communicates shared political and ethical beliefs, in particular the renunciation of manipulative techniques of persuasion in advertising and a commitment to social and public responsibility as professional values. Referring to Müller-Brockmann, Meggs/Purvis state the designer "sought an absolute and universal form of graphic expression through objective and impersonal presentation, communicating to the audience without the interference of the designer's subject feelings or propagandistic techniques of persuasion." The authors continue:

More important than the visual appearance of this work is the attitude developed by its early pioneers about their profession. These trailblazers defined design as a socially useful and important activity. Personal expression and eccentric solutions were rejected, while a more universal and scientific approach to design problem solving was embraced. In this paradigm, designers defined their roles not as artists but as *objective conduits for spreading important information between components of society* [italics added]. Achieving clarity and order is the ideal. (Meggs/Purvis, 2016)

And yet, when using the term "objective," authors seem to conflate technical practice with emotional restraint, as if "objectivity" was the natural, inevitable result of applying the formal principles of the Swiss style and the use of photography. Indeed, in his own *History of Visual Communication* (1971), Müller-Brockmann stated that "objectively informative designs are a socio-cultural task." And in commenting on the program at the Kunstgewerbeschule in Zurich, Müller-Brockmann tells his readers he has developed an "objectified course of training," that visual communication is a "means of conveying *objective facts* [my italics]," giving designers the ability to cope with "highly complex problems of human society." The section of his survey devoted to graphic design after the Second World War bears the subtitle "The Development of Objective Visual Communication after World War II."

Ethics, Advertising, Objectivity, and Politics

The relationship between Swiss style and ethics applies most directly and clearly to graphic design for advertising. Stemming from a long-standing mistrust of the advertising industry's goal of promoting sales and profits by exaggerating or misrepresenting the truth, designers and promoters of Swiss design renounced, both in practice and in professional writing, persuasive techniques that associated products with personal fulfilment and status, emphasizing instead "objectivity," translating visually as presenting commodities plainly through the use of "object" photography rather than employing techniques based upon consumer psychology and motivational research to play upon customers' hopes or fears. The designers who defined and practiced Swiss design believed that it was their professional responsibility to avoid the excesses of consumer-led advertising, long before government regulation and consumer activism (e.g. the Consumer Protection Organization of the Federal Trade Commission in the United States) assumed such a role politically or legislatively. In his *History of Visual Communication*, Müller-Brockmann wrote:

The way it [objective information] is tackled highlights the position of the designer in society. Does he feel responsible to society? Does he want to provide reliable information or to doctor facts? The business world along with the advertising agencies use their resources, including sometimes those of science, to speed up and promote the sale of goods. Often for the benefit of the producer. *An intention which is, however, resisted by people who think for themselves* [italics added]. They [the thinkers] expect impartial information about what comes on the market. They take a critical look at what they are offered. (Müller-Brockmann, 1971)

Equally telling is a passage on the subject of advertising in the 1956 book *The New Graphic Art*, by Basel-based artist and graphic designer Karl Gerstner. Illustrating examples of women's shoe advertisements, he contrasted a Lord & Taylor advertisement featuring two photographed views of a shoe with an I. Miller ad (Andy Warhol provided illustrations for I. Miller ads in the 1950s) in which a women's leg is photographed wearing a shoe, commenting:

> One way of advertising shoes is to show a picture of them. Another is to make the picture promise the fulfillment of a wish: If you buy my shoes you will have beautiful legs (the shoe itself seems to have become a minor consideration). It is all rather like a fairy story and nobody troubles to check the truthfulness of such promises. (Gerstner, 1959; see also the advertisements for women's stockings advertisements below in chapter 5, Figures 5.24 and 5.25)

Examples of advertising illustrated in Müller-Brockmann's *History of Visual Communication* also support this approach, whose origins are easily traced to the "Sachplakat" ("Object poster") pioneered by German designer Lucien Bernhard (1883–1972) in the early twentieth century. The journal *Neue Grafik*, beginning in 1958, echoed these views in numerous articles, promoting an ethical component in professional practice that resisted commercial and popular pressure and emphasized the graphic designer's "cultural responsibility," most clearly seen in advertising, where understatement and restraint reigned. Concluding an article from the trilingual journal *Neue Grafik* in 1959 titled "The Graphic Designer and his Training," designer and teacher Robert Gessner repeated the saying "moderation in all things." And in an article in *Neue Grafik* from 1959, Richard Lohse remarked, "This responsibility [of the designer to culture] is particularly obvious when the creative designer opposes the customary practice of persuading by false means and supports the opinion that he must convince the buying public by *purely objective means* [italics added]."

Müller-Brockmann's critical position toward advertising incorporated a political dimension that identifies advertising more generally with the dangers of manipulating public opinion. In the United States mistrust of the advertising industry intensified with the rise of television in the 1950s, with the sensationalist writings of journalist and social critic Vance Packard (1914–96), and with threats of congressional action to impose taxes on advertising or to eliminate corporate tax deductions for advertising as business expenses (see chapter 5, p. 174). In his popular 1957 book *The Hidden Persuaders*, Packard used the phrase "motivational research" to refer to the techniques advertisers employed to sway the buying habits of an unsuspecting and passive public, associating cigarettes with "masculinity" for instance, or suggesting more ominously that a public so easily manipulated by psychological means to purchase products or services could also be persuaded to elect or follow the promises of a demagogue or dictator:

> What the probers are looking for, of course, are the *whys* of our behavior, so that they can more effectively manipulate our habits and choices in their favor. This had led them to probe why we are afraid of banks; why we love those big fat cars; why housewives typically fall into a hypnoidal trance when they get into a supermarket; why men are drawn into auto showrooms by convertibles but end up buying sedans; why junior loves cereal that pops, snaps, and crackles.
>
> We move from the genial world of James Thurber into the chilling world of George Orwell and his Big Brother, however, as we explore some of the extreme attempts at probing and manipulating now going on. (Packard, 1957)

The menacing ring of Packard's prose connects consumer-led advertising with a public susceptible to the false promises or the flaming of popular fears and prejudices by politicians. For Europeans, interwar anti-Semitic and other fascist propaganda offered more chilling memories

of the persuasive power of propaganda imagery to arouse hatred or promote nationalist identity, emboldened by state control of mass media, providing an underpinning for the attitudes of graphic designers in Switzerland and their commitment to ethical responsibility through self-imposed safeguards and restraint, along with independence from the dangers of exaggeration in commercial practice. Linking such attitudes to standards of professional practice would help to create a healthy partnership (or checks and balances) between graphic design and the business community, curbing any tendency toward the excesses of advertising through self-control and "objectivity."

But if "schutzt das Kind!" is a paradigm of Swiss design, and if Swiss design is "objective," is it accurate to describe the poster as "factual" or "objective"? Using Müller-Brockmann's own criteria, how does the poster "convey objective facts" or address the "complex problems of human society"? Despite its frequent inclusion in survey texts, "schutzt das Kind!" appears to violate some of the Swiss graphic design's basic principles. While photography may appear more "objective" than drawing or painting, and while orderly arrangements of analogous shapes may be achieved through the application of consistent mathematical relationships, there is nothing "factual" about Müller-Brockmann's use of photomontage in "schutzt das Kind!," where a dramatic contrast in scale between motorcycle and child creates a sense of impending, even frightening danger and elicits a strong emotional response. "Schutzt das Kind!" makes a statement about the relationship between drivers and pedestrians, about the power and aggressiveness of the former and the vulnerability of the latter. Compare, for example, an example of pictographic public traffic signage in today's cities (Figure 1.5; for pictograms and the work of Otto Neurath, Marie Rademeister Neurath, Gerd Arntz and others for ISOTYPE, see chapter 3, p. 80; Neurath and his team in Vienna developed pictograms for use in charts to display quantitative information using symbols, later used as well for public service, e.g., as traffic warnings). Both poster and sign offer warnings to motorists, but the intervention of the designer differs: in the pictogram the artist avoids the particular in favor of the generic—repetition of triangular shapes and the black-on-yellow contrast breeds familiarity, comprehension, and alerts pedestrians and drivers

FIGURE 1.5 *Traffic sign (Caution-Pedestrian Walkway), 34th and Walnut Streets, Philadelphia, PA, 2018, photograph: author*

alike; the poster triggers a response as well, but the relationship between speaker (the poster or addresser) and driver (addressee) is anything but "neutral" or factual, less a reminder to "slow down for school children" or that children may be playing nearby with which today's drivers are more familiar than a frantic warning of an impending catastrophe. The traffic sign also includes a reminder of the role of the child/pedestrian by positioning the figure in the center of a crosswalk.

"Schutzt das Kind!" exemplifies the differences between the assumed "neutrality" of graphic design for advertising in Switzerland and graphic design for other purposes that sanctioned and even promoted stronger language and more persuasive rather than impersonal approaches to visual communication. And so the moral responsibility of the graphic design profession, as envisioned by Müller-Brockmann, was not in all cases equated with "facts": photography could be powerful and dramatic as well as emotionally neutral, demonstrating the relative, contextual meaning of the terms such as "subjective," "fact," or "objective." An earlier example of a similar emotional use of photography is Hans Neuberg's 1944 poster soliciting contributions to the International Red Cross to address the refugee and POW crises during World War II, superimposing photographs of fleeing refugees and prisoners of war (Figure 1.6); here too photography is highly charged emotionally, much like the handwritten plea for help in red below the courier font above it. In his 1971 book *History of Visual Communication*, Müller-Brockmann acknowledged both the power of Neuberg's photographic poster as well as the dire wartime circumstances that conditioned its appeal to emotion (Müller-Brockmann, 1971). Indeed, perhaps "realism" is a better word choice to describe this strain of Swiss style—factual in cases such as advertising, persuasive in other situations. Comparing Hans Thöni's 1955 poster "Vorsicht—Kinder" (Caution—Children, Figure 1.7 and color plate section) that uses cartoon-like drawings of a child passing in front of an automobile with Müller-Brockmann's photomontaged "schutzt das Kind!," the former looks almost playful and the vehicle less menacing in comparison to the latter: Thöni's approach, closer to the traffic sign, is a mild reminder, Müller-Brockmann's an urgent warning.

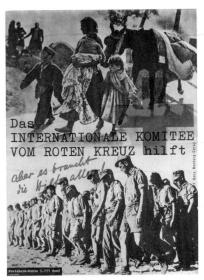

FIGURE 1.6 *Hans Neuberg, "The International Committee of the Red Cross Helps, but it needs your help too!," offset lithograph, 1944, 127 × 90 cm, Museum for Design, Zurich*

FIGURE 1.7 (and color plate) *Hans Thöni, "Vorsicht—Kinder!" (Watch out—Children!), poster, chromolithography, 1955, 128 × 90.5 cm, Plakatsammlung SfG Basel*

To be sure (or to be fair), that generalizations about "Swiss Style" fail to grasp or appreciate its contradictions or exceptions has not gone entirely unnoticed. In an article devoted to the graphic design work of Müller-Brockmann in the journal *Industrial Design* (1956), the designer stated the standard emphases upon technical perfection, typographical clarity and hierarchy, and simplicity of form, but also noted that while the graphic designer should respect the value of photography as documentation and the presentation of "real facts," the technique of photomontage makes it possible to combine one photo with another to convey inner connections that can *either* be "subtle or startling." In other words, the role of the designer is not uniformly "neutral," as Müller-Brockmann indicated: "where photography reaches its limits the task of the designer begins" (Dialogs on Graphic Design, 1956). Designer Ernst Scheidigger expressed a similar view in an article published in *Neue Grafik* (1959) titled "Photography and Graphic Design." Here Scheidigger offered examples of the varied functions of photography in graphic design, remarking that a photograph can record objects of events factually, but also can function persuasively and emotionally. Coincidentally, as an example, he writes, "a child playing in the midst of traffic symbolizes danger," bringing to mind Müller-Brockmann's "schutzt das Kind!" More recently art historian Gerry Beegan, in his entry on "Swiss Style" for the *Bloomsbury Encyclopedia of Design* (2015), reminds readers: "Swiss design has never been a homogeneous discourse, however. There was and continues to be many strains of design practice within Switzerland" (Beegan, 2015). In the same way in an unpublished lecture at the Alliance Graphique Internationale in 2015, Sarah Owens expressed a similar view: "the homogeneous canon of Swiss graphic design reduces a rich past with a vast number of different designers and approaches to a certain period and certain actors within that period" (Lizcar and Fornari, 2016). And in the caption accompanying their illustration of "schutzt das Kind!" in Drucker/McVarish's *Graphic Design: A Critical Guide* the authors note:

But claims that its [the "schutzt das kind!" poster's] design is entirely rational are contradicted by its emotional impact. The scale distortion between wheel and child, the lines of motion coming from the brakes, and the elevation of the exclamation point to the status of a separate word by the introduction of a space after "Kind" are all expressive elements. The poster is *emotionally manipulative* [italics added], and no grid or logical structure organizes its composition. Instead, the design makes use of a reduced and carefully managed set of elements for maximum effect. (Drucker/McVarish, 2013)

Despite these occasional reservations and objections most scholars accept an uncritical and homogenous view of Swiss graphic design that includes "schutzt das Kind!," one that rarely questions the equation among photography, technical precision, and "facts."

Social Welfare and the Poster in Switzerland

In analyzing Müller-Brockmann's "schutzt das Kind!" poster it is worthwhile to consider not only differences in purpose, but also less well-known aspects of the history of the poster in Switzerland in the twentieth century. In addition to shaping attitudes toward advertising, the ethical disposition of the Swiss School also emerges when we consider the historical role of social welfare within Switzerland and its strong visual expression in poster design. Beginning with the establishment of the International Red Cross Committee in 1863 in Geneva and gaining visibility during World War I, both government-sponsored and private initiatives to attend to wounded soldiers and displaced persons expanded to include establishing rights and economic assistance for society's neediest citizens. Poster campaigns grew to become an integral part of these kinds of relief efforts in public discourse, whether as appeals for private donations or to advocate for opposing positions in plebiscites to enact (or to reject) welfare legislation. In the interwar period, such welfare posters aimed at persuasion rather than "objective" information, focusing upon initiatives such as advocating (or opposing) working conditions (shorter working hours) for the laboring classes or sympathy for the rights and dignity of the elderly, homeless, women, refugees, and children (Richter, 2009).

In Switzerland the majority of these social welfare posters throughout the interwar period and stretching into the 1950s were illustrative. Rather than following the practices of the "New Typography" that emerged in the 1920s, established a foothold in Switzerland, and provided the foundation for the "Swiss Style" after World War II, social welfare posters often feature hollow-eyed mothers, needy children, or the care-worn faces of the handicapped, elderly, and destitute, dominating condensed narrative representational imagery—examples include posters for an annual "Winter Aid" campaign to feed and shelter the poor during colder months, borrowing figural types, poses, and gestures drawn from the history of Western art to identify with and elicit sympathy for suffering through pictorial means such as strong outlines, isolation of the subject, a somber color palette, deep shadows, and empty, introspective expressions and body language (Figure 1.8).

Among the most frequent targets of sympathetic appeals for social welfare initiatives in Switzerland between the world wars and stretching into the post war era were children (Figure 1.9).

They figure prominently not only in the annual "Winter Aid" campaigns mentioned above, but also for aid to refugees, the needy, and programs specifically directed toward safeguarding the rights of children such as the non-profit Swiss charitable organization "Pro Juventute" and

FIGURE 1.8 *Hans Beat Wieland, "Help the Elderly," poster, chromolithograph, 129 × 90.5 cm, 1931, Museum for Design, Zurich*

FIGURE 1.9 *Victor Rutz, "Pro Juventute," poster, 128 × 90.5 cm, 1941, chromolithograph, Museum for Design, Zurich*

"Aid for Children," usually emphasizing innocence, vulnerability, and the need for protection. The emotional nature of many of these poster campaigns provides a context for and continuity with Müller-Brockmann's "schutzt das Kind!," and it is not surprising that the ACS included posters as an integral component of their driver safety initiative. While in his own recounting of the process the designer remarked on his decision to use a motorcycle rather than an automobile, the choice of a child is also worth noting, as a natural, even obvious metaphor for vulnerability. While rejecting illustration in favor of photography, "schutzt das Kind!" communicates the urgency and emotional appeal of social welfare propaganda, substituting a newer set of means in support of liberal, persuasive ends.

And so, "schutzt das Kind!" is not an informational poster, nor does it adhere to the restrained approach toward "objective" advertising we associate with Swiss design—there is nothing "factual" or restrained about it. If traffic accidents are a "complex" problem for modern society, "schutzt das Kind!" presents the problem in a simplified, polemic rather than nuanced way, emphasizing driver responsibility rather than pedestrian caution or traffic regulation. It is propaganda, using modern forms of visual hyperbole (here photomontage) as a call to arms, dramatically exaggerating imminent danger, urgency, and the threat of motor vehicles to public safety through the manipulation of scale relationships, an extreme contrast in proportions, and the use of the trope of childhood to arouse universal feelings of compassion and protection. Müller-Brockmann didn't invent this approach to visual communication, but in "schutzt das Kind!" the designer's method operates at a particularly high level of technical attention whose achievement has tended to eclipse the poster's high emotional temperature.

Photography, Photomontage, and Graphic Design

Although under-represented in general surveys of graphic design history in Switzerland, the illustrative or pictorial poster tradition connected with welfare advocacy coexisted with the Swiss design that emerged after World War II: Müller-Brockmann was a skilled draughtsman and successful advertising illustrator early in his career, but eschewed the pictorialism of his training and early practice in the early 1950s in favor of the visual language he and a select group of designers were developing and championing.

To be sure, the photographic technique employed for the poster was remarkable for the time, even a virtuoso performance. Kerry William Purcell describes the working partnership between Müller-Brockmann and photographer E. A. Heiniger with great attention to process and technical mastery (all before Adobe Photoshop), using a double-exposure of the motorcycle rather than retouching:

> Müller-Brockmann was faced with the difficulty of how to realize an image of a fast-moving bike without the object becoming so blurred that the viewer would not recognize it … Heiniger's reply was to photograph the front wheel of a motorcycle and thus achieve the sense of velocity Josef Müller-Brockmann desired by positioning the wheel at a slight angle, so it appears to be gathering speed. This impression of velocity was further amplified by Heiniger in a second exposure that masked part of the wheel and moved the image during exposure, generating a trail of light from the bike's suspension and wheel trim. (Purcell, 2006)

Despite the exacting application of photography, the abrupt juxtaposition of wheel and child has more in common with photomontage than with "objective" photography. In particular it calls to mind the photomontage covers and images published in the communist magazine *AIZ* (*Workers' Illustrated Newspaper—Arbeiter Illustrierte Zeitung*) designed by John Heartfield (in collaboration with his brother Wieland Herzfelde) between 1930 and 1938 for distribution in Germany and printed by copperplate photogravure, forms of anti-Nazi propaganda aimed at discrediting the regime by exaggerating the gap between fascist leadership and working class experience in Germany. Müller-Brockmann described and illustrated examples of Heartfield's work in his 1971 book *History of Visual Communication*. An example is a 1936 *AIZ* photomontage juxtaposing a colossal carved head of the fascist dictator Benito Mussolini at the left (resembling the Great Sphinx at Giza) with a mound of skulls at the left with the centered tagline above that reads "Fascist Monuments of Glory" (Figure 1.10)

The image juxtaposes two photographs to create meaning, contrasting familiar symbols of god-like permanence with human transience. In addition, the smaller text to the lower left ("Denkmal des Duce in Abessinien"—Il Duce's memorial in Abyssinia) refers to one of Mussolini's strange if unrealized projects to create a monument celebrating the dictator's occupation of Ethiopia (1935–6 also known as the second Italo-Abyssinian War) out of the bones of fallen Italian soldiers. Here photography is clearly a tool of propaganda, using metaphor, exaggeration, and abrupt juxtaposition to present the belief that dictators portray themselves as powerful icons of authority but bring about human suffering on a monumental scale.

The Swiss designer and artist Herbert Matter (1907–84) used photomontage in the 1930s for a series of travel posters for the Swiss Tourism Bureau, reproduced using three-color gravure printing on a large scale. Müller-Brockmann also illustrated an example of Matter's

FIGURE 1.10 *John Heartfield, "Fascist Monuments of Glory: Monument of Il Duce in Abyssinia,"* cover for Allegemeines Illustrierte Zeitung, *no. 17, April 22, 1936, 15 1/8 × 11 1/8 in., photogravure, 1936, Museum of Fine Arts, Houston, Artists Rights Society, NY*

work from the tourism series in his *History of Visual Communication*, which featured drastic juxtapositions of scale for dramatic effect, precise relationships among shapes that create a unified composition across the poster's surface, a clear hierarchy of information, along with the careful manipulation of tone in the reproduction of photographs that creates, or preserves, a compelling lifelike quality to the aggregate image. These effects can be seen in Matter's 1935 Engelberg—Trübsee poster (Figure 1.11 and color plate section), featuring a young, smiling female addresser with a knitted glove blocking the left side of her face and a cable car and mountain in the background.

A series of three stars (white, red, blue from upper left to lower right) create eye movement and connect the elements of the asymmetrical composition, including the stars' similarity to the snowflake pattern on the young woman's glove. Matter's technique and careful control of photography serves a "persuasive" rather than "objective" purpose; again, the identification of photography with objectivity (or illustration with subjectivity), so frequently cited in the literature on Swiss graphic design, is a proverbial "red herring," a generalization that does not stand up to careful scrutiny of individual examples. Such generalizations were part of

FIGURE 1.11 (and color plate) *Herbert Matter, © Copyright. Poster: Engelberg, Trübsee/ Switzerland. Switzerland, 1936. Offset lithograph on white wove paper. 1019 × 637 mm (40 1/8 × 25 1/16 in.). Museum purchase from General Acquisitions Endowment Fund, 2006-15-1. Photo: Matt Flynn, Cooper Hewitt, Smithsonian Design Museum. Photo Credit: Cooper Hewitt, Smithsonian Design Museum/Art Resource, NY; Artists Rights Society*

the construction of Swiss design by the practitioners themselves; in championing the use of photography, the integration of image and typography, and a carefully composed formal unity, designers such as Müller-Brockmann and Hans Neuberg embraced a duality pitting "graphic design" against painting and drawing, objectivity against subjectivity, an "either-or" approach that belied subtlety and contradiction in favor of a selectivity and oversimplification. But it is time now to turn from Swiss "style" and the tradition of the welfare poster in Switzerland to the role of the client in "schutzt das Kind!"

The Automobile Club of Switzerland

The Automobile Club of Switzerland, sponsor of the competition that produced "schutzt das Kind!" was founded in 1898 in Bern to promote automobile travel and tourism nationally. The organization published an English version of an "Autoguide" (Handbook) in 1957 containing useful information for travelers that included maps, road conditions, population, history, art, geography, the economy, and climate, along with suggestions for travel routes, similar to today's Michelin guides, in an octavo format based upon and in conjunction with the international travel guide publisher Baedeker. Informative and straightforward in layout (without today's glossy photographs, foldouts, or inserts for particular destinations), the Autoguide's purpose was to facilitate individual or family leisure travel, akin to the weekend travel sections in today's metropolitan newspapers.

Like the American Automobile Association (AAA) in the United States, the ACS charged an annual membership fee for its services. Fees underwrote the cost of its benefits, including the organization's publications, the installation of roadside telephones and first aid stations on highways, and lobbying efforts to improve roads and other amenities for automobile travel.

As noted above, in 1952 the ACS commissioned a public display of statistics on automobile accidents and traffic deaths in Zurich's Paradeplatz, home to the central offices of the nation's prominent banking companies. Designed by Müller-Brockmann, the "Accident Barometer" (Figure 1.2) resembled an abstract Constructivist sculpture with rectangular components intersecting at right angles with a prominent black vertical slab that displayed and updated the number of traffic accidents and deaths, as well as enlarged photographs of accidents and other statistics. Switzerland saw a rising number of automobiles on the roads after the end of World War II, resulting in increasing numbers of road accidents. Between 1947 and 1954 the number of automobiles in the country rose from 82,000 to 238,000, an increase of close to 200 percent. Not surprisingly casualties also rose steadily over the same period both at the local and national levels. In Zurich, the number of traffic accidents increased at an average rate of 9 percent between 1946 and 1955. In 1952 there was a marked increase in traffic fatalities (fifty-eight as compared with thirty-seven in 1951), although this was followed by a decline in deaths as well as injuries for 1953. At the national level statistics show less fluctuation—over the same period of time accidents increased steadily along with the number of vehicles on the road. Statistically, drivers were injured more frequently than pedestrians (or passengers): the number of accidents involving both groups rose between 1951 and 1955, with injuries to drivers rising 15.5 percent compared with 13 percent for pedestrians. The Swiss government kept highly detailed records published annually in its *Statistisches Jahrbuch der Schweiz*. Reports in the *Jahrbuch* included numbers of accidents along with their causes, ranging from drunkenness, to excessive speed, to not following road signs, as well as casualties divided by age groups. The number of children 0–14 years of age injured in traffic accidents rose at a higher rate than the general population, an increase of 30 percent between 1951 and 1955, compared with an 18 percent rise in injuries for the general population during the same period (*Statistisches Jahrbuch der Schweiz*).

While the ACS promoted public awareness of these statistics through the Accident Barometer and Müller-Brockmann's poster series that includes "schutzt das Kind!," newspapers and other print vehicles also served as routine sources of public information and awareness. The daily *Neue Zürcher Zeitung* regularly reported stories of traffic accidents and also published comparative statistics on the number of accidents several times each year. In July 1952 the newspaper noted a decline in the number of accidents for the month of May of that year compared with the previous year, but noted an alarming number of traffic deaths (seventeen, almost double) as compared with nine in the same time period for 1951. The same article reported more than 74,000 motor vehicles on the roads in Zurich as of May 1952, in comparison to 61,000 in May 1951. Indeed, among the largest and most frequent advertisements in the newspaper during this time were those for automobiles whose manufacturers were seeking to expand their markets in Switzerland (BMW, Ford, General Motors, English Rover), often including illustrations or photographs of their latest models (no Swiss company manufactured automobiles). A sign of economic growth, higher per capita incomes, and the convenience of personal mobility, increasing automobile ownership brought with it a host of safety concerns, pitting individual freedom against the public interest.

Many of the accident reports that appear in the pages of the *Neue Zürcher Zeitung* offered personalized reminders to readers of the dangers that traffic posed to drivers as well as to pedestrians. Articles identified victims by name and age, and described in some detail the circumstances surrounding mishaps, including the particular injuries sustained, even the reactions of witnesses as well as causes ranging from excessive speed, joyriding, or drunkenness, and noting collisions between automobiles, motorcycles, trolleys, pedestrians, and bicyclists. On May 26, 1952, for instance, an article reported on a child who was struck by a car near Bätterkinden, sustaining broken bones while his mother looked on, and a motorcyclist who was seriously injured when the automobile in front of him stopped suddenly at a railroad crossing resulting in a rear to front-end collision. Another typical article dated November 9, 1952 reported on a fifty-one-year-old bicyclist who died when struck by a car whose driver lost control along trolley tracks in Zurich, and on the same day thirty-eight-year-old motorcyclist died when he crashed into a traffic island, leaving behind a widow and four children. Perhaps not surprisingly, the accident report articles in the *Neue Zürcher Zeitung* mirror to some degree the general themes of Müller-Brockmann's series of posters, as the posters reinforce visually the interaction among automobiles, bicyclists, trolleys, and pedestrians that are chronicled in the daily newspaper, along with motorcycles.

In addition to daily newspapers, the Fussgänger-Schutzverband Zürich (Zurich Pedestrian Safety Organization), founded in 1932, became more proactive in the early 1950s, publishing a bi-monthly newsletter beginning late in 1952 documenting concerns on the subject of traffic safety ranging from laws governing pedestrian movement (Figure 1.12), to advocating the redesign of public spaces with clearly marked intersections to minimize risk to pedestrians, to reports on traffic issues in other cities both in Europe and in the United States and their approaches to addressing the dangers resulting from increased automobile travel.

Alarmed by the congestion resulting from an increase in the number of automobiles on city streets along with trolley traffic, contributors to the magazine noted that crowded streets and the

FIGURE 1.12 *Cover for "Der Fussgänger," no. 1, December 1952, New York Public Library*

FIGURE 1.13 *Series of traffic signs adopted for use in Switzerland, "Der Fussgänger," no. 3, June 1953, p. 13, New York Public Library*

speed of vehicular traffic were contributing to higher numbers of accidents and traffic fatalities, while focusing their attention upon the increasing danger to pedestrians. To address the problem the organization took a multi-pronged approach, lobbying local police to monitor and help direct traffic at busy intersections, advocating for laws to institute and enforce speed limits and driver responsibility on city streets, as well as strongly encouraging more disciplined foot traffic through the clear marking of crosswalks, recommending the use of sidewalks, construction of pedestrian underpasses and overpasses, and endorsing a new series of triangular street signs in 1953 with pictograms that included warnings for dangerous road conditions, markings for pedestrian crossings, and alerts to exercise caution in areas around schools and playgrounds (Figure 1.13).

The Fussgänger-Schutzerband worked closely with local government and law enforcement agencies, viewing traffic safety as a shared responsibility among drivers, pedestrians, police, and local transportation authorities. The tone of the magazine was generally informational, reproducing aerial photographs that documented both safety measures such as crossing strips and traffic lights installed near areas of heavy traffic as well as images of crowded streets with pedestrians walking amid streetcars and automobiles rather than being restricted to sidewalks. But other articles were more alarmist, highlighting the dangers that increased traffic posed to pedestrians and the severity of injuries suffered as a result of collisions.

The poster competition that produced "schutzt das Kind!" was a highly visible effort by the ACS to promote driver safety, an alliance between a private enterprise and the public that promoted automobile use on the one hand but demonstrated on the other hand responsibility for civic welfare. The ACS poster campaign might be understood as an effort not only urging drivers to exercise caution, but also as a public relations endeavor to reduce the conflict between the ACS's interest in increasing its membership and demonstrating visually the statistical connection between numbers of vehicles on the road and increasing numbers of accidents and injuries. Awareness of this ambiguity may be seen in a 1955 editorial from the *Neue Zürcher Zeitung* (November 21) written by a Zurich police commissioner. Here the author disputed the ACS's claim to be working together with police and government to reduce accident rates, pointing out that the ACS opposed speed limits of 50 km per hour (about 31 mph) on particularly busy Zurich streets along with other restrictions or regulations to help ensure pedestrian safety. In other words, there was a gap or conflict of interest between what the ACS said and *displayed*, and what the ACS *did*, a conflict resolved in part through the medium of striking graphic communication.

Posters might be seen then as a form of "grandstanding," employing emotionally charged graphic visual language to promote traffic safety in the public interest while opposing legislation that would restrict driver freedom. While the efforts of the Fussgänger-Schutzerband dovetailed with those of the ACS, the role of graphic design in the latter, in posters such as "schutzt das Kind!," aimed to jolt the viewer, casting the driver in the role of aggressor and the child as unsuspecting victim. Rather than an isolated campaign, Müller-Brockmann's "schutzt das Kind!" poster and the Paradeplatz installation were highly visible, but still only a part of a wider effort of broad public awareness involving a variety of organizations, forms of communication, and a variety of motivations and activities, including legislation, along with the lobbying of and cooperation with law enforcement. Among these forms of communication "schutzt das Kind!" was perhaps the most insistent: stern warning rather than gentle reminder, its imagery and reductive design drew the attention of motorists and created a climate of crisis and a sense of imminent rather than latent danger (it was certainly *not* a public service announcement). Urgency was only occasionally the message of the "Der Fussgänger" newsletter. In the lead article for the June 1953 edition of the magazine, entitled "Full Throttle—in Death," author

J. C. Furnas repeatedly described in gory detail the sights and sounds of deadly accident scenes, warning readers that statistics, however alarming they may be, do not communicate the shock of witnessing (or suffering) a traffic accident or the tragedy of its aftermath. He noted that some judges in the United States forced drivers responsible for accidents resulting in deaths to visit morgues to see the bodies of their victims. Strangely perhaps, this author also doubted the ability of "graphic artists" to adequately represent the grim reality of collisions, suggesting that the medium of film was better suited to communicate the horror with a combination of movement and sound. As if in response, Müller-Brockmann's and Heiniger's expert use of photography and double exposure approximates the cinematic technique of montage to heighten movement and drama.

It is not possible to verify the success or effectiveness of the ACS's Accident Barometer or Müller-Brockmann's posters in reducing traffic accidents; after all, the ACS's campaign was part of a much broader and varied effort of public awareness and activism at the time. As noted above, statistics from the city of Zurich police records show that there were fifty-eight traffic deaths in 1952, a marked increase over relatively stable numbers of deaths from 1946 to 1951 (average of 33 per year), while the number fell to thirty-five in 1953, the year in which the posters were on view. On the other hand, the number of reported accidents and accidents per 1,000 vehicles on the road in 1953 barely declined in that year, and increased in subsequent years along with personal automobile ownership. Moreover, while the posters were directed primarily toward motorists and driver safety, evidence of improved traffic safety and lower accident rates in Switzerland might also have contributed to more disciplined pedestrian behavior, safeguards, traffic regulation, and enforcement. During the second half of the 1950s, legislative initiatives rather than poster or other propaganda campaigns, began to take hold, including signage, speed limits and their enforcement on city streets, as well as new laws governing drunkenness, the use of blood-alcohol levels of drivers to determine responsibility for causing accidents, and greater attention to disciplined pedestrian traffic through painted walkways, traffic police to regulate street traffic, one-way traffic on particular streets, and the redesign of busy intersections. Ultimately the legislation of traffic and speed restrictions along with other safeguards such as police enforcement, road safety measures, accommodations for pedestrian discipline, and safety design measures in the automobile industry all contributed to reduce the level, if not the number, of traffic accidents and fatalities. While practitioners of Swiss design took their sense of professionalism and social responsibility seriously, it would be difficult to demonstrate the degree to which their efforts produced change or made a difference, except in a very general relationship to the increasing awareness that eventually led to legislative reform. In the case of "schutzt das Kind!" Müller-Brockmann stimulated awareness with an appeal to emotion that contradicts our general understanding of Swiss "objectivity" in graphic design.

A related factor in traffic safety awareness at the time of the ACS campaign was a growing public concern for the dangers of automobile racing. Often dramatized in advertising posters during the interwar and postwar periods for the excitement and exhilaration of speed and competition, Grand Prix racing in Switzerland took place at the raceway in Bremgarten near Bern beginning in 1934 (Figure 1.14).

After a horrific crash resulting in deaths and severe injuries to drivers in 1948, another in 1952 that killed one driver and injured another, and a well-publicized disaster in 1953 at the Grand Prix race in Le Mans (northwest France) in which eighty persons died, the Swiss government declared the sport unsafe. The *Neue Zürcher Zeitung* reported these incidents, and the last Grand Prix race at Bremgarten took place in 1954. A law banning the sport nationwide was passed in 1958.

FIGURE 1.14 *Kasper Ernst Graf, Grand Prix Suisse race poster, chromolithography, 120 × 90 cm, 1934, Museum for Design, Zurich*

The problem I have tried to illustrate here, and elsewhere in these chapters, is the nature, and the danger, of "generalization" in the history of graphic design. While post-World War II graphic design in Switzerland may possess a set of coherent formal characteristics and technical methods, the meaning of those forms and technical methods can be quite varied, dependent upon the motivations of the client and the broader historical context of the commission. Moreover, the deeper problem is that the construction of Swiss design or a Swiss School is based upon the suppression of a tradition of pictorial graphic design with deep roots in the history of twentieth-century graphic design in Switzerland and the selective approach of designers, authors, and promoters who claimed an elusive and not always accurate or consistent concept of "objectivity" for Swiss design. Awareness of this selective construct and the false dualism it implied, as well as an investigation of the particular circumstances of the ACS campaign for traffic safety, informs our broader understanding and appreciation of Müller-Brockmann's "schutzt das Kind!," its meaning, and its impact.

As in post-World War II graphic design elsewhere in Europe and in the United States, the emerging profession was grounded in an unspoken partnership with both business and government—as the clients of graphic designers are not only presented as acting in the public interest, but the relationship between the profession and client places graphic designers in the role of custodian of the public trust. The role of graphic designers was to strengthen that relationship and to restore faith in it, to bolster it, through communicating a sense of responsibility in advertising and in support for social welfare. While "objectivity" might apply to advertising, it certainly does *not* apply to "schutzt das Kind!" Here, photomontage and exaggeration serve more overtly persuasive purposes—the hand of the designer is heavy, hidden to an extent behind the medium of photography-as-fact. Moreover, the role of the ACS is a complicated one: Müller-Brockmann's efforts on behalf of the organization in "schutzt das Kind!" promoted the organization's public image of social responsibility, while the ACS was not particularly pro-active at the time in backing legislation to impose speed limits and other safety restrictions upon drivers.

Coda: Designers and Designer's Writings

Müller-Brockmann's opinions on graphic design are well documented in his own writings about the field, including his 1994 autobiography. Few designers have played such a strong role in creating their own legacy, but Müller-Brockmann's many statements, arguments, and aphorisms are hardly without their contradictions, specifically in his use of the terms "objective" and "fact" to blur distinctions between technique and expression, and *create* some confusion between particular and general, and between information and persuasion. One is reminded of Adrien Forty's observations (in *Objects of Desire*, 1986) on the role of autobiography as evidence in constructing the history of design:

> there seems no particular reason why the often obscure and long-winded statements made by architects and designers should provide a complete or even adequate account of the buildings or artefacts they design. If political economy consisted only of the study of the economy in the light of the statements made by politicians, the subject would indeed do little to increase our understanding of the world. Clearly, it would be foolish to dismiss designers' statements altogether, but we should not expect them to reveal all there is to know about design. After all, they themselves are not the cause of design having become such an important activity in modern society, and we should not assume that they hold any superior knowledge about the reasons for its importance. (Forty, 1986)

The decisions designers make about their own work can be illuminating from the standpoint of understanding the creative process and the motivations behind design choices. But they do not exhaust, and sometimes do not even touch upon, the specific circumstances of production, reception, and mediation that communicate meaning in graphic design. "Schutzt das Kind!" reveals a complex rather than reductive understanding of "Swiss Style," one that departs from its canonical interpretation and reminds us of the dangers of perhaps too readily invoking terms such as "objective" in the study of graphic design history. It is perhaps to the style's credit that its means were flexible enough in the early 1950s to meet the demands of welfare propaganda and public safety as well as corporate communication, but it seems important *not* to associate its ethics with a single or even consistent approach to design.

Chapter 2

Koloman Moser's Thirteenth Secession Exhibition Poster (1902): Anatomy of a Work of Viennese Graphic Design

Preface

In 1988, Italian artist-designer Ettore Sottsass (1917–2007) exhibited his "Yellow Furniture," an homage to early twentieth-century Viennese design (Figure 2.1 and color plate section). The gilt veneered rectangular cabinet, almost five feet tall, featured identical rectangular drawers with large circular pullers, interrupted by a symmetrical shelf to each side that rests upon two wider drawers.

Sottsass's attraction to early twentieth-century Vienna was both aesthetic and personal: the designer's father was trained by Viennese architect Otto Wagner (1841–1918), and the younger Sottsass was attracted to the city's distinctive early modern design heritage. When displayed prominently at the entrance to an exhibition of Sottsass's work in 2017 at the Met Breuer Museum in New York ("Ettore Sottsass: Design Radical," July 21—October 8, 2017), the cabinet stood beside a photograph of Wagner's Steinhof Church (completed 1907) in Vienna. The prominent Viennese-based architects Josef Hoffmann (1870–1956) and Joseph Maria Olbrich (1867–1908) were among Wagner's more celebrated students; together with painter Gustav Klimt (1861–1918) and designer Koloman Moser (1868–1918; Moser designed the stained-glass windows for Wagner's Steinhof Church), and all were active members of an organization of progressive Viennese artists known as the Vienna Secession (Vereinigung der bildender Künstler Österreichs Secession) founded in the spring of 1897. The Secession staged exhibitions of its members' work (as well as the work of contemporary artists from abroad) that was underrepresented in the more conservative exhibitions of the Künstlerhaus, the association that exhibited the work and promoted the interests of living artists in Vienna. In addition to its steady diet of exhibitions, the Vienna Secession published a well-illustrated journal titled *Ver Sacrum* ("Sacred Spring"), issued monthly 1898–9 and twice a month beginning in 1900, though in smaller format. The aims, excitement, and optimism of the Secession members and their literary supporters for artistic renewal in Vienna may be gauged from an article in the

FIGURE 2.1 (and color plate) *Ettore Sottsass, "Yellow Cabinet," (Mobile Giallo), Burled maple, briar, ebonized oak veneer, gilded wood knobs, 57 ½ × 51 7/8 × 18 1/8 in., 1988–9, Bridgeman, Artists Rights Society*

journal's very first issue, penned by Max Burckhard, director of the Vienna Burgtheatre: "The spirit of youth that infuses the spring has brought the withdrawing group of artists together (i.e., the Secession); the spirit of youth that always turns the present into the 'modern,' that is, the driving force behind artistic creation; let it also give its name to these pages in the form of *Ver Sacrum*."

While the geometric precision and repeated circular shapes that characterize Sottsass's Yellow Cabinet may oversimplify the range of work produced by Secession artists and designers, circle and square have nevertheless come to connote a recognizably "Viennese" style of design around the year 1900, seen, for instance, in the interiors of Josef Hoffmann's Purkersdorf Sanitarium (1904–5) or in the guest room of the home Hoffmann designed for (and with) fellow Secessionist Koloman Moser in 1902 (Figure 2.2).

Circle and square also appear frequently in much of the work of other Secession members in various media for the Wiener Werkstätte (Vienna Workshops), a spin-off from the Secession founded in 1903 by Hoffmann and Moser to design and manufacture modern and original home furnishings and interior design, with financial backing from wealthy textile mill owner Fritz Waerndorfer.

FIGURE 2.2 *Josef Hoffmann and Koloman Moser, Guest Room of Moser's House, Vienna, 1902, Gustav Klimt installation view at Tate Liverpool 2008. Photo © Tate, London 2019*

Koloman Moser's poster for the Thirteenth Secession Exhibition (1902) is often reproduced in survey texts as an exemplar of this early twentieth-century modern Viennese design in the *graphic* arts, though, as I hope to demonstrate, it is in many ways an odd, even misleading choice when considered in relation to the development of graphic design more generally for the Secession and to the history of the advertising poster (Figure 2.3 and color plate section). It is this context that I hope to explore more fully in this chapter.

The Thirteenth Secession Exhibition Poster

Between its founding in the spring of 1897 and the autumn of 1902, the Vienna Secession mounted fifteen exhibitions (on average three per year), and regularly printed and circulated posters designed by Secession members as a form of promotion (as well as printed catalogs and post-card announcements). The exhibitions were also promoted through articles and illustrations in the Secession's journal *Ver Sacrum*, and announcements and reviews appeared regularly in Vienna's many daily and weekly newspapers, as well as through press coverage in cities in other parts of the Austro-Hungarian Empire and elsewhere in Europe. Moser's slender poster for the organization's thirteenth exhibition, held from January to mid-March 1902, measures 69 × 23 inches, printed on two attached (widthwise) sheets of paper in three colors, with areas of blue and black against a muted red background. The reproduction process is chromolithography, patented in France by Godefroy Engelmann in 1837 for color printing, requiring separate lithographic stones and careful registration for the printing of each color. The chromolithographic process was responsible for the flowering of large-scale color advertising posters beginning in the later 1850s.

FIGURE 2.3 (and color plate) *Moser, Koloman (Kolo) (1868–1918). Ver Sacrum, XIII, poster for the 13th Secession exhibition. 1902. Lithograph, 73 3/16 × 25 3/16 in. (185.9 × 64 cm). Printer: Lith. Anst. A. Berger, Wien. Gift of Joseph H. Heil, by exchange. The Museum of Modern Art Digital Image © The Museum of Modern Art/Licensed by SCALA/Art Resource, NY*

The poster's composition is strikingly geometric, consisting of repeated precisely drawn square, rectangular, and circular shapes that create a highly unified, and very austere, controlled design. The surface is essentially a grid divided vertically into twelve parallel and equal rectangular units. The vertical grid determines the widths of the elements of the surface design, from the white circle at the top (ten units) that intersects with the circles behind the busts of the heads (six units) of three female figures, to their shoulders (each one unit) and torsos (two units).

Horizontal bands intersect with the vertical divisions to create a system of squares in the poster's lower portion, some decorated with a checkerboard pattern, others entirely in blue, or divided and then subdivided into small triangular shapes. The grid mostly controls the height of letter forms, but letters vary considerably in width across bands and do not conform to the system of patterned square units. Overall, the letters for the words VER SACRUM ("Sacred Spring,") V JAHR (fifth year of publication for the journal) and SECESSION are more widely spaced than the other text and can be read most clearly (though clarity doesn't seem to be Moser's overriding concern; see pp. 49–50). In terms of color, a dark reddish-brown is used for the background, for some of the letters, for the outline of triangles within the three teardrop shapes that adorn the three female figures' torsos, and with a spattered effect (crachis) for the bodies of those figures; blue, along with a lighter spattered blue fills in the circles above the heads of the three female busts toward the top, and the more saturated blue fills the blue squares, checkerboards, and triangles inscribed in the poster's lower portion. In addition to the pale white of the paper in several horizontal bands and again in the shoulders and arms of the three female figures, a soft reddish-tan color, also produced by spattering of both red *and* blue, provides the background of those figures' torsos, with small areas of black used for their wing-like hair. A. Berger, a Leipzig-born printer who opened a printing shop in Vienna in 1887, printed the Thirteenth Secession Exhibition poster and served as the organization's "house printer" for several of its exhibition posters. Berger also printed illustrated books of student and faculty designs for the School of Applied Arts in Vienna (Kunstgewerbeschule) where Moser was appointed professor of decorative painting in 1899 and where other Secession members also served as faculty.

An Icon of Modern Graphic Design?

Moser's Thirteenth Secession Exhibition poster has become a standard, recognized part of the graphic design history canon and by extension a prominent icon in the history of the advertising poster; it is found in the collections of major museums in Europe and the United States and has been reproduced in virtually every available survey text in the field since the early 1980s (including Josef Müller-Brockmann and Shizuko Müller-Brockmann's 1971 *History of the Poster*), whose authors note the contrast between its severe geometry and restrained decorative vocabulary and the more fluid, expressive style of the contemporary Jugendstil in Germany or practiced earlier in France as L'art nouveau; it also marks a shift in Moser's own graphic output, for instance, in comparison with the designer's earlier and more sinuous graphic work, including a poster for the Secession's fifth exhibition (1899; Figure 2.4 and color plate section) or his cover for the second issue of the Secession's journal *Ver Sacrum* (1898; Figure 2.5—the design "wraps around" to include the spine and the issue's back cover) and numerous drawings, decorative borders, and other embellishments printed in *Ver Sacrum* and other publications.

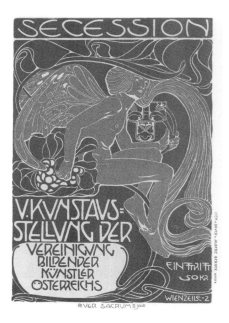

FIGURE 2.4 (and color plate) *Koloman Moser, Fifth Secession Exhibition Poster, 98.4 × 66.7 cm, chromolithography,1899, MAK–Österreichisches Museum für angewandte Kunst/Gegenwartskunst*

FIGURE 2.5 *Koloman Moser, cover illustration, Ver Sacrum, Jahr I, February, 1898, Courtesy of Marquand Library of Art and Archaeology, Princeton University*

As to the place the poster occupies generally within graphic design history, Meggs/Purvis write:

Moser's poster for the Thirteenth Vienna Secession exhibition is a masterpiece of the mature phase. When Vienna Secession artists rejected the French floral style, they turned toward flat shapes and greater simplicity. Design and craft became increasingly important as this metamorphosis culminated in an emphasis on geometric patterning and modular design construction. The resulting design language used squares, rectangles, and circles in repetition and combination. Decoration and the application of ornament depended on similar elements used in parallel, nonrhythmic sequence. This geometry was not mechanical or rigid but subtly organic. (Meggs/Purvis, 2016)

Terms such as "metamorphosis" suggest an internal process of graphic simplification and abstraction traced from the later nineteenth to the early twentieth century across several media including architecture as well as painting, graphic design, and interior design, but the Meggs/Purvis narrative doesn't offer a motivation behind the change or consider local context as an explanation. Instead, they and other writers point to comparisons between the "flat shapes and greater simplicity" of Moser's poster and the oeuvre of architect and designer Charles Rennie Mackintosh (1868–1928) and a small group of Scottish artists associated with the Glasgow School of Art including Mackintosh's wife Margaret MacDonald, Herbert McNair, and Frances MacDonald. Indeed, Secession members admired this group of Scottish artists and designers; Mackintosh contributed a furnished interior at the Eighth Secession exhibition held in November and December 1900 (Figure 2.6) and was invited to Vienna to prepare for the show. While there he was commissioned to design a music room for the home of Fritz Waerndorfer that was completed in 1902.

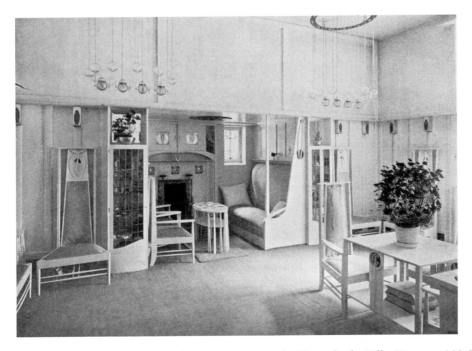

FIGURE 2.6 *Charles Rennie Mackintosh, Music Room at the Waerndorfer Villa, Vienna, 1902,* The Studio, *57, 1912, p. 72, Courtesy of Marquand Library of Art and Archaeology, Princeton University. Photographer: John Blazejewski*

The austerity of the music room interior, the emphasis upon the empty areas (negative spaces) of wall and interior floor space, the repeated rectilinear rhythms and restrained abstract decoration, all demonstrate visual similarities with the contemporary work of both Moser and Josef Hoffmann, and it's clear from *Ver Sacrum* and the works selected for display at Secession exhibitions that the artists affiliated with the Secession looked beyond Austria as validation of and inspiration for their own efforts to create a "modern," original art and design (see p. 59).

But to say that something looks like something else doesn't explain *why* something looks the way it does. And so such comparisons and similarities, against a general background of a shared desire for renewal and originality, remain vague, offering scant explanation for Moser's decision to employ abstract, geometric shapes and a severely controlled composition for his Thirteenth Secession exhibition poster; writers also tend to ignore the choice of an exhibition poster to illustrate this new approach to design. Indeed, from the standpoint of advertising, Moser's poster violates virtually every tenet of what contemporary critics felt constituted a successful approach to the chromolithographic poster as a new and persuasive form of promotion—namely to arrest the attention of the pedestrian viewer ("the man in the street") from a distance with "audacious color and broad execution," to project a mood of gaiety, and to "sell" something; as critic Charles Hiatt commented in the periodical *The Studio* as early as 1893, "the advertisement that doesn't advertise is a contradiction in terms" (Hiatt, 1893; see also pp. 64–6). Considering the poster in relation to advertising, one has to wonder precisely *what* Moser's poster is promoting. Is it the Thirteenth Exhibition? The Secession? The *Ver Sacrum* journal? Koloman Moser? More importantly perhaps, why should we have to guess? I believe that these basic questions have not been asked, and that their answers lie in a more detailed consideration of the poster's design, its iconography, the exhibition building itself, the interior design of the Thirteenth Exhibition's display rooms (for which Moser was responsible), and the role of posters within the broader activities of the Secession and within Viennese culture and society.

Moser, Book Arts, and *Ver Sacrum*

Although Moser trained as a painter at the Vienna Academy of Fine Arts, his father's death in 1888 forced him to turn from academic painting to commercial illustration in order to earn a living. As an illustrator he contributed sketches to Austrian as well as German publications, including the fashion magazine *Wiener Mode* and a witty weekly illustrated satirical newspaper entitled *Meggendorfers Humoristisches Blätter* published in Munich. Moser's popular illustrations featured fashionably dressed men and women in parlor and other social settings engaged in conversation or other middle-class leisure pastimes (Witt-Dörring, 2013), as seen in a cover illustration from the magazine in 1896 (Figure 2.7).

Many of these same characteristics, including the artist's focus upon the human (mostly female) figure are also found in Moser's colorful advertising posters, for the newspaper *Illustrierte Zeitung* as well as for "Richardsquelle" mineral water (printed in reduced size as black and white line drawings for quarter-page ads in *Ver Sacrum*; Figures 2.8 and 2.9 – see also color plate section).

In both examples a young woman dominates the space of the compositions and commands the viewer's attention from a distance, generally with little distraction from competing elements such as the rampant, even wild decorative elements (such as the figure's hair and the lozenge shapes that surround their bodies) found in Moser's fifth Secession exhibition

FIGURE 2.7 *Koloman Moser, cover for* Meggendorfers Humoristisches Blätter, *vol. XXVII, no. 12, 1896, MAK– Österreichisches Museum für angewandte Kunst/Gegenwartskunst*

FIGURE 2.8 *Koloman Moser, "Illustrierte Zeitung," advertising poster, c. 1897, chromolithograph, 94.6 × 110.23 cm, MAK–Österreichisches Museum für angewandte Kunst/Gegenwartskunst*

FIGURE 2.9 (and color plate) *Kolomon Moser, "Richardsquelle" Mineral Water advertising poster, c. 1897, chromolithograph, 56.8 × 68.58 cm, Albertina Museum, Vienna*

or the 1898 *Ver Sacrum* cover (see Figures 2.4 and 2.5). For instance, a diagonal movement dominates the advertising poster for the *Wiener Illustrierte Zeitung*, moving from upper left to lower right, and embellished with subdued decorative patterns both on the clothing of the reading figure as well as suggesting patterns for wallpaper of a study or dressing room. A clear hierarchy prevails, beginning in importance with the casually reclining reader, moving to the left with the tagline "Lesen Sie" (Read!), and then to the title of the newspaper, price, availability, and decorative elements. In the "Richardsquelle" poster, the water-sprite's orange hair is strewn with flowers and seashells, as she swims effortlessly against a background of deep blue sprinkled with lighter blue and violet floating bubbles from the upper right of an asymmetrical horizontal composition. Her arms lead the eye toward the right and frame the product's brand name of in off-white, while the remaining texts are paler in tone and less prominent. The arrangement of information again emphasizes the dominant female figure and product name, moving diagonally from upper left to lower right, balanced by ancillary text, stimulating eye movement further echoed in the free placement of the floating bubbles. Both compositions reduce or de-emphasize detail and are unified in terms of color, following the successful format for the chromolithographic advertising poster as practiced by Jules Chéret in Paris and emulated throughout Europe in the later nineteenth century. This Art Nouveau/ Jugendstil poster formula also appears in Carl Müller's 1903 watercolor and chalk study of a street in Vienna (Figure 2.10 and color plate section), where an advertising poster designed by Italian artist Giulio Angelo Liberali for the shoe manufacturer Paprika Schlesinger features a fashionably dressed woman in bold yellow against a blue background and stands out in the center of Müller's composition.

Also in the 1890s, Moser followed in the footsteps of fellow Viennese artists Franz Matsch and Max Klinger who had provided illustrations for two lavishly printed books titled *Allegorien und Embleme*, replete with personifications of familiar subjects, akin to today's "clip art," including representations of the seasons, the arts, sciences, and trades, for use in print and other media for promotion and identity, published by the Viennese publishing firm of Gerlach & Schenk in 1882–5 (Figure 2.11). *Allegorien und Embleme*'s illustrations were fairly traditional, with naturalistically and idealistically rendered figures based upon Renaissance compositions and decorative motifs.

Moser's contribution of several sketches to a third volume of Gerlach's series (titled *Neue Folge*, 1895) were more graphic, with broader areas of flat, contrasting color, an integration of figural and decorative elements, and simplified, linear drawing, as seen in Figure 2.12.

FIGURE 2.10 (and color plate) *Carl Müller, "Street in Vienna", 1903, 27.3 × 37.7 cm, watercolor and chalk, Vienna Museum. Karlsplatz, Bridgeman*

FIGURE 2.11 *Gerlach, Martin, ed., Title page*, Allegorien und Embleme, *Vienna 1882, New York Public Library*

FIGURE 2.12 *Koloman Moser, "Spring," plate from Gerlach, Martin, ed.*, Allegorien und Embleme. Neue Folge, *Vienna, Gerlach & Shenk, 1895, MAK–Österreichisches Museum für angewandte Kunst/Gegenwartskunst (also reproduced in Gerlach, Martin, ed.,* Allegorien: Wein, Tanz, Liebe, Musik, Gesang., Serie 1, *Vienna, Gerlach & Schenk, 1896)*

In contrast to his advertisements and illustrations for *Allegorien und Embleme* and *Neue Folge*, Moser's poster for the Thirteenth Secession exhibition eschews the monumental figures, fluid drawing, spontaneity, and asymmetrical compositions of those efforts in favor of strict symmetry and a composition tightly controlled by a horizontal and vertical grid. The new approach appears to have much more in common with publication design than with poster advertising (or easel painting); and indeed, the Thirteenth Secession Exhibition image was reproduced twice in color as the title page and again on an interior page for the sixth issue of *Ver Sacrum* in 1902 (Figure 2.13), centered with ample margins, timed to coincide with the opening of the exhibition and followed by reproductions of works on view, along with photographs of the exhibition rooms Moser designed and accompanied by a descriptive essay (see p. 60).

The difference in scale is significant: posters are meant to be seen by pedestrians on the street while magazine illustrations are read close at hand—Moser's detailed and disciplined approach to design in the poster and *Ver Sacrum* illustration undermines the advertising poster's appeal to immediacy and its function to inform and persuade. The contradiction was not lost on journalists and critics at the time of the exhibition, who were bewildered by Secession designers' abandonment of the poster's basic "duty" to inform its audience, and commented that Moser's originality and refinement produced effects that were both "bizarre and eccentric" (Mascha 1915, see also p. 65).The failure of modern-day authors to acknowledge the commercial function of

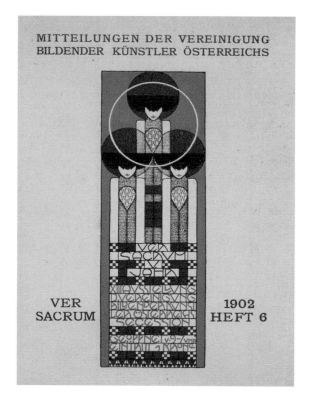

FIGURE 2.13 (and color plate) *Koloman Moser, title page,* Ver Sacrum, *Jahr V, no. 6, 1902, Courtesy of Library of Art and Archaeology, Princeton University. Photographer: John Blazejewski*

advertising in their treatments of the poster blurs differences between art and design that relate directly to the meaning of Moser's Thirteenth Secession Exhibition poster.

The connection between the Thirteenth Secession Exhibition poster and publication design rather than advertising finds support not only in the image's inclusion (twice!) as an illustration in the same issue of *Ver Sacrum* but also in relation to Moser's activities as graphic designer and art director for the journal that included the emblem he designed for the organization (Figure 2.14), cover images, illustrations, and decorative borders, patterns, headpieces, initials, tailpieces, and numerous inventive graphic accompaniments to poems, plays, and even musical scores.

While *Ver Sacrum* documented its series of exhibitions with half-tone photographic reproduction of paintings and sculptures on display and the gallery interiors (designed by Secession members, including Moser, as well as Josef Hoffmann and Alfred Roller), the journal also included original woodcut and chromolithographic prints by Secession artists and was in effect a showcase for original work in a variety of print media included as a respected branch of artistic practice. The Secession sponsored an "International Exhibition of Graphic Art" in 1900, featured in *Ver Sacrum*'s February issue of that year. These activities dovetailed with Moser's appointment to the faculty of the Vienna School of Applied Arts, first as instructor in 1898 and then as professor of decorative painting beginning in 1899 where he taught classes in design

FIGURE 2.14 *Koloman Moser, emblem for* Ver Sacrum, *Jahr I, January, 1898, Courtesy of Marquand Library of Art and Archaeology, Princeton University. Photographer: John Blazejewski*

FIGURE 2.15 *Jutta Sika and Franz Burian, print designs from* Die Fläche, *Vienna, A. Berger, 1901, MAK–Österreichisches Museum für angewandte Kunst/Gegenwartskunst*

for publication, wallpaper, fresco, and textiles. The school served two purposes for Moser, providing opportunities for him, for his colleagues (Josef Hoffmann and Alfred Roller) and for his students to publish their original patterns and illustrations as pattern books in a series of handsome volumes titled *Die Fläche* (The Surface) and *Die Quelle* (The Source), and second, to demonstrate and reinforce the unity and close relationship among the various branches of design including interior design, graphic design, painting, decorative painting, and typography (Figure 2.15). In addition to encouraging individual creativity and originality among students and faculty alike, the School of Applied Arts' publications promoted the commercial potential of modern pattern design for the manufacture of wallpapers and textiles in Vienna and beyond.

Squares and Circles

The abstract square and circular motifs that appear in the Thirteenth Secession Exhibition poster occur earlier in several of Moser's page designs in *Ver Sacrum*, beginning in 1901. The title page to issue no. 2 of the journal in that year (Figure 2.16), repeated as a tailpiece that brackets an article on the Secession's eighth exhibition featuring the work of Belgian sculptor George Minne (1866–1941) as well as Mackintosh's interior, employs an abstract design constructed from a simple repeated vocabulary of hand-drawn square shapes and closely placed comb-like parallel lines.

A modern, original form of page decoration (part of a tradition in book printing sometimes referred to as "printers flowers" and used for frames and borders), Moser's design is a reductive interpretation of a flowering tree, treated in purely graphic terms on the page. The blossoming tree, in a variety of forms, was a frequent, even dominant symbol for the Vienna Secession. Alfred Roller's cover for the very first issue of *Ver Sacrum* illustrates a tree whose roots are breaking the planks of its barrel container (Figure 2.17), and the same issue includes a vignette by Moser labeled "book decoration" that appeared at the conclusion of an introductory essay by Max Burckhard and illustrates a nude female figure whose raised arms turn into the branches of a tree (Figure 2.18).

Variations on the image of a verdant tree, often morphing from the outstretched arms of a female figure, occur throughout Moser's page layouts for *Ver Sacrum*, including a design for a book cover in February 1898 (Figure 2.19), where the figure's arms suggest either branches of a tree or the wings of a butterfly.

Several graphic variations on this theme by Secession artist Wilhelm List (1864–1918) appear in 1900 (issue 6) with bundled vines in the center of the page branching out into bud-like leaves toward the top (Figure 2.20) accompanying an article entitled "Masks."

Both trees and variations on a budding female figure (whether suggested by hair or branch-like arms) may be interpreted as images of fertility in keeping with the journal's title "Sacred Spring" (they also bring to mind the Greek myth of the nymph Daphne who escaped the advances of Apollo by being transformed into a tree). The substitution of patterns of abstract lines and squares beginning in 1901 for representational or freely rendered imagery indicates Moser's respect for the letterpress process, that is, for the flatness of the printed page and discipline the type forme imposed upon the designer. Within such practice-based restrictions the modern designer was free to construct arrangements of simple shapes that respected the rectangular shape of the page but also permitted invention and variety. A final example further demonstrates Moser's interest in the grid and use of repeated square patterns as a rhythmic graphic accompaniment to text: it is a short

FIGURE 2.16 *Koloman Moser, title page with abstract flowering tree for* Ver Sacrum, *Jahr IV, 1901, no. 2, Courtesy of Marquand Library of Art and Archaeology, Princeton University. Photographer: John Blazejewski*

FIGURE 2.17 *Alfred Roller, cover of* Ver Sacrum, *Jahr I,1898, January, Courtesy of Marquand Library of Art and Archaeology, Princeton University. Photographer: John Blazejewski*

FIGURE 2.18 *Koloman Moser, illustration, ornament,* Ver Sacrum, *Jahr I, 1898, January, Courtesy of Marquand Library of Art and Archaeology, Princeton University. Photographer: John Blazejewski*

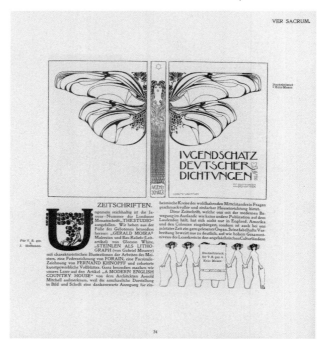

FIGURE 2.19 *Koloman Moser, design for a book cover with binding, from* Ver Sacrum, *Jahr 1, 1898, February, Courtesy of Marquand Library of Art and Archaeology, Princeton University*

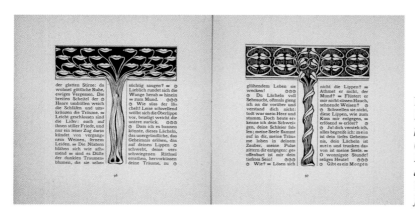

FIGURE 2.20 *Wilhelm List, book decoration from* Ver Sacrum, *Jahr IV (1900), no. 6, Courtesy of Marquand Library of Art and Archaeology, Princeton University. Photographer: John Blazejewski*

play by German poet and playwright Arno Holz (1863–1929) entitled "The Tinsmith" ("Der Blechschmied") printed in *Ver Sacrum* in 1901 (issue 18, cover and 297ff; Figure 2.21).

The Holz layouts are entirely in black against the white page. Square shapes dominate Moser's page designs beginning in 1901, but he did not abandon a simple hand-drawn spiral as a decorative accompaniment to the printed page: they continue to appear, for instance, in 1901 (issue no. 4, Figure 2.22) in a series of regular delicate patterns, again aligned with the tradition of book printing.

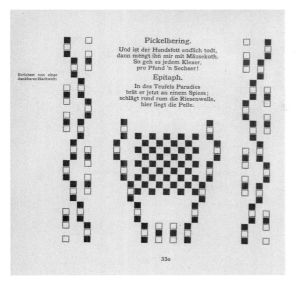

FIGURE 2.21 *Koloman Moser, graphic accompaniment to Arno Holz, "Die Blechschmiede,"* Ver Sacrum, *Jahr IV, 1901, no. 18, Courtesy of Marquand Library of Art and Archaeology, Princeton University. Photographer: John Blazejewski*

FIGURE 2.22 *Koloman Moser, Title page,* Ver Sacrum, *Jahr IV, 1901, no. 4, Courtesy of Marquand Library of Art and Archaeology, Princeton University. Photographer: John Blazejewski*

It is his work in print for *Ver Sacrum* that aligns most closely with Moser's poster for the Thirteenth Secession Exhibition; reproduced as a poster in a larger scale the image appears almost like an afterthought that addresses neither the demands of advertising nor basic concerns with legibility that are treated directly below. Its frequent reproduction in surveys and other books on the history of graphic design obscures its appearance at the same time on a scale suited to private reading rather than casual pedestrian viewing.

Letters

Discussions of Moser's Thirteenth Secession Exhibition poster regularly note the overall unity of the design, not only through color and the organizing grid structure, but also in its integration of lettering with image, where the thin, ribbon-like strokes of the letter forms match the color scheme of muted reds and blues and harmonize with the regular circular and rectilinear shapes found throughout the design.

But few descriptions of the poster in introductory books discuss (or criticize) Moser's very curious letter forms (see Figure 2.3). The exclusively upper case letters are indeed quite odd, constructed from strokes of a single width (or weight) rather than with variations between thick and thin strokes as in more traditional calligraphy for the letters of the Roman alphabet, employing awkward spacing between several of the words, and introducing rather bizarre letter forms themselves, which may be highly original but are also quite difficult to read from close at hand and especially frustrating to discern from a distance.

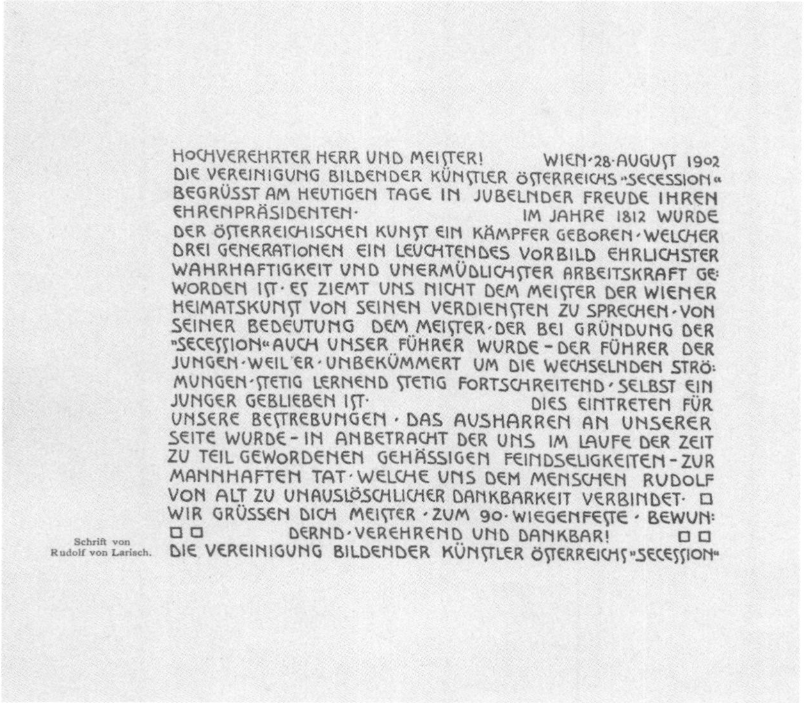

FIGURE 2.23 *Rudolf Larisch, Lettering, in* Ver Sacrum, *1902, no. 16, Courtesy of Marquand Library of Art and Archaeology, Princeton University. Photographer: John Blazejewski*

Before describing the lettering further it's best to translate them into a more legible body text:

VER
SACRUM
V
JAHR
XIII AUSTELLUNG
D [ie] VEREINIGUNG
BILDENDER KUNST [-]
LER ÖSTERREICHS
SECESSION
GEOFFNET V. 9–7 V[U]HR
EINTRITT 7 KRONE
(Sacred Spring, 5th year, Thirteenth Exhibition of the Association of Visual Artists of the
Austrian Secession, Open 9–7, Entrance 7 Kroner)

The announcement of the exhibition itself *follows* rather than precedes the title of the group's journal *Ver Sacrum* ("Sacred Spring"), which was in its fifth year of publication (1898–1903). The result is an inverted hierarchy of information that foregrounds the journal ("Ver Sacrum

V JAHR") at the expense of the exhibition itself ("XIII AUSTELLUNG D[IE] BILDENDER KUNST"). Together with the organization's series of exhibitions and Joseph Maria Olbrich's Secession building that opened in November 1898, *Ver Sacrum* was the Secession's most visible means of disseminating the work of its members and promoting the cause of modern art and design in Austria, and the words also appeared in gold on the left front wall of the Secession building. The journal was well illustrated with half-tone photographic reproductions of works of art by Secession members and artists from abroad, as well as prints in the media of woodcut, engraving, and chromolithography, along with essays, poems, and short plays by the leading literary figures of the time.

Most letter forms in the Roman alphabet balance the designers' interest in making clear distinctions among letters for recognition with the use of similar strokes for rhythm in reading, between efficiency in writing (or cutting letter forms for printing fonts) and the needs of readers to easily distinguish one letter from another. While one might argue that Moser's lettering in the Thirteenth Secession Exhibition poster and illustration employ a consistent line weight and small number of repeated shapes, the results are eccentric and often puzzling. In particular, "A"s resemble "R"s, so closely as to produce confusion for the reader; the "K" tends to resemble an "N," and while all letter forms are in the upper case, Moser makes several of them smaller than others, or elevated rather than resting on the base line. Umlaut accents are placed atop, below, or even inside of the vowels (a, e, o, u), and Moser opts for square periods rather than round ones. While a journal reader might find time to enjoy the Moser's clever and playful deviations from traditional Roman letter forms, a pedestrian would easily become either frustrated or merely indifferent looking for information to facilitate a visit to the exhibition.

Courses in lettering and typography were among those offered at the Vienna School of Applied Arts where Moser was professor of decorative painting. Although Moser's training was in painting and later in illustration, he took a strong interest in letter forms, stemming from an embrace of all areas of art and design as inherently creative and united as vehicles for individual expression and in their relationship to one another, aimed at realizing the goal of the "total work of art" (see p. 60) and shared by fellow Secessionists.

Lettering was the lifelong passion of Rudolf von Larisch (1856–1934), who taught courses in lettering and typography at the School of Applied Art and maintained close contact with the artists of the Vienna Secession. Larisch's courses were an integral component of design education at the school, and he published examples of his own work as well as that of other students and faculty, including Moser, in a series of books on the subject of decorative and artistic lettering, including *Über Zierschriften als Dienste* (Decorative Writing as Service, 1899), and *Unterricht der künstlerischen Schrift* (The Study of Artistic Lettering, 1905). At the School of Applied Art, Moser as well as Alfred Roller shared Larisch's interest in the unity of the arts and in lettering as a form of individual expression. Larisch encouraged his students to treat lettering as a serious art form, and there are several elements of Moser's lettering that demonstrate a connection to Larisch's teaching and writing. Larisch favored monoweight (monoline) strokes for letter forms to create clear contrast between figure and ground, rhythms among straight and curved letter forms, and harmony between letter forms and drawing to emphasize surface planarity. He believed that legibility was a relative term, and while he could be critical of letter forms that were difficult to read, he also questioned rules and practices that hindered experimentation and creative expression (Thomas, 2015). Turning again to Moser's Thirteenth Secession Exhibition poster, the similarity among curved (C, O, E, G, A, D) straight (T, I, N, R), and diagonal lines (V, crossbars of A and E, X) create rhythms that enable the eye to perceive "word pictures." Larisch also recommended that the horizontal crossbars of letters be placed either above or below their mid-point, and that varying the height of letters (as Moser does with the letter "D") facilitates rhythmic flow. Another aspect of Larisch's teaching concerned the "optical" rather than measured or standardized spacing between letters. Here again the issue was legibility: Larisch argued that attention to spacing encouraged students to be aware of negative space, to think of letters as "islands in the sea" rather than as "soldiers in a row," thus encouraging experimentation (Lee, 2015). While the lettering in Moser's Thirteenth Secession Exhibition poster creates confusion both in the design of the letter forms themselves and in their spacing (or lack thereof, more so in the poster version rather than the version published in *Ver Sacrum*), their relationship to Larisch's preference for monoweight strokes, his interest in rhythm, unity, and figure-ground contrast all suggest he was the source for Moser's practice of letter forms in the Thirteenth Secession Exhibition print and poster. An example of Larisch's lettering was reproduced in *Ver Sacrum* in 1902 (Figure 2.23).

For body text, Larisch admired the first printers of Roman letter forms in Venice in the later fifteenth century such as Nicholas Jenson (also praised, and collected, by artists and printers in the Arts and Crafts movement in England such as William Morris).

Moser's experimentation with artistic letter forms is found throughout the layouts in *Ver Sacrum* in his design of decorated initials, culminating in a series of distinctive artist monograms in woodcut on display at the Secession's fourteenth exhibition (1902), all based upon the square, and reproduced in the exhibition catalog (Figure 2.24). Here too Larisch's insistence upon equal attention to negative space, invention, and contrast may be felt, and as Jeremy Aynsley noted, Larisch also claimed that lettering played an important role in creating distinctive, unified trademarks or graphic identities for businesses (Aynsley, 2013).

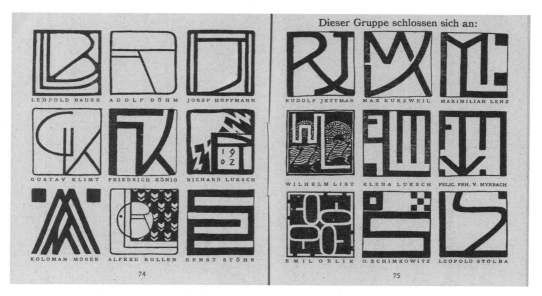

FIGURE 2.24 *Koloman Moser and other Secession artists, artist monograms, exhibited at the XIVth Secession Exhibition, 1902, MAK–Österreichisches Museum für angewandte Kunst/Gegenwartskunst*

Iconography: Symbols—Myth and Nature

From the outset, the activities of Secession artists were steeped in idealism and optimism for the renewal of the visual arts in Vienna, replete with mottos, aphorisms, and a pervasive visual symbolism. The group's first president was the painter Gustav Klimt (1862–1918). Klimt worked with his brother Ernst (1864–92) and fellow painter Franz Matsch (1861–1942) on an important commission for a series of wall and ceiling frescoes for the foyer and staircase of Vienna's Kunsthistorisches Museum (completed 1891), but his later public commissions proved controversial, most notably a series of three paintings ("Philosophy," "Medicine," "Jurisprudence" 1899–1907, destroyed near the end of World War II) for the University of Vienna that were rejected by the faculty while ardently defended as a statement of modern artistic freedom by critics committed to the cause of the Secession. "Medicine" was on display at the Tenth Secession Exhibition in 1901. While Klimt's painting challenged prevailing conservative standards of propriety in the treatment of the nude figure and faith in rationalism, the artist's less contentious allegorical, landscape, and portrait paintings found acceptance among private collectors in Vienna and beyond in exhibitions outside of Austria, including a prize for the artist's "Philosophy" painting when it was exhibited at the Paris World's Fair in 1900. He was an important figure among the artists who formed the Secession and their supporters, admired for his originality and the psychological depth and complexity inherent in his treatment of subjects that challenged the constraints of decorum and tradition.

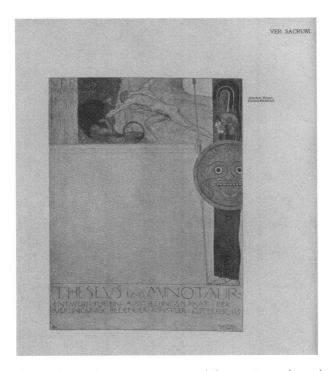

FIGURE 2.25 *Gustav Klimt, Poster for First Secession Exhibition, Gartenbau, chromolithography, 63.5 × 46.9 cm, Vienna, 1898, also reproduced in black and white in* Ver Sacrum, *Jahr 1, 1898, March, Courtesy of Marquand Library of Art and Archaeology, Princeton University*

FIGURE 2.26 *Hans Makart, Poster for First International Art Exhibition of the Kunstlerhaus, chromolithograph, 1882, reproduced in Ottokar Mascha, Österreichische Plakatkunst,* Vienna, J. Löwy, 1915, color plate 1, New York Public Library

FIGURE 2.27 (and color plate) *Alois Hans Schram, poster for Thirty-Fifth Kunstlerhaus Exhbition, Vienna, 1902, Albertina, Vienna, reproduced in Ottokar Mascha, Österreichische Plakatkunst,* Vienna, J. Löwy, 1915, color plate 4, New York Public Library

FIGURE 2.28 *Theophil Hansen, Parliament Building with sculpture of Athena,* ®Shutterstock

The Secession organized its first exhibition in late March 1898 and a second exhibition in November of that year to mark the opening of the organization's new building on the Ringstrasse. For the first exhibition a sketch by Klimt (Figure 2.25) was chosen over a design by Moser to be reproduced as a poster in red, gold, and black on an off-white ground; its graphic character contrasts sharply with earlier, more illustrative posters for the Künstlerhaus such as Hans Makart's design for the 1882 exhibition depicting armored male and crowned female figures framing symbols of the arts and the Austrian flag and emblem (Figure 2.26), or even a later (and similar in its depiction of Athena) Künstlerhaus poster from 1902 by Alois Hans Schram (1864–1919; Figure 2.27).

Klimt's poster emphasizes line and flat shapes rather than modeled forms depicting Athena standing beside a frieze-like scene with lettering below identifying its subject as Theseus and the Minotaur, a metaphor drawn from Greek mythology that suggests a struggle between youth and a repressive authority. The design was reproduced as a sketch in *Ver Sacrum* (1:2, March, 1898, p. 2, Figure 2.25) with a nude Theseus, but for the more public and large-scale poster version a tree covered the hero's genitals to avoid public criticism of indecency. Athena was a familiar presence in Vienna: her image loomed large in the city, and was the subject of a monumental sculpture and fountain in front of the Vienna parliament building (not far from the Secession building on the Ringstrasse, Figure 2.28) constructed 1898–1902, combining the intellectual and physical attributes of wisdom, craft, and war.

Looking more closely, in the contemporary Künstlerhaus poster (Figure 2.26), three gold escutcheons appear beside Athena; the escutcheons (also seen at the bottom of Makart's 1882 poster, see Figure 2.26) are a traditional emblem of the art of painting from the later Middle Ages onwards in representations of trades on shop signs and in print, repeated several times in the volume of allegories and emblems published in Vienna in 1882 (for example, see Figure 2.11). The three escutcheons also appear in Moser's emblem for *Ver Sacrum* in 1898 with the title of the journal enclosed in a circular wreath interrupted by the three shields (see Figure 2.14) and on the cover of the very first issue of *Ver Sacrum* (see Figure 2.17). There Alfred Roller invoked nature (spring) rather than the heroes of Greek mythology as a visual metaphor for the Secession (see p. 46 and Figure 2.17). Referencing the ideas of growth, spring, youth, and energy bursting the constraints that hold it back—appearing at the same time as Klimt's Theseus poster for the First Secession Exhibition, both images communicate the theme of a struggle with authority. We might also see a variation on the escutcheons in the teardrop shapes in Moser's Thirteenth Secession Exhibition poster, though their placement is inverted in comparison with the examples cited above.

Iconography: The Secession Building

The use of the number three, seen in the three escutcheons for the *Ver Sacrum* emblem or Roller's tree for the cover of *Ver Sacrum*, is repeated above the doorway to Olbrich's Secession exhibition building, opened in November 1898 (Figure 2.29), where three female heads represent the arts of architecture, sculpture, and painting. As a friend of Secession artists and literary contributor to its journal, Hermann Bahr (1863–1934) connected the group's aspirations with artistic (and personal) freedom: Bahr was responsible for the Secession's motto, displayed in letters above the doorway: "To every time its art, To every art its freedom" (Der Zeit Ihre Kunst, Der Kunst Ihre Freiheit, Figure 2.29) and penned the following phrase linking modernity with originality and the uniqueness of the individual: "the artist shows his world, the beauty, which was born with him, which never was and never will be again." ("Seine Welt zeige der Künstler—die Schöhnheit, die mit ihm geboren wird, die niemals noch war, die niemals mehr sein wird"; the same heady aphorism appears in the circular border of the window [now lost] that Moser designed for the foyer of the Secession building).

And yet there was an inherent contradiction in these idealistic pronouncements: Secession artists may have been struggling or striving for a voice in matters artistic in Vienna, but they also seemed quite cognizant of a shared past as well, freely invoking and interpreting in their own terms time-honored themes and symbols from nature and from a common Western classical artistic and literary heritage—it was neither possible, nor desirable, to entirely escape the tradition against which they rebelled as they pursued the goal of modern cultural renewal, a dialogue with rather than a rejection of the past.

Indeed, this shared symbolic visual language operates as well in Moser's Thirteenth Secession Exhibition poster: its design features three simplified female figures in a unified decorative scheme that includes a checkerboard and three lozenge or shield-shaped patterns. Most noticeably, the three abstract female figures correspond to the three heads (identified as the arts of painting, sculpture, and architecture) above the Secession building's doorway (see Figure 2.29). The white circle that intersects the blue circles above their heads references the prominent gilt circular "bird's nest" dome with schematized laurel leaves that crowns the exhibition building, known popularly as "The Golden Cabbage," reinforcing associations with spring and renewal. A clear echo of the circle is also found in period photographs of the building as well as Olbrich's drawing for the cover of *Ver Sacrum* that features a sketch of the façade, used for the Second Secession Exhibition poster, with carefully cropped round bushes placed in the urns at either side of the entrance (Figure 2.29), creating, with the dome, a triangle that repeats the number three (Figure 2.30).

The building's plain white exterior appeared shocking to viewers and critics at the time, especially in comparison with nearby buildings located on the perimeter of the city (the "Ringstrasse,") whose rich sculptural programs and columned porticoes recalled the Greco-Roman and Baroque past (see, for instance, above, the Greek Revival Parliament Building, Figure 2.28).

While Olbrich was the architect for the Secession exhibition hall, Moser played a prominent role in designing the building's accompanying decorative scheme. The three identical half-length female figures in Moser's Thirteenth Exhibition poster are arranged in a triangle, each appearing to look downwards toward the text below (Figure 2.2). They have black wing-like hair framed by blue circular haloes (nimbuses), further unified by the outline of the white circle that connects them. As noted above, they recall the female heads representing the visual arts above the building's entrance, often identified with the classical "muses" who inspire the creations of mankind in the arts and sciences (or "genies" according to one contemporary writer). Unlike the controlling geometry that governs the figures in Moser's poster, the unkempt hair of the façade figures gives them the powerful, destructive character of the "furies," mythological beings whose association with instinct appealed to the Secession artists' embrace of unbridled artistic and individual freedom.

The white circle and blue circular shapes that frame the female figures' heads echo the three shapes formed by the circular dome of the Secession exhibition hall and the neatly trimmed circular bushes to either side of the entrance. Intersecting circles are also found in a now lost frieze (see Figure 2.31) of standing female figures ("wreath-bearers") located at the rear of the building. Moser also designed a circular stained-glass window (also lost) for the foyer of the Secession building featuring a standing winged female figure with arms crossed, appearing to hold up a patterned garment with the words "VER SACRUM" in a band at the top above three

FIGURE 2.29 *Joseph Maria Olbrich, Entrance, Secession Building, Vienna, 1898, photo: author*

FIGURE 2.30 *Joseph Maria Olbrich. Poster for the Second Secession Exhibition. 1898. Lithograph, 57.8 × 50.9 cm Printer: Lith. Anst. A. Berger, Wien. Acquired by exchange. The Museum of Modern Art, New York, NY, USA. Digital Image © The Museum of Modern Art/Licensed by SCALA/Art Resource, NY*

FIGURE 2.31 *Joseph Olbrich (and Koloman Moser), mosaic frieze (Wreath-bearers) at rear of Secession Building (now lost), 1898, MAK–Österreichisches Museum für angewandte Kunst/Gegenwartskunst*

shields (a line drawing of the window was reproduced in *Ver Sacrum*, 2 [1899], no. 4, p. 37 and it appears in the same volume in a photograph).

The blue-and-white checkerboard squares that are interspersed with the lettering are also found on the building itself on the piers that frame the dome (see Figure 2.29), and the three teardrop-shaped lozenges that adorn the torsos of the female figures also echo the arrangement of the three shields (escutcheons) that Moser designed as the Secession's first emblem, used on their stationery and in the decoration of *Ver Sacrum* (see Figures 2.14, 2.17). Finally, the words "VER SACRUM," more prominent than the lettering for the exhibition itself in the poster (and illustration), also appear to the left of the building.

Taking into account these various architectural references to the Secession building together, Moser's 1902 design (in *Ver Sacrum* and as a poster) emerges as a *graphic* abbreviation, a condensed image of the building that hosted the Secession's exhibitions, concentrating upon essential elements of its design in a reduced, elementary form, distilling figural and decorative features that stand for the organization's home and exhibition hall. And it was not the first time the building appeared in a Secession exhibition poster. As noted above, Olbrich himself had supplied the drawing for the group's second exhibition in November 1898, the first held in Secession's new hall (see Figure 2.30), and the architect supplied the cover illustration for the January 1899 issue of *Ver Sacrum* that also celebrated the building's recent opening.

There are several reasons why Moser chose to graphically represent the Secession building in his poster for the association's Thirteenth Exhibition. Not only was he a founding member of the organization, but he played a significant role in designing the building's decorative program. As mentioned above, he designed a stained-glass window for the building's foyer, the frieze of standing interlocking female figures (wreath-bearers) at the rear of the building, and also the

FIGURE 2.32 *Joseph Olbrich and Koloman Moser, Three owls from the Secession Building, Vienna, 1898, ®Shutterstock*

overall exterior details, including a relief of three owls that appear at each of the corners of the building's façade (Figure 2.32), and whose round eyes make a witty play on the scrolled volutes of an Ionic capital. Moser's decorative articulation of the building's structure also included patterns and repeated circular and square motifs such as checkerboards, also found in the Thirteenth Exhibition poster.

Beyond Vienna

As noted above (see p. 39), references to Moser's Thirteenth Secession Exhibition poster invariably offer comparisons with Scottish architect and designer Charles Rennie Mackintosh and a small group of Glaswegian artists, whose work exhibits a similar geometric character and linear austerity and was on view in 1900 at the Secession. But the role of Mackintosh and his circle raises the broader issue of the relationship between the Secession and modern approaches to design internationally. While primarily representing Austrian and German artists, Secession exhibitions consciously featured the work of foreign artists whose efforts were illustrated or reproduced photographically in *Ver Sacrum*. These included not only Mackintosh, but Belgian sculptor George Minne, Javanese-Dutch painter Jan Toorop, Moravian illustrator and artist Alphonse Mucha (who for a short time was a Secession member), English designers Charles Ashbee and Walter Crane, and even an exhibition devoted to the arts of Asia including Japanese woodcut prints. Indeed, members of the Secession found a more receptive audience for their own work abroad, in Germany, for instance, than they did at home, and were eager to make Vienna part of a wider network of artists with shared interests in subjectivity and originality, and a willingness to challenge prevailing conservatism and traditional historicism.

With a desire to compete with contemporary publications in Germany and in England, such as *The Studio* (beginning 1893), *Pan* (Berlin, 1895–1900), and *Jugend* (Munich, beginning 1896), the dissemination of original works of art in woodcut, engraving, and chromolithography, the photographic reproduction of works of art and exhibition installations, and the publication of art criticism were essential aims of the Secession from its inception, all intended to stimulate a modern artistic renewal in Austria, asserting a place, an identity for the city in a modern, international avant-garde. In addition to promoting the organization's own exhibitions and illustrating the work of artists outside of Austria, *Ver Sacrum* proclaimed the printed page and the graphic image as works of art in their own right, worthy fields for aesthetic experimentation and freedom of expression.

The Thirteenth Secession Exhibition and *Gesamtkunstwerk* (The Total Work of Art)

In addition to alluding in its imagery and design to the Secession building, Moser's poster (and illustration) for the Thirteenth Secession Exhibition also references the design of the exhibition itself. The exhibition featured work by Secession artists, including paintings and sketches by Gustav Klimt, Rudolf Alt, prints by Emil Orlik based upon his recent visit to Japan, and works by Munich-based painter and founder of the Munich Secession Franz Stück, as well a group of younger Munich artists known as "Die Scholle." Moser designed the exhibition galleries, including a specially constructed display to highlight a large mythological painting on wood by the well-established Swiss-born painter Arnold Böcklin (1827–1901), entitled "Sea Idyll" (1882), on loan from the German Ministry, depicting a Nereid, Triton, and their two small children on a large rock in the midst of turbulent sea and foreboding sky. Böcklin's "Sea Idyll" was the subject of a lengthy interpretive essay in *Ver Sacrum* by writer Ludwig Hevesi that commented on the theme of the harmony between man and an often unpredictable, menacing nature. Böcklin, who had died in January, 1901, had also been the subject of an article in *Ver Sacrum* (no. 4, 1901, pp. 67ff).

There is little evidence to connect Moser's poster with any of the eclectic works in the Thirteenth Secession exhibition and certainly not with Böcklin's featured "Sea Idyll." But Moser, along with fellow members Josef Hoffmann and Alfred Roller, took an avid interest in the aesthetic arrangement of the works in Secession exhibitions, how pictures were hung in relation to one another, and how the individual rooms were arranged and furnished to complement one another as well as to create a unified, coordinated ensemble. Earlier Secession exhibitions featured patterned wallpapers, architectural decoration, and furniture that suggested harmonies between works of fine art on display and other design elements of the exhibition rooms. An example is Moser's "grey and silver" room (Figure 2.33) that was photographed for *Ver Sacrum* from the Secession's fifth exhibition in 1900; he also designed the poster for that exhibition (see Figure 2.4). The "grey and silver" room featured curving wooden frames for the doorways, strange vines and leaves that stretch towards ornaments in the corners of the room where walls meet the ceiling, stenciled plant-like patterns as a repeated alternating border on the upper walls, and a patterned leaf design for the walls themselves.

For the Thirteenth Exhibition Moser placed the paintings and sculptures at eye level and side-by-side rather than salon-style (pictures placed in rows above one another). To judge from photographs of the exhibition reproduced in *Ver Sacrum*, the poster echoes elements in the exhibition design. In general interior design elements were restrained: rather than compete with the work on display, Moser limited decoration to geometric motifs that serve as accents to the horizontal and vertical elements of the architecture and rectangular frames of pictures, such as the squares framed in black that frame the display for Böcklin's "Sea Idyll," or the square panels and painted motifs (Figure 2.34), also framed in black, that decorate a short stairway leading from one exhibition room to another (Figure 2.35).

FIGURE 2.33 *Koloman Moser, Grey and Silver room, Fifth Secession Exhibition, Vienna, 1900, from* Ver Sacrum. *Jahr III, January (no. 1), Courtesy of Marquand Library of Art and Archaeology, Princeton University*

FIGURE 2.34 *Koloman Moser, Interior from the Thirteenth Secession Exhibition, with constructed display for Arnold Böcklin's "Sea Idyll," Vienna, 1902, Ver Sacrum, Jahr V, 1902, Courtesy of Marquand Library of Art and Achaeology, Princeton University. Photographer: John Blazejewski*

FIGURE 2.35 *Koloman Moser, Interior from the Thirteenth Secession Exhibition, Vienna, 1902, Austrian National Library Picture Archive, Vienna*

Moser's poster and illustration makes good visual sense when viewed as a succession of pages in *Ver Sacrum*, while once again it would appear unlikely that all but an uninitiated pedestrian viewing the poster on a street would appreciate the visual connections between poster and exhibition design.

Moser's interest in aesthetic unity, whether the equality among lettering, image, and decoration in his Thirteenth Secession Exhibition poster, the relationship between text and image in page layout, or in the design of exhibition spaces that united works on view with elements of interior design and decoration, touches upon the later nineteenth-century concept of the "total work of art" (*Gesamtkunstwerk*) that combined the belief in both the equality *among* the arts (fine and applied) as well as their essential unity and power to create an enhanced, immersive experience for the viewer, whether in a gallery, a musical performance, a stage play, or a public space or in the home. Usually credited to the German composer Richard Wagner (1818–83), the *Gesamtkunstwerk* (Wagner published his views first in 1849) was an engaging "performance" that intensified the experience of art through the combination of sensory aesthetic stimulation embracing the spoken word, music, and visual presentation. The concept may be flexibly extended to the issues of *Ver Sacrum* as sort of unified "performance" and also to exhibition design or to the domestic interior, where works of art were carefully coordinated with interior design to create a unified whole. Also known for his creative stage designs and exhibition designs as well as frequent contributions to *Ver Sacrum*, Alfred Roller (1864–1935) adopted the *Gesamtkunstwerk* idea: "I insist upon the fact that every issue of *Ver Sacrum* is a small, and *Ver Sacrum* in its entirety, a *large* exhibition." The *Gesamtkunstwerk* concept extended to artistic control over the advertisements at the beginning of each issue, which were reproduced as line drawings or in flattened colors to harmonize with graphic quality of text and prints. Moser was one of a group of Secession members who served on the editorial team as art directors of the journal that included Roller and Olbrich. An example of an advertisement for Pelikan inks and paints from 1902 (one of the years in which Moser's name appears in the credits as an editor) makes use of borders composed of small squares (Figure 2.36)

The "total work of art," embracing the unity and equality of the arts, may be easily extended to all manner of artistic production, from the relationship between architecture and its embellishment through sculptural and mosaic decoration or stained glass, to stage design, to the

FIGURE 2.36 *Advertisement from* Ver Sacrum, *Jahr V, 1902, no. 17, Marquand Library, Princeton University*

ornament applied to the printing of musical scores, or even to program notes that were provided to concert-goers at orchestral concerts, who expected some sort of written accompaniment from the composer to enrich the listener's experience. When composer and conductor Gustav Mahler premiered his First Symphony in Vienna in 1900, critics praised the score's inventiveness but were puzzled by a perceived lack of organization in the flow of its musical themes and sections, lamenting the absence of programmatic notes to provide some sort of narrative to explain Mahler's intentions and enhance the listener's experience.

From its beginnings, the Secession's journal *Ver Sacrum* and its series of exhibitions advocated an inclusive attitude toward the arts, one that embraced their unity rather than reinforcing a hierarchy of prestige that privileged the fine over the applied arts. In addition to the three main branches of architecture, sculpture, and painting, the Secession promoted prints, stage and interior design, and performance in its journal. Dancers such as American-born Isadora Duncan (1887/8–1927) and Löie Fuller (1862–1928) performed in staged spaces during the exhibitions in the Secession building, and *Ver Sacrum* included articles devoted to book decoration and "art in the street." The journal frequently included the reproduction of wallpaper and textile design, lettering, monograms, and emblems designed by Moser, Roller, Auchentaller, and others (see Figures 2.15 and 2.24); such efforts culminated in the founding of the Wiener Werkstätte in 1903. For a combination of reasons stemming from the cost of artisanal labor, the use of expensive materials, and matters of taste, the Wiener Werkstätte efforts depended upon a wealthy clientele and private commissions, though its range of products, from ceramics and glass to metalwork jewelry, tableware, printed textiles, wallpapers, and fashion, was extensive— while Moser ceased to be involved after 1907, the Werkstätte survived in Vienna until 1932 amid increasing financial difficulties (Witt-Dörring and Staggs, 2017).

The Secession and Viennese Art: Revolt or Reform?

The terms "secession" and "rebellion" are not synonymous. The artists who seceded from the Association of Fine Artists in Vienna and their exhibits at the Künstlerhaus (completed in 1868 with regular exhibitions occurring from 1871, see p. 33) were hardly an "underground" or subversive movement. Meeting from the early 1890s in two popular cafés in the city, this group of mostly younger artists, all eventually accepted as members of the Künstlerhaus, lamented the selection process for the organization's exhibitions, desiring stronger representation of more progressive approaches to art, claiming the Künstlerhaus selection was both conservative and geared toward sales (of which 10 percent went to the organization's coffers), and also less open minded toward including the applied as well as fine arts. The artists took their cue from a similar movement in Munich, where a supportive writer had identified the group as a "Secession." The term was borrowed from an ancient Roman practice known as "secessio plebis," whereby ordinary citizens would abandon the city to the patrician politicians in political power, refusing to work until concessions were granted and demands for representation met. In Vienna, the threat of withdrawal was in a sense quite real and politically sensitive. Several talented and progressive Viennese artists were working in Germany and their work was recognized and accepted elsewhere in Europe, where commercial opportunities were ample and lucrative. The artists forming the Vienna Secession appealed to the city government for a grant of land upon which to build their own alternative exhibition hall, received the grant with the support of the local government and the blessing of Emperor Franz Joseph, and solicited donations from a group of wealthy businessmen with an interest in supporting the arts and providing a worthy home for the group's exhibitions. Vienna's reputation as a modern city (the city had hosted a world's fair in 1873) had something to gain by encouraging younger artists to remain there rather than relocate abroad. The city's mayor, Karl Lueger (1844–1910), a popular figure in the city, initially opposed the Secession on behalf of a working-class constituency who resented its internationalism and its appeal to the city's educated and wealthier business and professional class, but capitulated to the artists' request in order to gain recognition from Emperor Franz Joseph, whose support was essential to Lueger's own political ambitions. In approving the Secession's petition, local authorities affirmed a connection between the arts, civic pride, and identity, acquiescing to political pragmatism and a liberal economic policy that acknowledged concerns for the potential loss of talented artists, architects, and designers, in effect the fear of a "brain drain."

Moser and Advertising

Moser's younger colleague and fellow Secessionist, Josef Hoffmann, admired and respected his friend not just for his imagination and versatility as an artist, but also because he had worked "in the real world," having been a commercial illustrator whose work reached a wider readership through the medium of print. This was an ultimate, if elusive aim of the Secession, and, from 1903, its applied arts arm, the Wiener Werkstätte, which both men initiated together with financial backing from Fritz Waerndorfer. Yet what is remarkable is how removed the Thirteenth Secession Exhibition poster is from Moser's earlier illustrations and advertisements, for example his poster for "Richard's Source (Bohemian) Mineral Water" or the "Illustrierte Zeitung" (see p. 40 and Figures 2.8 and 2.9). Moser's ads absorb the lessons of the chromolithographic advertising poster as pioneered by Jules Chéret and Alphonse Mucha in Paris (Mucha was briefly a member of the Secession and examples of his work were featured in an issue of *Ver Sacrum*, Jahr I, November, 1898), commanding the viewer's attention through contrast and simplification that reads easily and quickly from a distance, and appealing to viewers through buoyant, attractive images of young women at leisure.

Moser's advertising posters, along with the commercial work he did for *Wiener Mode* and *Meggendorfer's Blätter*, demonstrate an easy familiarity and facility with images that were immediate and spontaneous, attracting attention whether in print *or* on the street. Idealized images of young women (clothed or nude) and casual interactions between the sexes in relaxed social situations exemplified a direction in visual communication for popular print circulation that provided expanded, often lucrative opportunities for artists in the field of commerce, beyond the walls of museums, exhibition halls, and the private collections of wealthy patrons. But those opportunities were also in part subject to restrictions conditioned by function: that is, advertisements were commissioned by clients who wanted to market and sell their products and services. The vocabulary for the disposition of text and image, brought about by the technology of chromolithography and public spaces provided in cities for the display of large-scale posters (property owners received payment for renting the walls of their buildings to printing companies), needed to capture the attention not of a museum goer or connoisseur, but of a pedestrian (the "man on the street") on their way somewhere else, and command it quickly with imagery that was direct and appealing, communicating pleasurable outcomes connected with an advertised product or service. In other words, the purpose of an advertising poster was to *sell* something.

The English critic Charles Hiatt (d. 1911) published an essay in *The Studio* in 1893 (with elaborations in the journal *The Poster* in the later 1890s), stating the conditions and restrictions imposed by this new form of visual communication (see p. 40). One of Hiatt's intentions was to encourage English artists to follow the example of the French, specifically Jules Chéret, in designing and producing posters that could be collected as prints (he even gave instructions for how to mount and store them), expanding the market for art in a new medium suitable for display in the home or in galleries. But he also recognized the features of the new art form itself, namely, that it was created under the conditions of street-viewing rather than private viewing, that it needed to be bold, reductive, and aggressive in design and in color; its message benefited from stimulating eye movement and a "broad" rather than detailed execution. Hiatt included references to the "hottest colors" such as "bitter red" and "burning crimson," and concluded that the advertising poster's primary mood was one of gaiety and unbridled hedonistic pleasure, for which Chéret was the unequaled master. As noted above, Hiatt asserted the primacy of persuasion in the new poster art form.

Viennese architect Gustave Guglitz expressed similar views in an article on contemporary posters that appeared in *Ver Sacrum* in November 1898, writing that "what would be a glory in an interior … is only a link on the street where it has to be all the more powerful to emerge from its surroundings." And what allows it to emerge from its surroundings are simplicity, bold colors, "without graphic detail." Here again Moser seems to ignore the advice that he'd followed for his advertising posters in the 1890s.

Hiatt's analysis of the advertising poster accords with American writer Susan Sontag's assessment of the genre in an oft-reproduced article first published in 1970 (Sontag, 1970 and 1999). Sontag recognized and emphasized the public nature of the advertising poster, and the hoardings, kiosks, and other public spaces for which posters were designed and where they were experienced as a "theatre of persuasion." While it is unlikely that Sontag was familiar with Hiatt's views of advertising posters, her views correspond with the earlier critic's assessment of the advertising poster's raison d'être: the conditions of its production and viewing demand brevity, legibility, condensation, and asymmetry to garner the attention of passersby. Such commercial considerations conflicted with nineteenth-century notions of artistic independence and autonomy, reinforcing a hierarchy among the visual arts in the West that favored the free expression of ideas against the role of commerce that set limits and conditions on artistic freedom. Sontag recognized the inherent duality and conflict of the advertising poster: a living and public art with an ability to reach a mass audience on the one hand, and yet commercial considerations and constraints that curtailed free artistic expression but were underwritten by a new class of patrons, namely manufacturers, entertainment venues, and the diverse audience (customers) they hoped to attract and entice.

The inherent tension between these competing points of view produced distinctions within the expanding field of the advertising poster. By the second decade of the twentieth century the "art poster" had emerged as an entity in its own right, identified by artist rather than by product or manufacturer, and disseminated in journals and displayed in exhibitions aimed at collectors and devoted exclusively to the subject, such as Hans Sach's *Das Plakat* (from 1910) or in articles that appeared in journals such as *Pan* or *Kunst und Handwerk* and *Kunst und Dekoration*. In Austria, a poster exhibition was held in 1915 with a heavily illustrated catalog and history written by collector and writer Ottokar Mascha (1852–1929). There Mascha noted the distinction between the art poster and advertising (Gebrauch; Reklame), and commented that the exhibition poster is unique in that the designer and "client" (in this case the Secession exhibition hall) were one and the same and not compromised by the more commercial arrangement between artist and manufacturer or promoter (Mascha, 1915). Mascha remarked that the Secession exhibition posters often neglected their "duty" to inform their audience, and stood out for their eccentricity and bizarre, peculiar lettering and forms. Such peculiarity earned the attention of illustrators whose humorous cartoons in newspapers poked fun at them. One

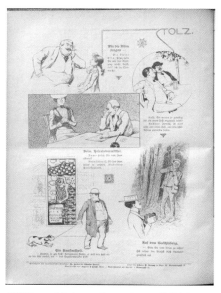

FIGURE 2.37 *Anon., cartoon, 1902, satirizing a Secession exhibition poster,* Figaro *(Vienna), June 14, 1902, p. 8, lower left.*

such cartoon satirizes Alfred Roller's poster for the Fourteenth Secession Exhibition, the so-called "Beethoven Exhibition" also held in 1902 (Figure 2.37, lower left).

It depicts a cigar-smoking burgher whose dog has stopped in front of the poster and won't move (the artists altered Roller's image by adding a large checkerboard shoe above the head of the female figure depicted in the poster). Titled "an art critique," the dog-walker scolds his pooch: "Come on … Damn (it); he doesn't want to go around the corner from where the Secession poster is (put up) (Floderl, so geh doch! Verdammter …, er will mir halt nicht an der Ecke vorbei, wo—das Zezessionsplakat pickt!"). The gist is that the man's dog is scared of the Secession poster, or perhaps, that the image has a stronger impact upon canines than upon people!

Another issue that emerges in the study of posters-as-advertising rather than as "art" has to do with differences in exactly "what" is being advertising or sold. With Chéret as a paradigm, the entertainment industry and "soft" goods such as alcoholic beverages and packaged foods were among the earliest objects of poster advertising. Thus the exhibition poster constitutes a specific "type" or genre of poster, with considerably more latitude on the part of the designer to deviate from the character of the poster as defined by Hiatt and others. Examining Moser's Thirteenth Secession Exhibition poster, it seems quite apparent that it lacks the immediacy, the ease of recognition, the aggressive design, and the strident colors that were understood at the time as the conditions for a successful advertising poster.

Summing Up: Moser, the Secession, and Vienna

Moser's Thirteenth Secession Exhibition poster, the exhibition itself, and the Secession's contributions generally to the art scene in Vienna are but a part of a rich flowering of the arts and culture that took place in the city at the turn of the twentieth century. The Viennese author

Stefan Zweig (1881–1942), writing his autobiography in exile during World War II, recalled the excitement of the period, particular its youthful vigor and sense of adventure:

> Happily it [youth] enjoys its age with that vivacity, that freshness, that ease, and that carefreeness which are fitting to this age. But the loveliest thing about this happiness seems to be that it need not lie to others, and may be honest with itself, honest to its natural feelings and desires (pp. 90–1) ... The streets became broader and more showy, the public buildings more impressive, the shops more luxurious and tasteful. Everything manifested the increase and spread of wealth ... New theaters, libraries, and museums sprang up everywhere; comforts such as bathrooms and telephones, formerly the privilege of the few, became the possession of the more modestly placed, and the proletariat emerged, now that working hours had been shortened, to participate in at least the small joys and comforts of life. There was progress everywhere. Whoever ventured, won ... Never had Europe been stronger, richer, more beautiful, or more confident of an even better future. None but a few shriveled graybeards bemoaned, in the ancient manner, the "good old days." (Zweig, 1943, pp. 192–3)

The city not only nurtured Moser, but also was home to Gustav Klimt, Josef Hoffmann, Otto Wagner, Oskar Kokoschka, and Egon Schiele, to name only a few of the better-known artists and architects of the period up to World War I. The city's reputation extended from the fine arts to design and fashion through the Wiener Werkstätte (founded 1903), including the efforts of a gifted if lesser-known group of designers, women as well as men, who collaborated with craftsmen and manufacturers in the production of original furniture, furnishings, and personal items ranging from book plates to textiles and table decorations. Many of the artists were students, as well as faculty, at the Vienna School of Applied Arts, the educational wing of the Museum of Applied Art (MAK—Museum für angewandte Kunst), founded in 1863 to promote the decorative arts (manufactures). In philosophy Vienna was home to Ludwig Wittgenstein, in medicine, Sigmund Freud and Emma Eckstein, in literature Stefan Zweig, in science, Albert Einstein and Karl Menger, and in music, Gustav Mahler and Richard Strauss. Vienna also benefited from being the capital of an empire that included Hungary and the modern-day Czech Republic, whose own artistic and musical traditions contributed to Vienna's own cultural identity along with the efforts of the Secession to bring art and design from abroad to the city through its ambitious series of regular exhibitions and the publication of *Ver Sacrum*.

As many writers have noted, Viennese identity benefited from the contributions of the city's Jewish population, many of whom were secularized and felt comfortably assimilated, identifying primarily as Austrian rather than Jewish. And yet there was something precarious, not only about Jewish identity in prewar Austria but about Viennese culture more generally. Beneath the city's impressive achievements in so many fields, its urban renovation through building, public monuments and parks, pedestrian-friendly streets and the convenience of public transportation: amid its outwardly welcoming diversity, lay working-class resentment toward the uncertainties of liberal economic policy that found expression in the populist anti-Semitic politics of Vienna's mayor Karl Lueger, who viewed Jews as outsiders whose banking and commercial (retail) interests aroused working class insecurities. Anti-Semitism in Europe was hardly limited to Vienna, but the newspaper editor and writer Theodor Herzl (1860–1904) recognized and worried about the limits of religious and racial tolerance, planting the seeds of the Zionist movement, encouraging European Jews to envision a Jewish homeland in Palestine as a refuge from discrimination and persecution (Schorske, 1979).

What has drawn scores of later twentieth- and twenty-first-century scholars and writers to turn-of-the-century Vienna is not only the city's rich visual, musical, scientific, and literary achievements, but also the particular if fragile intellectual climate that made that richness possible. Australian writer and poet Clive James made early twentieth-century Vienna the touchstone of his 2007 book *Cultural Amnesia*, in which he argued that the flowering of Viennese culture was built upon the foundation of a "café society" in which a rising and diverse middle class met and mixed with the traditional aristocratic elite to produce a vibrant artistic and intellectual milieu outside of the official and more restrictive enclaves of court, salon, or university, more casual, livelier, more public, more democratic, in a word, more "modern." For James, the informality of the café and the discourse that resulted from its unofficial status and diverse make-up were the keys to the creativity that energized the city. He praised Vienna's cultural legacy, and like Stefan Zweig's memoir *The World of Yesterday* (that James recommends reading), lamented its passing (James, 2007).

Cafés and Exhibitions

FIGURE 2.38 *Koloman Moser (at right) with Otto Wagner (left) and Josef Hoffmann at the Café Bristol, Vienna, c. 1905, Austrian National Library*

A photograph (Figure 2.38) shows Moser, Hoffmann, and Wagner seated at the Café Bristol in Vienna, the two groups of younger artists who joined forces to create the Secession in 1897 both held their meetings at cafés in the city, the Café Sperl (for the Siebener Club to which Moser and Hoffmann belonged), and the Hagengesellschaft, named for its owner and the site of the Secession's first exhibition. The Hagengesellschaft exhibition of the works of German Impressionist painter Max Slevogt (1868–1932) in 1897 was the subject of a poster designed

FIGURE 2.39 (and color plate) *Alfred Roller, Exhibition Poster (Max Slevogt), chromolithograph, 47.9 × 49.3 cm, Vienna, 1897, MAK–Österreichisches Museum für angewandte Kunst/Gegenwartskunst*

by Alfred Roller (Figure 2.39), an asymmetrical composition with loosely drawn lettering in the upper right balanced in the lower left by the bloody severed head of Medusa in dark reddish-brown against a uniform pale blue background.

Roller's striking if gruesome image appears to be a reference to Slevogt's painterly brushwork, but curiously, Slevogt's subject matter is generally contemporary and Impressionist rather than dramatic or historical. Art historian Werner Schweiger wrote that Roller's Slevogt poster marks "the beginning of the modern exhibition poster [in Vienna]" quoting contemporary critics who remarked that it caused a sensation and was the subject of discussion in newspapers at the time, recalling Gustav Guglitz's essay (see p. 65) and remarking that "grotesque, distorted forms" were advantageous for effective posters. The Slevogt poster and the public attention it received is all the more striking in contrast to Moser's tightly controlled and subdued poster for the Secession's Thirteenth Exhibition in 1902. Roller's poster seems more suited to the street and to capturing the attention of the pedestrian with a sensational, grisly image that frightens and appeals at the same time, while Moser's poster, composed of numerous interrelated parts, demands the careful attention of a reader with time on their hands.

This broader discussion of early twentieth-century Vienna is not simply a postscript to Moser's narrow poster and illustration for the Thirteenth Secession Exhibition: Moser benefited directly from being part of an ambitious circle of young artists who pushed the boundaries of traditional artistic practice in Vienna in the hope of contributing vitality and excitement to the city's art and design scene with a greater degree artistic freedom as well as with an awareness of contemporary developments outside of Austria. Vienna's casual, inclusive "café society" not only provided the physical setting for Moser and his colleagues to put talk into practice, but also the space to engage more freely, more "socially," with their public, garnering notice in local newspapers, engendering public debate, provoking comment from defenders as well as skeptics, but in an atmosphere of lively debate and controversy centered around the economic, social, and political purposes of visual culture in early modern Vienna.

Most scholars credit historian Carl Schorske (1915–2015) with renewing (if not igniting) the academic and broader public debate centered upon turn-of-the-century Vienna in the 1970s and 1980s. Schorske's cultural history of Vienna (*Fin-de-Siècle Vienna: Politics and Culture,*

1979 but preceded by scholarly articles beginning in the 1960s) included the city's art and offered an interpretation of the Secession that centered upon the career of Gustav Klimt, focusing upon the medical school faculty's rejection of his paintings for the University of Vienna as a sign of increasing marginalization of the Secession and its circle of friends and patrons, and their withdrawal from political and economic discourse (the relevant chapter is entitled "crisis of liberal culture"). Moser's poster for the Thirteenth Secession Exhibition might support Schorske's point of view, but only at the risk of oversimplification: a generation of scholars have argued that liberalism survived in Vienna despite the challenges its defenders faced politically and socially. Indeed, James argued that the quotas imposed upon Jews, for instance, for official appointments to professorships in universities or civil service jobs stimulated their broader public and social engagement. In other words, the relationship between retreat and engagement need not be an either-or choice. One might argue that because Moser's 1902 poster did not easily inform its audience, or even persuade them to visit the exhibition it signifies that Moser's interests lay with the better educated and informed clientele of the Secession, its exhibitions, and its journal, indifferent to the views or approval of a broader public. And yet the Thirteenth Exhibition did not go unnoticed in Vienna's newspapers and weeklies, and *Ver Sacrum* reported that the sale of work from the exhibition was strong. Even criticism, at times humorous, at least acknowledged an ongoing public dialogue without antagonism or dismissive rhetoric. The *Wiener Abendpost* (February 7, 1902) featured a lengthy review in its "Feuilleton" section that described the Thirteenth Secession Exhibition in detail, recognizing the break in tradition that many of the works on display represented in their stronger "decorative" character (i.e. emphasizing line and the flatness of the surface) and in the variety of media including caricature and illustration, as well as the display of artists from outside of Austria. The reviewer deems some works "bizarre" or simply "not pretty," but other works receive praise, including Böcklin's "Sea Idyll" and the work of landscape painters, some praise for the introduction of new faces including a local female artist named Ilse Conrat, along with the work of Belgian sculptor George Minne and the Swiss painter Ferdinand Hodler. The reviewer commented that the work aroused some indignation among those in the public who oppose a working program that at times may go too far in its stance against tradition—but, the writer adds, the public "takes notice," and the exhibition is not so marginal as to not register in the public's mind and offers much that remains appealing.

A single poster is hardly sufficient to reveal the complexities of Viennese graphic design in 1900. The available primary source material and secondary literature suggest numerous avenues of approach to Moser's iconic poster. This case study began with questioning the choice of this particular and frequently reproduced poster to represent the Secession's modern approach to design without considering the work's function, its reproduction in a smaller scale for the Secession journal *Ver Sacrum*, and its formal and iconographic relationship with the Secession building, especially in light of Moser's role in the exhibition building's design. Exploring the poster's design and imagery demonstrated in turn the importance of thinking about graphic design in relation to advertising, to scale, and to the experience of the viewer. The poster's questionable status as advertising hardly diminishes its significance: on the contrary, it demonstrates Moser's involvement with and respect for architecture and letterpress printing, both labor-based practices rooted in pragmatic technical considerations that balanced unbridled invention with workshop tradition and the collaborative, integrated, and inclusive nature of the design enterprise. This was an underlying theme in Moser's artistic trajectory (as well as in the teaching of his colleague at the School of Applied Arts, Rudolf von Larisch), establishing a link between fine and applied art, between the individual and society, that found expression in the concept of the "total work of art," and also equating "the modern" with practical values that embodied comfortable middle-class rather than ostentatious living. This approach was well-suited to the design of interiors and to the book or journal, but was less suitable to the demands of public advertising. It is found, for instance, in Moser's home on the Hohe Warte neighborhood in Vienna in 1902, designed by Hoffmann and furnished with furniture designed by Moser (see Figure 2.2), and displaying the same severe rectilinear elements and restrained decoration found in the Thirteenth Secession Exhibition poster, in accordance with the simple lines of the room's basic tectonic (box-like) structure. And it also found expression in the pages of *Ver Sacrum* beginning in 1901 with the use of the square as a modest decorative accompaniment to the journal's layouts.

By the time photographs of Moser's 1902 home were published in the German periodical *Kunst und Dekoration* in 1907, the direction of his professional activity had changed. In 1905 Moser ended his involvement with the Vienna Workshops (Wiener Werkstätte), the same year that there was a rift within the Secession when several members, including Hoffmann and Moser, withdrew their membership over the group's decision to separate the exhibition of fine art from the decorative arts. For the remainder of his career (he died in 1918 at the age of fifty) Moser turned almost exclusively to the more private and individual art of easel painting rather than the collaborative and commercial field of decorative painting (and design) that he had embraced and taught at the Vienna School of Applied Arts. In 1907 he married graphic artist Editha (Ditha) Kautner-Markhof, the daughter of a very wealthy Viennese family and an artist/designer in her own right. Freed from financial worries (that very early in his career prompted his work as an illustrator after his father died) and as the father of two young children, Moser could pursue painting without the pressures of commissions or the constraints imposed by clients or manufacturers; yet he is best remembered for his work as a gifted and highly respected versatile designer and active contributor to the Vienna Secession. His Thirteenth Secession Exhibition poster from 1902 may not be the most representative example of his oeuvre, but its study reveals the degree to which the arts of printing and architecture informed his approach to graphic design at that time.

Chapter 3

Cassandre and Dubonnet: Art Posters and Publicité in Interwar Paris

Indeed one of the things that made him such a delightful person
was his ability to contradict himself.
—HENRI MOURON, *A.M. CASSANDRE*, NEW YORK, RIZZOLI, 1985

Cassandre was the adopted name of the Ukrainian-born French artist Adolphe Jean-Marie Mouron (1901–68), whose advertising posters during the period between World War I and World War II are among the most celebrated of the twentieth century. Despite being frequently represented in museum collections, exhibitions, and illustrated in surveys and monographs on the history of the poster (Mouron, 1985), there have been few if any in-depth studies of Cassandre's individual works. As a result, neither the specific circumstances nor the broader context of particular commissions have been the subjects of investigation, in terms of their iconography, their connection to the artist's many statements about his own work, in comparison to the observations of contemporary critics, or in relation to the complex relationships among art, publicity, and business during the interwar period. "Dubo-Dubon-Dubonnet," a series of three monumental lithographic posters designed in 1932, provides the basis for such a case study (Figure 3.1 and color plate section). The series is certainly one of the best-known of Cassandre's poster campaigns. It is celebrated as an example of the appropriation of elements from the avant-garde fine art styles of Cubism and Purism for advertising, and as a borrowing from both modern cinematic *and* cartoon sequencing to appeal to a broader audience, but little attempt has been made to address and reconcile the varied and even occasionally contradictory assessments of Cassandre's methods, sources, and attitudes toward his medium.

The tension between art and advertising seen in contemporary critical writing, in Cassandre's own views of his work, in the emerging field of market research, and in early debates about the commercial use of public spaces in France, constitutes the major theme of the present chapter, which argues that Cassandre's "Dubo-Dubon-Dubonnet" oscillates between salon and street and between art and commerce. It argues that an increasingly uneasy balance was forged that began to unravel in the later 1930s as companies increasingly embraced "scientific" approaches to product promotion, emphasizing the relationship between poster advertising and sales rather than supporting its critical reception in exhibitions and art journals as a form of "peoples' art" and its role in raising the standards of public taste. While the study of Cassandre and the

FIGURE 3.1 (and color plate) A. M. Cassandre, "Dubo-Dubon-Dubonnet," 1932, chromolithograph, 120 x 160 cm and 240 x 320 cm, Alliance Graphique, TM & © Mouron. Cassandre License no. 2019-20-08-02 www.cassandre.fr

art poster has focused upon the "spectacle of the street" and Cassandre's appropriation of the practice of avant-garde artists, the economic and political foundations of such a narrative seem to demand a more nuanced, even skeptical examination, one that acknowledges more aggressive advertising in response to the newer mass medium of radio, declines in consumer spending in the wake of the stock market crash and resulting economic depression beginning in the autumn of 1929, along with restrictions and taxes that curtailed investment in poster advertising. After all, Cassandre died in 1968 (more than thirty years after the Dubonnet campaign), but designed very few posters after 1937, only a year after his solo exhibition at the Museum of Modern Art celebrated the (art) critical acclaim of his work. In order to present and test our thesis, let's look more carefully at Cassandre's achievement in "Dubo-Dubon-Dubonnet."

Dubonnet and Cassandre

Dubonnet is a fortified wine that contains quinine, a bitter substance obtained from the bark of the cinchona tree (native to South America), effective in combating the malaria that threatened the health of French soldiers stationed in colonial North Africa. The drink was invented by Joseph Dubonnet in 1846, and won a competition sponsored by the French government to solicit ways of making quinine more palatable to soldiers. To promote the product beyond its medicinal use, Dubonnet marketed his beverage more generally as an aperitif and publicized its new use through advertising, including a series of posters designed by Jules Chéret dating to 1895 (see Figure 3.4 and color plate; p. 78), including one that features a young woman wearing a low-cut striped dress, with outstretched arms against a red oval background (she appears to float, as it's difficult to say whether she is seated or suspended from a swing of some sort) holding a bottle of Dubonnet in one hand and a glass in the other.

Cassandre's 1932 posters for Dubonnet feature a reductive rendering of a single male figure seated at a round café table, engaged in three successive stages of holding, drinking, and pouring a glass of the beverage. The deft combination of repetition and variation to attract and maintain viewer attention is remarkable. There are subtle variations in pose, as well as in color. Cassandre's "little man" (aka "Monsieur Dubo") is composed entirely of straight and precisely drawn semi-circular curved lines, whose regular contours are repeated from part to part in each of the three variations, creating a strong sense of visual unity within each poster and as a sequence that is "read" left to right. The little man's torso and legs remain in the same position while the upper body, head, and right arm reveals slight variations in the sequence. Straight lines are generally parallel or drawn at a 90-degree angle. Other angles create parallel lines, such as the pouring bottle in the third of the three images, which matches the angle of Dubo's head and his bent left leg. The angle of the head is at 90 degrees in the first image in the series, turning more acutely in the middle "drinking" image. In each of the three posters the viewer's eye follows a diagonal path downward from upper right to lower left and then continues across horizontally with the letters of the word "Dubonnet," echoed in the numerous horizontal contours and shapes of the little man, table, and chair. Circular and semi-circular shapes are found in Dubo's tightly fitting bowler hat, and find echoes in the shapes of the wine glass, elbow, eye, eyeball, sleeve buttons, and the fingernails of the left hand. They are also found in the counters of the geometric sans serif upper-case letters and the shapes "U," "B," "O," and "D."

Repetition is certainly a key element in the design of "Dubo-Dubon-Dubonnet." It creates movement and establishes narrative continuity and coherence simply, easily, and without distraction. The use of repetition as a narrative device has a parallel in contemporary cartoon strips, and writers have often invoked the popularity of the comic-strip form as a source for Cassandre's Dubonnet posters, connecting it to an accessible and familiar form of visual communication. Yet sequences in cartoon strips generally lack the monumentality of "Dubo-Dubon-Dubonnet"; and comics also regularly contain text bubbles or "speech"; moreover they are meant to be seen and read at close range rather than from a distance.

Treatment of the poster in surveys and monographs also often includes a reference to film. Cinema was a popular form of entertainment in France beginning in the early twentieth century, competing with live theatre after the introduction of feature-length movies in 1911. In the journal *Art et métiers graphiques* (roughly translated as *Professional and Graphic Art*) the Dubonnet poster series was featured as a double page spread with short description in 1933. There the anonymous author noted the series' "cinematic technique," observing that successive use of word and image recalled animated cartoons. Meggs/Purvis wrote that "the iconography of his cinematic sequence of word and image was used to advertise the liquor Dubonnet for over two decades" (Meggs/Purvis, 2016). A cinematic candidate for comparison may be Fernand Léger's 1924 experimental and non narrative animated film "Ballet Mécanique," which begins with a sequence featuring a fragmented and toy-like Cubist figure reminiscent of the jumpy movements of comic film star Charlie Chaplin and includes shots of bottles and eyes, as well as hats (Figure 3.2; Vallye, 2013). Despite these similarites, however, Cassandre's sequence of three images proceeds with a slow, almost stately movement in contrast to the frenetic rhythms of the "Ballet Mécanique."

Another source for the sequence of monumental figures in "Dubo-Dubon-Dubonnet" is mural painting, a tradition Cassandre himself cited in an article published in December, 1926 in the monthly journal *L'Affiche*, referring to the stock poses and repetition found in ancient Egyptian frescos and the narrative cycles of medieval illuminators and fresco painters, examples of "anonymous arts that flourished in the Middle Ages and in Antiquity" (Andrin, 1926, and translation in Mouron, 1985). Indeed the analogy is a helpful one: it reinforces references to the

FIGURE 3.2 *Film Still of "Chaplinesque" collage in Fernand Léger's "Ballet Mécanique," 1924, Anthology Film Archives*

past (also combining word and image) as precedent and justification for Cassandre's approach to poster design as a form of public and commonly understood visual communication, not only for the composition of "Dubo-Dubon-Dubonnet" but also for the upper-case lettering that he saw as monumental and "architectural" in the manner of Roman epigraphy (see p. 88).

Cassandre's "Dubo-Dubon-Dubonnet" also anticipates the development of modern trademarks with its preference for reductive graphic symbol rather than illustration, and the equality and integration of word (or slogan) and image that are so much a part of modern corporate graphic identity and branding. For "Dubo-Dubon-Dubonnet" Cassandre expanded on a slogan already in use by the company, "Dubon Dubonnet" or "Good Dubonnet," adding "Dubo" but read in French as "du beau" or "beautiful." Some writers have interpreted the first part of the slogan ("Dubo") as a colloquial phrase meaning "doubt." If correct, this second translation allows some interpretive connection with the first of the three posters, associating "doubt" with the "incomplete" painting of the little man, who has not yet finished his glass of Dubonnet (Brown and Reinhold, 1979). Such branding had a respectable history in France from the beginnings of the twentieth century in the beverage industry, with Nicolas Wine Company's bottle-wielding "Nectar" from 1914; in the travel industry, "Bibendum" was an equally recognizable mascot for the Michelin Tire Company beginning in 1894.

While the literature on Cassandre often notes and provides demonstrations of the artist's use of mathematical proportions and constructive modules to create his compositions, such procedures do not seem to have been employed rigorously in "Dubo-Dubon-Dubonnet" (for the use of a controlling grid, see chapter 2 on Koloman Moser's poster for the Thirteenth Vienna Secession Exhibition). Neither the width of Monsieur Dubo's torso, profile head, leg, nor arm constitute units out of which the other elements of the poster are built by any sort of mathematical formula. Certainly formal unity or formal relationships are achieved in each of the three related posters and strengthened by repetition collectively; the thickness of the table, pedestal, and high-backed chair approximates that of the strokes of the upper case sans serif letters of the brand, but the shapes themselves appear to be determined more by sensibility than by mathematical calculation or the application of the proportions of the golden section. The repetitive, orderly arrangement of shapes creates a sense of regular, soothing movement, certainly unlike the dynamic energy of Cassandre's earlier "Au Bucheron" poster or other Au Bucheron displays (see pp. 89–90).

The regular contours and draughtsman-like precision of "Dubo-Dubon-Dubonnet" are also often seen as an aesthetic analogy to the efficiency of machines, and an ideal, reductive geometric purity, seen also in Cassandre's railway advertising posters (Eskilson, 2012); but Cassandre's use of compass and straight edge in "Dubo-Dubon-Dubonnet" and elsewhere also had a practical advantage: it helped to guide the hands of workers in the printing shop who executed his designs, leaving less to chance in the process of reproduction. The artist had stated that posters were designed *to be reproduced* rather than as unique paintings, and the draughtsman-like character of "Dubo-Dubon-Dubonnet" was a means to ensure faithful execution of his ideas by a team of assistants: the notion of the "anonymous workshop" appealed to Cassandre, who praised the working methods of the late medieval atelier as a group of able workers who carried out large fresco commissions or the lengthy picture cycles of illuminated manuscripts from the instructions of a master or lead designer. Cassandre's use of landscape motifs and other naturalistic human figures and animals in his destination-oriented travel posters from the later 1920s and 1930s certainly posed a challenge to his working method, but even in his 1934 "Écosse" (Scotland) poster, the contours of the mountains tend to be smooth rather than irregular or jagged, and strong contrasts among the various overlapping shapes reduce the complexity of the scene and simplify the process of reproducing the design on a large scale (Figure 3.3).

FIGURE 3.3 *A. M. Cassandre, "Écosse," poster, chromolithograph, 240 x 320 cm, 1934, TM &*
© Mouron. Cassandre License no. 2019-20-08-02 www.cassandre.fr

Iconography

Despite its reductive approach to drawing and overall compositional unity, "Dubo-Dubon-Dubonnet," is comprised of several parts, and each element contributes to our understanding of the series. In the first place, "Dubo-Dubon-Dubonnet" departed from the most common approach to advertising alcoholic beverages. Jules Chéret's Dubonnet posters dating to 1895 are typical of the genre: an attractive young woman, dressed in a striped dress with puffy sleeves, low neckline and black stockings, emerges energetically, if somewhat off-balance, from a red oval background, holding a glass in one hand and a bottle of Dubonnet in the other, accompanied by a white cat "dressed up" with a ribbon and bell on its collar, inviting the viewer to imbibe (Figure 3.4 and color plate). By the time Chéret produced his Dubonnet posters, the association between young, attractive women and cats was not uncommon in modern French painting and prints. As art historian James H. Rubin notes, cats were a frequent subject for modern artists (and poets) in nineteenth-century France, included in numerous paintings as a metaphor for independence as well as sexuality. Rubin quotes from writer Florent Prévost, who noted that "in spite of living in our houses, one can hardly say cats are domesticated." Rather, "they are entirely free, they do as they please [...] Their natural opposition to constraint makes them incapable of systematic education." And the French poet Champfleury (the pen-name for Jules François Felix Fleury-Husson, who wrote a book about cats), reminded his readers of "the oriental notion that of all female animals, the cat most resembles woman in her cleverness, deceit, seductiveness, inconstancy, and fury" (Rubin, 2003).

Movement, gaiety, and conviviality pervade the image, an enticement to carefree pleasure in the company of the (implied) opposite sex, to which a glass of Dubonnet contributes an added note of festivity and casual informality. More suggestive than Chéret but along the same gendered lines, the Italian poster artist Leonetto Cappiello's (1875–1942) poster for Absinthe Pernot

FIGURE 3.4 (and color plate) *Jules Chéret, "Quinquina Dubonnet, Apéritif, Dans tous les Cafés." 1895. Lithograph, 49 1/16 × 34 5/16 in. (124.6 × 87.1 cm). Printer: Imp. Chaix (Ateliers Chéret), Paris. Given anonymously. The Museum of Modern Art, New York, NY, USA. Digital Image © The Museum of Modern Art/Licensed by SCALA/Art Resource, NY*

FIGURE 3.5 (and color plate) *Leonetto Cappiello, "Absinthe extra-supérieure J. Edouard Pernot, lithograph," 152 × 105 cm, Bibliothèque nationale de France*

(*c.* 1900–3) portrays an "unequal" couple—middle-aged man and younger woman—seated at a table in a café (Figure 3.5 and color plate). While the young woman is depicted in profile, the man faces the viewer as well as his companion, affecting an admiring, even lascivious grin.

In both of these posters, drinking is a social event, a pastime enjoyed in the company of others, whether for carefree enjoyment or as a prelude to a sexual encounter (even the Nicolas Wine Company's "Nectar" generally holds several bottles of wine, connecting wine with a social gathering); a good time implies a public space shared with other people, including members of the opposite sex. The situation is not much different from beer advertisements on television today, whether they are set in bars, discos, or a living room with the invited guests watching a football game—in short, at least for the purposes of advertising, people rarely if ever drink alone.

Monsieur Dubo shares the geometric reduction of pictograms but is not quite as generic as, say, a highway safety sign, and elements of his attire identify a more specific "type" of addressing figure, along with pale colored backgrounds that also suggest time and space (see p. 82). The approach, however, is certainly contemporary with the development of pictograms designed for display in charts for the "International Picture Language" (Isotype) initially developed in Vienna under the direction of Otto Neurath (Neurath, 1936; Neurath, M. and Kinross, 2009) for the city's Social and Economic Museum to promote the free dissemination of quantitative statistical information in a consistent and accessible form (the museum opened in 1932 but was closed in 1934; see also chapter 1 on Josef Müller-Brockmann's "schutzt das kind!" poster, p. 12). The Neuraths' work continued, however, first in the Netherlands at The Hague, then England, and through his colleague Rudolf Modley in the United States. Figure 3.6 provides an example of Isotype's reductive approach, while Figure 3.7 illustrates the use of a similar pictogram for present-day traffic signage in the United States.

Unlike Cappiello's protagonist in "Absinthe Pernot," Cassandre's Monsieur Dubo wears a tight-fitting bowler rather than a top hat, and hats of one sort or another frequently appear in the artist's posters as signifiers of group identity or social position (Figures 3.8 and 3.9).

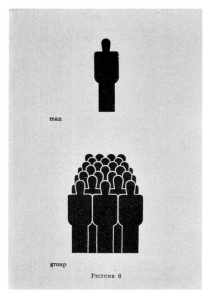

FIGURE 3.6 *Otto Neurath,* International Picture Language: the First Rules of Isotype, *London, Kegan Paul Trench and Trubner, 1936, p. 31*

FIGURE 3.7 *Flagger sign, United States Department of Transportation, Federal Highway Administration,* Manual on Uniform Traffic Control Devices (MUTCD), *2004, Brimar Industries*

FIGURE 3.8 *A. M. Cassandre, "Triplex" chromolithograph, 480 × 120 cm and 120 × 160 cm, 1930, Alliance Graphique, TM & © Mouron. Cassandre License no. 2019-20-08-02 www.cassandre.fr*

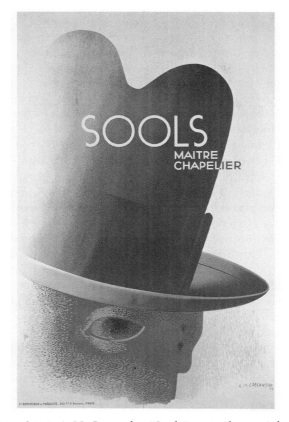

FIGURE 3.9 (and color plate) *A. M. Cassandre, "Sools" poster for men's hat shop, chromolithograph, 160 x 240 cm, chromolithograph, 1929, TM & © Mouron. Cassandre License no. 2019-20-08-02 www.cassandre.fr*

Neither formal attire nor working-class cap, the bowler was a practical and unpretentious head covering without clear class associations. The same might be said for the little man's clothing. Indicated only minimally, Cassandre's drawing indicates a plain suit coat or jacket by its lapel and sleeve buttons. He is neither gentleman nor laborer, dressed but not "dressed up." And more significantly, perhaps, he is by himself, addressing his glass of Dubonnet primarily and secondarily communicating with the viewer.

The round table and varied atmospheric backgrounds (pale yellow, greyish-blue, and more saturated yellow, most likely rendered using airbrush) with pedestal base signifies an outdoor café, a standard part of urban public space in Paris and other European cities, recorded time and again by contemporary artists and photographers. The café table-as-still life was a frequent subject in the early twentieth century for Cubist painters Picasso, Braque, and others, and was captured from above by André Kertész in a photograph from 1927–8 (implying the presence of a writer composing a poem, and reproduced in a book of poetry by the Hungarian writer Endre Ady, published in 1934 under the title *Az Igazi Ady*—The Real Ady). The café table was also photographed by René-Jacques in 1932 (the same year as "Dubo-Dubon-Dubonnet," with a Dubonnet company placard on the wall and two middle-aged men, one with a bowler and both wearing suit jackets). In another photograph (Café du Dome, 1925) from the same period Kertész captured the café at a busier time of day, with lone customers immersed in their dailies and others congregating in groups, whether seated, arriving, or departing (Figures 3.10, 3.11, and 3.12).

These and other images, whether photographs or cartoons, all emphasize the democratic, quotidian, and familiar nature of the posters' subject—the café was a quite ordinary, socially diverse, and a regular part of everyday urban life, whether as a place to work by yourself (like wi-fi-enabled tables and counters in Starbucks today), to take a short or even rushed mid-morning or afternoon break in between tasks or appointments (whether to enjoy the weather or escape from the cold—indoors—or heat—outdoors), or to relax after work with friends over coffee, or in this case, an aperitif.

Typical and yet at the same time remarkable, even personal when triggered by one of its attending objects, the café celebrates an aspect of our experience of modern "time," offering a respite (whether private or social) from the demands and obligations of work (when time is *not our own*) and the hurried pace of the day, a small indulgence that reminds us of our autonomy, lending significance to unimportant moments rather than dramatic or climactic ones. In a review of an exhibition in Paris in 2016 devoted to the art collection of Russian businessman Sergei Shchukin (1854–1936), art critic Jason Farago (*New York Times*) commented upon a preparatory version of Claude Monet's "Luncheon on the Grass" (1866) that was one of the highlights of the show. Less celebrated than Edouard Manet's 1863 painting of the same subject on view in the Musée d'Orsay, Farago described the painting as an outdoor scene "in which a dozen Parisians practice the new bourgeois art of *doing nothing* [italics added]," an apt description of "Dubo-Dubon-Dubonnet" (Farago, 2016). Cassandre's Dubonnet poster series modernizes, urbanizes, monumentalizes, and democratizes such moments as simple pleasures—the sequence of images, focusing upon the word "good" and resulting in the "Dubo's" completeness or fulfillment (somehow he is "incomplete" until the final of the three images)—something as transient as an afternoon glass of wine acquires significance and lends meaning to the average and ordinary, triggering an immediate association between image and a shared, satisfying experience, and the product that brings it to mind.

FIGURE 3.11 *René-Jacques, "Two Policemen, Rue de la Verrière," 1932, negative, 2.4 x 3.6 cm, 1932, Ministère de la Culture*

FIGURE 3.10 *André Kertész, "A Poem by Ady," silver gelatin print, 1927–8, 24 x 20 cm, Agence photographique de la Réunion des Musées Nationaux et du Grand Palais; Art Resource, NY (also reproduced in Az Igazi Ady, by Endre Ady, 1934)*

FIGURE 3.12 *André Kertész, © André Kertész—RMN.Tihany, Café du Dome, 1925. Silver gelatin glass plate negative, 6 x 9 cm, Ministère de la Culture. Art Resource, NY*

L'oeil

Throughout his career as a poster artist, Cassandre frequently employed the image of the human eye. We see it in Monsieur Dubo's circular frontal white eye and black pupil, where the artist changed the position of the pupil to achieve a balance between continuity and the maintenance of visual interest through variety rather than strict repetition. A similar simplified rendering of a circular frontal eye against a profile head appears in one of the artist's earliest posters, the magpie of the PiVolo wine poster dating to 1924, as well as in the advertising poster for the newspaper "L'Intransigeant" from 1925. More naturalistic eyes and pairs of eyes also appear regularly in Cassandre's posters from the 1930s, addressing the viewer frontally for the beauty products of "Dr. Charpy", or again for Triplex safety glass, both dating to 1930, and eyes also appeared frequently in the series of covers he designed for *Harper's Bazaar* in 1938, under art director Alexey Brodovitch, either in pairs on a human face or disembodied (Figures 3.13, 3.14, and 3.15 – color Plate).

The culmination of Cassandre's fascination with the eye was the enormous 1937 "Watch the Fords Go By" billboard-sized poster for the Ford Company's new "V-8" (eight cylinder) engine. Cassandre designed the poster during the two years he lived and worked in the United States (Figure 3.16 and Color Plate). It measures more than nineteen feet across and features a single frontal eye whose pupil is inscribed with the V-8 insignia.

FIGURE 3.13 *A. M. Cassandre, "PiVolo," chromolithograph, 220 x 134 cm, 1925, Hachard & Cie, Paris, TM & © Mouron. Cassandre License no. 2019-20-08-02 www.cassandre.fr*

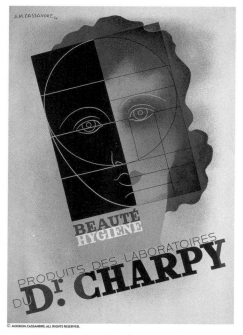

FIGURE 3.14 *A. M. Cassandre, "Dr. Charpy," poster, 160 x 240 cm, chromolithograph, 1930, Cie Artistique de Publicité, TM & © Mouron. Cassandre License no. 2019-20-08-02 www.cassandre.fr*

FIGURE 3.15 (and color plate) *A. M. Cassandre, cover from* Harper's Bazaar, *September (or October), 1938, TM & © Mouron. Cassandre License no. 2019-20-08-02 www.cassandre.fr*

FIGURE 3.16 (and color plate) *A. M. Cassandre, "Watch the Fords Go By," billboard advertisement, offset lithograph, 264 x 594 cm, 1937, N. W. Ayer & Sons, TM & © Mouron. Cassandre License no. 2019-20-08-02 www.cassandre.fr*

FIGURE 3.17 *Alfred Leete, Britons, "Lord Kitchener Wants You. Join Your Country's Army!" lithograph and letterpress, 74.6 × 51 cm, 1914. Private Collection, HIP/Art Resource, NY*

FIGURE 3.18 *Christ in Majesty, San Clemente de Tahull, Spain, fresco, c. 1123 (now in the Museum of Catalan Art, Barcelona), 620 × 360 × 180 cm (entire apse), Museum of Catalan Art, Barcelona*

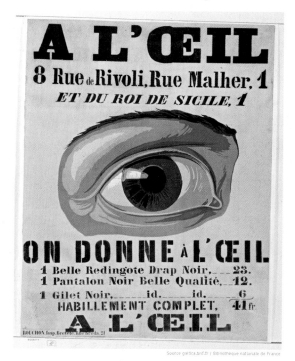

FIGURE 3.19 *Anon., "A L'Oeil," printed by Jean-Alexis Rouchon, 125 × 98 cm, 1864, Bibliotheque Nationale de France*

Whether naturalistic or abstract, disembodied or contained within a face, a frontal eye, or pair of frontal eyes, the eye *confronting* the viewer was a frequent device used in advertisements, as well as in propaganda. As in World War I recruiting advertisements, or for that matter the frontal image of "Christ in Majesty" found in the apses and tympana of Romanesque churches, the frontal eye imposed a certain authority upon the viewer, a visual assault that fixed the viewer's attention and was hard to escape, especially when treated on a monumental scale (Figures 3.17 and 3.18).

As such the disembodied eye was employed in a painted commercial poster in France, designed by Jean-Alexis Rouchon in 1864 for a clothing store called "At the Eye" (Figure 3.19; Rouchon, 1983). Cassandre's use of the eye on the cover of the catalog for his 1936 exhibition at the Museum of Modern Art is yet another instance of its importance and persistence in the artist's oeuvre. To this image we'll return below (p. 92 and Figure 3.27).

Letters and Words

Among the many statements Cassandre offered about his posters, those relating to lettering and words are prominent and merit further attention. First, Cassandre's interest in letters supports the integration of word and image that we associate with the development of the graphic design profession. Cassandre stated that his posters *began* with words rather than images, and that words command the viewer's attention rather than being an afterthought. "The design should revolve around the text," he wrote in 1926 (Mouron, 1985); elsewhere he wrote that "a poster is not a picture, it is first of all a word." His interest in letters also included the display typefaces he designed for the French type foundry Deberny Peignot: Bifur (1929) and Acier (1935) (Mouron, 1985).

Cassandre's preference in letter forms was for sans serif and the upper case. Used in titling since the early nineteenth century, sans serif fonts were bold and could be closely spaced to form tight units, even overlapping at times, as in a travel poster for Étoile du Nord (North Star Line) dating to 1927 (Figure 3.20).

His letter forms for "Dubo-Dubon-Dubonnet" are mono-weight and geometric, and the thickness of the uniform strokes with repeated right angles and semicircles matches that of the café table, pedestal, and chair in the poster's illustration. The mono-weight lettering brings to mind the

FIGURE 3.20 *A. M. Cassandre, "Étoile du Nord," poster, 75 x 105 cm, chromolithograph, Hachard & Cie, Paris, 1927, TM & © Mouron. Cassandre License no. 2019-20-08-02 www.cassandre.fr*

FIGURE 3.21 *Pantheon, Rome, 125 CE (or Base, Column of Trajan, Rome, dedicated 113 CE),*
®*Shutterstock*

typeface Futura, designed by Paul Renner in 1927, and distributed widely through the German type
founding firm Bauer (Frankfurt-am-Main). The typeface reached France soon after its commercial
release and was the subject of an article in the journal *Arts et métiers graphiques* in 1927.

As to his preference for the upper case, Cassandre cited historic precedent: he praised
the upper case lettering used on the buildings as well as on triumphal arches and columns
during the Roman Empire, where they proudly proclaimed their dedication to an emperor or
deity, commanded attention, and were an integral part of a monumental architectural setting
(Figure 3.21).

Indeed, one should remember the architectural scale of Cassandre's posters, including "Dubo-
Dubon-Dubonnet": they were meant to be seen as part of the building, walls, and tunnels on
which they were posted, and the stately letters and right angles were indeed architectonic, or
in Cassandre's own words "lapidary." Cassandre invoked history elsewhere, comparing, for
instance, the simplified shapes of his products and reductive human subjects to the painted figures
on ancient Greek vases, presumably seeing a connection in the contrast of their figure-ground
relationships and the ease with which their audience could identify a figure and comprehend a
narrative (Andrin, 1926; Mouron, 1985).

The Poster and the Street

With each of its three images measuring three-and-a-half feet wide (ten-and-a-half feet if placed
side by side) and four feet tall, the panels of "Dubo-Dubon-Dubonnet" were larger than life,
placed on the walls of buildings or along the pedestrian tunnels of Metro stations in Paris, as

FIGURE 3.22 *Photograph of Paris Street with posters, c. 1931, from Alfred Tolmer,* Mise en Scene, *1931, courtesy Philadelphia Museum of Art Library and Archives*

FIGURE 3.23 *Maynard Owen Williams, Paris Street with Advertising Posters, photograph, 1935, National Geographi Image Collection*

captured in photographs by André Kertész (1894–1985) and other visual chroniclers of the urban scene (Figure 3.12).

Their size, monumentality, multiple postings, and frequent step-wise rhythm illustrate a common theme among many writers in contemporary art magazines who saw advertising posters as an integral part of the "spectacle of the street," works designed for reproduction to be seen by a socially diverse public, communicating aesthetically the boldness, rhythm, and "vitality of today's man" as observed by the poet Blaise Cendrars in 1936, who called Cassandre one of the "most fervent animators of modern life: the director (mise-en-scène) of the street" (Cendrars, 1936).

French printer and designer Alfred Tolmer voiced a similar optimistic view of the happy relationship between advertising and "art" in his 1931 book *Mise-en-Scène*, and included an unidentified photograph of two women walking in front of a hoarding of monumental posters (Figure 3.22): "From the picture gallery formed by the walls of a great city, publicity fires at the public, at close range. Only novelty will permit the layout of a poster to triumph over the medley of advertising appeals amidst which it struggles, and really to do its job in spite of its *unruly neighbors*" (italics added; Tolmer, 1931). In 1935, photographer Maynard Owen Williams captured a scene of Parisians strolling on a crowded street crossing with a group of over-life-size posters as a backdrop against a façade (Figure 3.23).

But not all artists and writers at the time endorsed or welcomed the "poetry" of the street. The Swiss-born architect Charles-Édouard Jeanneret (1887–1965), who adopted the pseudonym Le Corbusier in 1920, was a harsh critic of the traffic, congestion, and general chaos of the urban scene, which he disparaged as cacophony, and to which the modern advertising poster only contributed additional unwanted visual noise. In a 1924 article for the journal *L'esprit nouveau* that he edited with his colleague Amadée Ozenfant (1886–1966), Le Corbusier singled out for criticism (and illustrated with a photograph) a series of striking chromolithographic street displays designed by Cassandre (though he didn't mention the artist by name) for the furniture store Le Bucheron (the Lumberjack).

Le Corbusier did not aim his criticism at the better-known "Le Bucheron" poster (1923) that shows the silhouetted wood-cutter felling a large tree, with the viewers' attention focused on the apex of an inverted triangle formed by the contour of the lumberjack's body, the tree, and a

FIGURE 3.24 *A. M. Cassandre, "Au Bucheron," poster, chromolithograph, 150 x 400 cm, Hachard et Cie, Paris, 1923, TM & © Mouron. Cassandre License no. 2019-20-08-02 www.cassandre.fr*

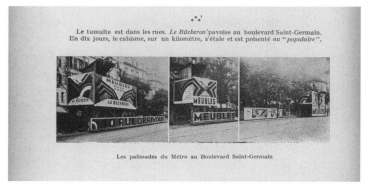

FIGURE 3.25 *A. M. Cassandre, Street displays for Le Bucheron, illustrated in* L'esprit nouveau, *no. 25, 1924 (unpaginated), courtesy Anne and Jerome Fisher Fine Arts Library, University of Pennsylvania*

series of converging triangular forms illuminated by a sunburst in the center of the composition (Figure 3.24), but rather at the large, colorful and predominantly abstract sign with converging diagonal shapes and curved, overlapping target-like shapes displayed prominently on the Boulevard St. Germain (Figure 3.25), in which the lumberjack figure appears far less prominently. It was the more simply constructed poster that received a grand prize at the 1925 Paris exhibition of decorative and industrial art. Corbusier complained that the poster he illustrated in *L'esprit nouveau* was gaudy and excessive, an inauthentic perversion of Cubism that disrupted what should rightly be a more rational, unified, and restrained organization of public space. Rather than the stimulating "spectacle" championed by Cendrars and other writers and artists, Le Corbusier criticized the "tumult" of the street, likening its heightened "temperature" to a "fever," that is, an illness demanding a cure. Indeed, Le Corbusier was, after all, an architect, and the broader context for his criticism was the control of urban space and the threat posed to the architectural environment by unregulated commercial expansion and invasiveness: the text of his article in *L'esprit nouveau*, for instance, was followed by a collage consisting of a series of newspaper clippings that mentioned automobile traffic, accidents, congestion, crowding, and other problems associated with city life. Whether vibrant spectacle or sickness, celebration or critique, the street mediated the meaning of the advertising poster. For some observers the visual and aural excitement of urban life and urban space was intoxicating and poetic, for others it was disruptive and dangerously chaotic, inducing effects akin to a nervous disorder and interfering with the city dweller's mental and physical health. It's possible that Cassandre's more simplified and geometric approach in the Dubonnet series and other posters from the mid-1920s was in part a response to this criticism, as the two artists were on friendly terms; they were members of the avant-garde Union des Artistes Modernes (UAM, founded 1929), and the architect proposed a design for Cassandre's home in Versailles built in 1925 (though he chose the architects Auguste and Gustave Perret).

"Art" and Commerce

Cassandre's "Dubo-Dubon-Dubonnet" raises an issue central to the history of the poster, namely, the differences between the "art poster" and the commercial advertising poster that emerged with the advent of chromolithography in the later nineteenth century. As Ruth Iskin notes in her book *The Poster: Art, Advertising, Design, and Collecting 1860s–1890s* (Iskin, 2014), the distinction between the art poster and the commercial poster is fundamental for a critical understanding of poster history. This distinction applies not only to the *fin de siècle*, but

FIGURE 3.26 *Paris. Affiches Bébé Cadum, c. 1925,* © *Albert Harlingue/Roger Viollet*

is also relevant to poster advertising both during and after World War I and includes the oeuvre of A. M. Cassandre. In particular, artists and writers who celebrated Cassandre's achievements in poster design in the 1920s frequently contrasted his posters with their commercial "other," criticizing the ubiquitous and enormous posters and painted billboards in Paris and throughout France advertising Cadum soap and their outsized images of "Bébé Cadum" (Figure 3.26).

Such a distinction was fundamental to Ernestine Fantl, curator of architecture and design at the Museum of Modern Art in New York from 1933 to 1937, who mounted an exhibition of Cassandre's posters at the museum in 1936, the first exhibition of posters to be held there. "Dubo-Dubon-Dubonnet" was among the examples of Cassandre's posters selected for that exhibition (it remains in MoMA's collection). Fantl remarked upon the connections between the poster and the movements of modern fine art, noting the wit and sophistication that the modern poster imparted in contrast to the majority of public advertisements in the United States, which she judged to be vulgar, misleading, and appealing to the lowest common denominator of mass taste: "Advertising in general is geared to the intelligence of a child in order to insure universal comprehension. In America the main emphases are apparent: Sex Appeal (young ladies of fabulous face and figure); Statistics (different but equally fabulous figures); Fear (will your best friends tell you?) ... None of these formulae appear in Cassandre's designs" (*Posters by Cassandre,* 1936).

Fantl reasoned that the modern poster could be tasteful, universal, *and* commercially successful, attracting viewers' attention by capturing the essence of forms and eliminating the unnecessary. She compared Cassandre's Dubonnet "little man" to Walt Disney's Mickey Mouse in its ability to communicate with a mass audience. It was the notion of the poster as a popular form of modern art mediated by the street rather than the museum, salon, or gallery that presented a persistent, "high art" interpretation of Cassandre's posters during the 1920s and early 1930s, one that viewed the poster as an agent of reform and the elevation of public taste, a "people's art."

Yet the artist was himself ambivalent about such a view, and on occasion contradictory in his statements regarding the poster as a form of "art for the street." In fact, in comments published in 1929, Cassandre included "Bébé Cadum" as part of the visual excitement of urban publicity without reference to a qualitative aesthetic judgment between the worlds of commerce and art (Cassandre, *Art et métiers graphiques*, 1929; Mouron, 1985). Indeed, reconciling art and advertising presented a challenge: Cassandre's catalog cover for the 1936 Museum of Modern Art exhibition illustrates quite directly the uneasy relationship between an aggressive sales pitch and the loftier goals of art! A male figure stands against a bright red background, outlined in white with areas of complementary green/chartreuse to suggest contrasting shadows (Figure 3.27 and color plate). The figure appears to stride toward the right, but his head tilts awkwardly backwards, his oversized eye pierced by an arrow, the vulnerable victim of an assault by an armed advertiser. This striking image might be seen as an illustration of several of Cassandre's statements about his approach to poster design. In the first place the artist often reminded those who asked him, that posters were *not* paintings, that painting was a "goal in itself" while the poster was a "means of communication between the public and the seller," in which the designer has "no right to express himself." While Cassandre's references to himself (the poster designer) as a telegrapher or "dispatcher" and to his posters as "Morse code," may be most easily understood in relation to his reductive, direct, and efficient means of communication in a crowded visual environment, the artist made other statements that can only be interpreted as an acknowledgment of the poster's invasive and blatantly commercial function. Cassandre often used military metaphors to describe the relationship between poster and viewer, stating, for instance, that the goal of the poster was to "hold the viewer in its grip." In comparing painting to the poster, he wrote that the former was an act of "love," while the latter was a form of "rape," and that the goal of the poster artist was to "conquer the public like a Hussar" (Andrin, 1926). The notions of violence and assault used by Cassandre to describe the relationship between viewer and advertisement are a far cry from soft selling and aesthetic uplift, and such statements have more in common with the artist's Museum of Modern Art 1936 catalog cover or the Rouchon "A l'Oeil" poster than with the tradition of the "art poster" celebrated in arts magazines and praised by contemporary artists and writers such as Léger and Cendrars (see p. 98), as well as by curators such as Ernestine Fantl. It's not surprising that exhibitions of Cassandre's posters, as well as their treatment in surveys and monographs, focus upon their aesthetic qualities rather than upon the tradition of the commercial poster and its association with violence, vulgarity, the disruption of public space, and the threat it posed to refined taste. Such a separation underscores the conflicted position the poster occupied, and the shifting allegiances of the poster artist, between the demands of clients' commercial interests and the aesthetic associations of the art poster tradition and the artistic independence and technical experimentation it implied. Indeed, the indeterminate status of the poster also surfaces in other of Cassandre's comments: he admitted that discerning the role of the poster in the arts is "no easy matter"; and while he stated that his favorite commissions were those that were "spontaneously" accepted by his clients, he also commented that designing posters requires "total self-effacement" (Andrin, 1926; Mouron, 1985). Repeatedly in interviews Cassandre distinguished fine art from the poster and minimized the importance of the individual artist in poster design, utilizing the

FIGURE 3.27 (and color plate) *A. M. Cassandre, Exhibition catalogue for "Posters by Cassandre" January 14-February 16, 1936 (cover). Publisher: The Museum of Modern Art, New York, NY, USA. TM. & © MOURON. CASSANDRE. Lic 2019-20-08-02 www.cassandre.fr*

metaphor of a "telegrapher" as intermediary to describe his function, and the poster a "machine for announcing" in the manner of a town crier (a phrase used by Alfred Tolmer in his book *Mise-en-Scène* in 1931), and his process akin to solving a technical and commercial problem, designing with the objective that the final result is created and "reproduced" as an anonymous, serial object in the manner of many of the products he advertised rather than as a unique work of art. At the same time he signed his work in the manner of an easel painter, acknowledged and praised Cubist abstraction, formal relationships in composition, the simplicity and precision found in the work of other contemporary artists connected with the avant-grade movement of Purism (Eskilson, 2012), was a member of the progressive Union des Artistes Modernes (UAM), and was proud of the degree of creative freedom and independence he enjoyed with some of his clients (Mouron, 1985). Posters might be sophisticated in their carefully orchestrated visual organization and pared down, reductive approach to representation, but they needed to make an impact, to stand out, to startle, to penetrate, suggesting visual metaphors of violence reflected in Cassandre's exhibition catalog cover as well as in several of the artist's remarks cited above.

At the level of publicity, Cassandre's Monsieur Dubo and the artist's views on the primacy of the word in his poster relates to the branding of the products he advertised. Branding was acknowledged in the advertising industry as a means of making products "known," not directly as a means to persuade viewers to buy them. Advertising executives and marketing researchers in the United States considered slogans to be effective in gaining product recognition, with Morton Salt's "When it rains, it pours," or even names such as "Cream of Wheat" cited as successful examples (in the United States) of branding that were responsible for achieving product distinction among

FIGURE 3.28 *Mural advertisement, photographer unknown, Paris c. 1932, from Mouron, H., A. M. Cassandre, NY, Rizzoli, 1983*

similar products and leading to substantial increases in sales. "Dubo-Dubon-Dubonnet" built upon an existing branding slogan (Dubon-Dubonnet) that connected the product name with the word for "good" that Cassandre emphasized with his bold geometric sans serif and repeated letters. While posters with Monsieur Dubo gained notice on walls and the Metro tunnels, the name also appeared on its own in signs or in poster compositions without the little man, seen for instance in a photograph by René-Jacques from 1932 entitled "Two Policemen, Rue de la Verrerie" (Figure 3.11) as well as other posters that were purely typographic (Figure 3.28).

Writing from a more scientific and commercial standpoint, advertising experts acknowledged that posters could help to build brand loyalty, but only when the brand, whether the product name, logo, or trademark, was reinforced in print, packaging, and other forms of print promotion. In other words, the poster *alone* was not sufficient to impact sales, the ultimate goal of an advertising campaign, toward which advertising investment should be directed. To that end, for "Dubo-Dubon-Dubonnet," the company reproduced Cassandre's lettering and little man in a number of merchandising displays in a variety of media, including hand-held fans (Sauvage, 2005). As advertising, branding was a benign form of promotion, immediate, insistent, but generally low key or "soft," distinct from the more aggressive forms of persuasion endorsed by scientific advertising executives, who favored celebrity endorsements, testimonials, advice, and melodrama as more effective means to appeal to consumer insecurities and motivate them to buy products. Such views naturally threatened the autonomy of individual poster artists who enjoyed their independence and those printers or agencies that valued a balanced relationship between art and commerce.

Cassandre and the "Moment" of the Art Poster after World War I

Cassandre's success as a poster artist coincided with efforts of economic recovery in France after World War I that included the promotion of domestic products nationally and internationally. Such patriotically inspired efforts (including "Bébé Cadum" and its association both with improved hygiene and concerns with increasing the national birth rate) culminated in the 1925 international Exposition des arts décoratifs et industriels in Paris. At that exhibition the four major French department stores erected pavilions to display their goods, while French magazines such as *Art et decoration* and *Le monde ilustrée* (and *Feminina*) also sponsored their own pavilions; each used signage, interior design, and window display to draw attention to fashion and other luxury goods on display to promote commerce. In each of these pavilions graphic design figured prominently and the attention it attracted was noted by visitors.

The host nation also sponsored a pavilion devoted to the printing industry that celebrated the advertising poster and acknowledged the medium's effectiveness as propaganda for campaigns to sell loans and bonds during World War I. Cassandre's poster for the "Au Bucheron" (see Figure 3.24) furniture store was awarded a grand prize. The exhibition organizers emphasized originality and progress in all the areas of the exhibition, stipulating that submitted designs be "modern" rather than traditional or historicizing. Cassandre's muscular woodcutter referenced youth and health, and celebrated the theme of physical culture that surrounded the 1924 Olympic Games held in France, the first games held after a gap of eight years. Physical culture also played a part elsewhere in the 1925 exhibition, in the sparsely decorated "Physical Culture" room designed by Pierre Chareau and Francis Jourdain for the residence of an ambassador, sponsored by the Société des Artistes Décorateurs (Figure 3.29).

FIGURE 3.29 *Pierre Chareau and Francis Jourdain, Physical Culture Room, Residence of an ambassador, Exhibition des arts décoratifs et industriels, Paris, 1925*

Observers at the time recognized the increasing role that advertising was playing in the lives of city dwellers, whether in the street through posters or more recently by illuminated displays, signage on storefronts and store windows, in magazines and newspapers, and in the new medium of radio, all forms of popular communication and part of the fabric of city life (Cheronnet, 1925). In an illustrated book published at the time of the 1925 Paris exhibition, author Charles Imbert stated, in a section entitled "L'art dans la Publicité," that commerce was the "god(dess)" of the modern world, publicity its "prophet," speaking with a thousand voices, and that no surface or space lacked publicity of one kind or another, and where no one who traversed city streets could fail to notice and retain their images. Today's reader may be struck by the repeated references to the all-embracing, unifying religion of the Middle Ages, intertwined with people's daily lives: store windows are "chapels for wandering pilgrims (shoppers)," chromolithographic posters are "the stained glass windows of cathedrals; they sing to us like the jongleurs who greeted pilgrims on their holy journeys." The tone of these religious metaphors was upbeat and optimistic: technology expanded the "voices" of publicity; commerce helped to bring art into the streets, it announced the goods that bring happiness into our lives, it provided talented individuals with a "mission," it brought light into darkened streets—in short, the author concludes, "What time was ever more abundant in miracles?" (Imbert, 1925)

Léger and Cassandre: The Art Poster and Modern Art

Cassandre's advertising posters were celebrated in journals such as *L'Art vivant, Art et métiers graphiques*, and *L'Affiche*. The authors of graphic design surveys and monographs also often note that the reductive simplicity and formal unity found in "Dubo-Dubon-Dubonnet" constitutes Cassandre's original contribution to the history of the poster, and is the result of a creative "borrowing" from the Cubist-inspired fragmentation of form and conceptual rather than optical approach to representation, as well as a fascination among avant-garde artists in the interwar period with the smooth surfaces, regular shapes, functional precision, and accuracy associated with machines and mechanized mass production, seen also, for instance, in the 1934 exhibition "Machine Art" held at the Museum of Modern Art and curated by architect Philip Johnson.

Among the modern artists most supportive of Cassandre's posters was Fernand Léger. After World War I, Léger transformed his own prewar abstract Cubist style with the introduction, in an often fragmented form, of the human figure and a more easily recognizable subject matter of figures and objects. In a 1926 article for *L'Art vivant*, written by Louis Cheronnet but based upon interviews with painters Léger and Robert Delaunay, Léger applauded the simplified representational vocabulary of Cassandre's posters, and celebrated the city as a feast for the eyes and speed as the "law" of the modern world (Cheronnet, 1926). Léger contrasted Cassandre's "modern" approach to the poster with the more commercial poster advertisements for "Cadum" soap—Léger admitted to not being able to offer an opinion as to which was most effective as *advertising*, but described the commercial poster as a "hole in the wall," arresting and yet irritating at the same time. Cassandre's sense of composition could "calm" as well as "excite" the nerves, that is, be both dynamic and yet soothing at the same time. Curiously, it was American businessman Michael Winburn who partnered with a French chemist to manufacture and market Cadum hand soap, introducing the new product with a massive billboard advertising campaign in France featuring "Bébé Cadum" beginning in 1912 and expanding after World War I (Wlasssikoff and Bodeux, 1990).

Borrowing a musical analogy, Leger likened "Cadum" to jazz and the 1923 "Le Bucheron" poster to orchestration, a structured rather than unbridled and undisciplined "spectacle of the street" (Cheronnet, 1925). The approach is seen in Léger's own work from the period, for instance, the large 1927 "Composition with Hand and Hats" featuring wine bottles, a profile head, a bowler and other hats, a pipe and what appears to be smoke rings, using familiar subject matter, repetition, relationships among rectangular and circular shapes, and color harmonies to structure the disjointed array of ordinary objects (Figure 3.30).

While it has been common in the literature of graphic design history to note the dependence of the advertising poster upon contemporary avant-garde fine art, Léger's paintings, such as

FIGURE 3.30 *Fernand Léger,* © *ARS, NY. Composition with Hand and Hats. 1927. 248 x 185.5 cm Inv. AM1982-104. Photo: Georges Meguerditchian, Musee National d'Art Moderne.* © *CNAC/MNAM/ Dist. RMN-Grand Palais/Art Resource, NY*

Composition with Hand and Hat, and others from the 1920s, suggest a more open-ended exchange between salon and street. In Léger's view, the poster was part of the street's "plastic serenity" and the special "landscape of the city," organizing rather than impeding the "flow of life."

And yet despite the praise for advertising and its civilizing role in modern life, Léger's arguments were primarily aesthetic rather than commercial. Posters were an opportunity for modern artists to engage with the rhythms of contemporary life to reach a mass audience: the connection between art and advertising was essential, and yet at the same time tenuous. It depended ultimately not upon the support and opinions of artists, poets, and magazine editors, but upon the patronage of clients as well as upon the views of a public whose tastes were difficult to predict or easily control. After all, Cassandre's career as a poster designer lasted little more than a decade, and his abandonment of the form after 1937 offers some evidence for the difficulty that poster artists encountered in successfully navigating the turbulent seas of commercial advertising.

Publicité Versus "Scientific" Advertising

Cendrars, Léger, and even Le Corbusier all viewed the poster as a form of public art, for better or for worse. In *Le spectacle dans la rue,* Blaise Cendrars selected a sampling of pairs of Cassandre's posters with accompanying phrases to show the range of their themes, from nature to still life, escape to arrival (*conquête*), and ending with three images of "Dubo-Dubon-Dubonnet" and a final image in color of Cassandre's large poster (1935) for the wine retailer Nicolas and its mascot "Nectar," accompanying the following phrase: "Cassandre uses all of the gifts [*données*] of the world to SING at the reaches [*portées*] of the light of day [*de la lumière*]." (Figure 3.31)

But during the 1920s French advertisers began to acknowledge the findings of "scientific advertising" as advanced in business schools and within the wider business community in the United States. Having achieved maximum economy and efficiency through the application of scientific management to industrial production with the research of Frederick Taylor, Frank

FIGURE 3.31 *A. M. Cassandre, "Nicolas," 1935, chomolithographic poster, 240 x 320 cm, Alliance Graphique, TM & © Mouron. Cassandre License no. 2019-20-08-02 www.cassandre.fr*

and Lillian Gilbreth, and Henry Ford's moving assembly line for automobile manufacturing, business leaders and educators turned their attention to *consumption* efficiency (a shift from supply to demand), in which advertising would play a major role. Rather than the somewhat limited concept of "*publicité,*" scientific advertising judged success in terms of sales, and depended increasingly upon the understanding and *control* of human behavior. If production could be managed and streamlined by reducing time-on-task in the manufacture of serial commodities such as watches, appliances, soaps, and automobiles, business leaders were determined to discover what laws of consumer behavior could be ascertained and managed to increase desire and lead to higher levels of consumer spending. American scientific advertising, pioneered by academics at the University of Michigan and Harvard University and adopted by advertising agencies such as J. Walter Thompson, endorsed market research to compile statistical information on demographics, income levels, advertising expenses, viewer attention, and the desires, as well as the fears and insecurities, of consumers. This approach tended to favor testimonials, endorsements, and the negative effects of *not* using a product (for example the social stigma of body odor or perspiration used in advertisements for deodorant or bad breath for toothpaste). In his 1923 book *Principles of Advertising*, Harvard University business professor Daniel Starch defined the difference between publicity and advertising: the purpose of the former was to make a product known, of the latter to *sell* it, by adopting those advertising strategies that proved most effective to a company's bottom line (Starch, 1923).

Scientific advertising constituted a challenge to the business model that sanctioned and promoted the advertising poster. Poster designers sometimes worked under contract to printers, whose agents solicited business from manufacturers, or to service providers such as railroads or resorts who commissioned advertising from individual artists. Cassandre worked under contract to the Parisian printer Hachard between 1923 and 1927, then formed his own graphic design agency in 1931 under the name Alliance Graphique, in partnership with his close friend Maurice Moyrand and fellow artists Charles Loupot and Paul Colin, both of whose posters had also been singled out for praise in the pages of *L'Art vivant* and other publications. Moyrand had been the representative for a printing company based in the city of Lille and was the son of the owner of the Chemin du Fer du Nord Railway company, who commissioned travel posters (e.g. "Étoile du Nord," see Figure 3.20) from the newly formed agency. Moyrand died in an automobile accident in 1934, and Alliance Graphique disbanded in the following year. Cassandre then worked under contract to printers in France, Switzerland, and Italy to produce his posters.

As historian Marc Martin noted, business investment in poster advertising declined in the 1930s (from 25 percent in 1901 to 8.1 percent in 1938), the result of national and local efforts to regulate the use of public urban space for advertising through the imposition of taxes and surcharges that increased the cost of poster advertising. As a result, businesses turned increasingly to newspaper and magazine advertising for promotion (along with the newer medium of radio). Despite the decline in the use of the poster as an advertising medium and the increased costs and restrictions, French companies, and in particular beverages such as Dubonnet, continued to support poster advertising, particularly in Paris with its celebrated tradition of poster art from the fin de siècle (Martin, 1992).

Conclusion

"Dubo-Dubon-Dubonnet" stands just past the middle of Cassandre's career as a poster artist and at the height of his success. By 1932 his posters had received prizes, he had a long list of

FIGURE 3.32 *A. M. Cassandre, Logotype, Yves St. Laurent, 1963, TM & © Mouron. Cassandre License no. 2019-20-08-02* *www.cassandre.fr*

clients willing to pay for his services, was a partner in his own advertising agency, and lived comfortably in a home he commissioned in Versailles built of reinforced concrete and designed by the architect brothers Auguste (1874–1954) and Gustave Perret (1872–1952). Cassandre's designs were the subject of journal articles, and in 1936 he was the subject of a one-person show at the Museum of Modern Art, the first at the museum to feature the advertising poster. In the same year he was the featured artist in a book (Blaise Cendrars, *Le spectacle de la rue*). He attended the Museum of Modern Art exhibition and received commissions for posters and other work (a series of magazine covers for *Harper's Bazaar* under art director Alexey Brodovitch, and a four-page insert of color designs for advertisements in *Fortune* in March (*Fortune*, 1937)), but despite this recognition, Cassandre was disappointed in his North American reception. In 1938 he abandoned poster design for costume and set design for the theatre, and returned to France in 1941 for military service. He devoted the last two decades of his life to easel painting and occasional work on new typefaces; in 1963 he designed the logo for the fashion designer Yves St. Laurent (founded 1961) that remains in use today (Figure 3.32). He committed suicide in 1968.

We may conclude that at heart there was a tension between Cassandre's interest in articulating and practicing "principles" of effective advertising in poster design as a new form of artistic practice with its own rules, and a growing realization that the nature of advertising, demanding ever-new ways of engaging its audience, meant that "principles" of any kind were bound to be short lived, subject to the increasing input of market research, the vagaries of fashion, viewer attention, and novelty rather than practices validated by history or the poetic pronouncements of high-minded modern artists, writers, and curators. Cassandre's desire to reach the "common man" presumed a stable and universal vocabulary of forms, such as Monsieur Dubo, that would readily communicate ideas to a mass audience, command attention, and arouse collective emotions; while such a view gained recognition and financial success for Cassandre in the 1920s and early 1930s, by the mid-1930s his approach failed to secure many commissions in the United States, and what seemed universal and accessible in the 1920s or early 1930s became more exclusive, or at least less "sociable" and persuasive later in the same decade. The nature of advertising was ephemeral and the means of achieving its aims elusive; as attention shifted from designer to consumer, there was little beyond the pragmatism of sales results and market research to sway the manufacturers and printers who paid the fees and increasing production costs of poster advertising. The business needs that gave birth to the advertising poster and underwrote its success also determined its future and navigated the uncertainties of the form as an agent of promotion in what Susan Sontag termed "the theater of persuasion." Cassandre was both the beneficiary as well as the victim of those uncertainties. Curiously, in the United States the pendulum that oscillated between scientific market research and "art" in advertising began to swing back toward intuition after World War II with designers such as Paul Rand and advertising executives such as William Bernbach who looked at interwar Europe for inspiration and touted the advantages of brevity and sophisticated wit in the "New Advertising" amid concerns about truth in advertising and consumer manipulation. It was Rand who resurrected Cassandre's Monsieur Dubo in the early 1940s for the wine company's United States market (Figure 3.33). To this subject we'll return in the chapter on Doyle Dane Bernbach's early 1960s campaign for Levy's "real Jewish rye" bread (chapter 5).

FIGURE 3.33 *Paul Rand, magazine advertisements for Dubonnet wine,* Life, *October 25, 1943, courtesy Paul Rand Foundation*

Chapter 4

Frank Zachary at *Holiday*: Travel, Leisure, and Art Direction in Post-World War II America

Travel and tourism occupy a conspicuous place in the history of twentieth-century graphic design. The travel advertising posters designed by Herbert Matter for the Swiss Tourist Office, by Roger Broders for the sunny Mediterranean coast, or by A. M. Cassandre for train travel, as well as McKnight Kauffer and Tom Purvis for London Transport, are among the most celebrated examples of graphic communication in the period between the two world wars. The travel-related work of these and many other designers and illustrators figure prominently in surveys of graphic design; culturally they attest to the increasing economic, social, and political roles played by tourism (and advertising), emerging with greater personal mobility via train and automobile travel in the early twentieth century, and expanding with the growth of commercial air travel, improved systems of government-sponsored interstate highways, rising incomes, and lower unemployment in the United States after World War II.

While the advertising poster remained a vehicle for communicating the pleasures of travel in print during the second half of the twentieth century, the tourism industry also invested considerable capital in newspaper and magazine advertising as well as in commercials using the new medium of television, the latter beginning in the early 1950s. Advertising revenues supported *Holiday*, a large-format monthly magazine published by the Curtis Publishing Company in Philadelphia and launched in March 1946. Curtis also published the successful mass-circulation magazines *Ladies Home Journal* and the *Saturday Evening Post*. In response to initial mixed reviews and disappointing subscriptions for *Holiday*, the publisher named writer and advertising executive Ted Patrick (1901–64) as the journal's new editor in 1947 with the goal of giving the magazine a stronger identity and impact. Patrick hired Frank Zachary (1914–2015) as an associate editor in 1951 and as graphics editor in 1952. In 1954 Zachary appeared in the magazine's credits as art director. Beginning in 1953 and under Zachary's art direction the journal began to gain recognition in the graphic design community for its cover design and feature layouts in the Art Director's Club *Annual of Advertising and Editorial Art*; in 1958 (for the 1957 calendar year) *Holiday* garnered eight mentions for cover as well as editorial and advertising art—during that same year Zachary's name began to appear more prominently below Patrick's in the credits, in larger type and on a separate line, acknowledging the contribution that visual communication was making to the success of a monthly magazine devoted to the subject of leisure travel.

While lacking formal educational background or professional training in the visual arts, and not as widely celebrated as his mentor Alexey Brodovitch or contemporaries Alexander Liberman and Henry Wolf, Zachary and *Holiday* also merit inclusion in surveys of graphic design history (Meggs, 2012), and his contributions as art director have been acknowledged along with better-known large-format magazines of the interwar and postwar eras such as the fashion-oriented *Harper's Bazaar, Vogue,* and the short-lived *Portfolio* (1950–1), which Zachary edited together with Brodovitch and George Rosenthal (Heller, 2017).

Ted Patrick died in 1964 and Zachary left the journal shortly afterward when he was passed over for the job of managing editor. He was later named managing editor of the journal *Town and Country*, a position he maintained until his retirement in 1991; Zachary died in 2015 at the age of 101. An obituary in the *New York Times* (June 14) included a photograph of Zachary peering out from a porch atop the Cathedral of Notre Dame in Paris, his cheeks playfully resting on his hands mimicking the pose of a nearby gargoyle (Figure 4.1).

The *Times* obituary kindled my curiosity to learn more about Zachary (like me a native Pittsburgher) and his connection with *Holiday*, to explore the role of travel and leisure in American life and the close connection among tourism, advertising, and graphic design. Articles

FIGURE 4.1 *Frank Zachary at Notre Dame, photograph by Slim Aros, c. 1958, Getty Images*

in *Vanity Fair* and the *Paris Review* from 2013 (as he reached the age of 100) celebrated Zachary's achievement at *Holiday*, and Steven Heller reminded me of his own earlier appreciations of Zachary in *Print* and elsewhere, based upon Heller's personal friendship with the art director/ editor himself (Heller, 2015). Neither of the articles for the *Paris Review* and *Vanity Fair* were written by designers or art critics. Their authors were more interested in the magazine's literary content and the impressive stable of gifted writers its editor corralled—this in turn suggested to me that an appreciation for Frank Zachary depended upon a holistic approach to the magazine and its place in post-World War II America, integrating rather than isolating its layouts from the features and advertisements they accompanied, and thinking about the commercial as well as aesthetic motivations of the publisher and editing team. In fact, as a student in Pittsburgh, Zachary had aspired to be a writer, and in addition to being a newspaper journalist he contributed articles to magazines that included *New Yorker*. Through its editorials, features, advertisements, photographic essays, and illustrations, *Holiday* provided its readers with practical advice for travelers, editorial perspectives on a variety of tourist destinations, colorful illustrations and photographs of travel venues and related activities that helped to broadly shape, promote, and to defend the increasingly prominent place of leisure and the cultivation of taste in an age of rising white, middle-class incomes and affluence, along with fueling curiosity about the wider world upon which an expanding tourist industry depended. In effect then, for more than two decades *Holiday* was the monthly voice of the booming travel and tourism industry, whose substantial investment in advertising subsidized the ample space and creative freedom with which the magazine's editors explored more sophisticated aesthetic layouts, hired established photographers and illustrators along with a group of recognized authors, promising (and delivering) an expanding readership of travelers and armchair tourists to advertisers who underwrote the editorial staff's high-priced services and production costs, all at a newsstand price of fifty cents per issue or five dollars for an annual subscription (eight dollars for two years). Patrick and Zachary's contributions were part of the expansion of magazine art direction beyond the subject of fashion into the burgeoning business of leisure in post-World War II America.

A careful study of *Holiday* touches upon the history of the profession of art direction, upon modern and more traditional approaches to cover art and advertising, as well as upon the broad range of meanings and associations of travel in post-World War II America that the magazine communicated and championed. With his background as a journalist, writer, and publicist, Zachary contributed to a team effort involving photographers, artists, and illustrators, and editors, some of whom also received credit in the citations for the *Annual of Advertising and Editorial Art*. The editorial team also negotiated input from market research that closely monitored subscriptions, advertising revenue, along with reader response and interest.

The advent of network television, the role of location in the modern cinema, and the growth of the Internet more recently along with a myriad of DIY travel apps available for mobile phones and tablets have eclipsed the medium of print as the primary source of advertising and promotion that sustained *Holiday* until its demise in 1977 after nearly a decade of steady declines in circulation and advertising revenue. While the vehicles for promoting travel may have changed, the tourism industry itself continued to expand and to prosper; moreover, the motivations of today's travelers, along with the means of communicating and stimulating those motivations, whether for adventure, status, relaxation, or curiosity, were forged with text and image during *Holiday's* heyday.

Holiday, July 1952: Cover

An overview of an issue of *Holiday* under Patrick and Zachary reveals the interrelationship among text, photographs, illustration, advertising, and layout in which we can appreciate the role of art direction within the overall organization of the magazine. The July 1952 issue was devoted almost exclusively to travel in the United States; under Patrick's editorship, *Holiday* frequently featured a particular city, country, or continent as a tourist destination whose cover and tagline helped to attract attention and offer a quick take of the issue's theme for the would-be traveler. The July 1952 issue featured one of the journal's first "modern" covers, substituting abbreviation and abstract symbol for more traditional illustration or landscape photography (Figure 4.2). Designed by Robert Geissman with the tagline "TRAVEL USA" in sans serif typography to the lower left (like the larger sans serif masthead), the July cover featured a tapered red, white, and blue striped zig-zag band moving upward from the lower right to the upper left against a black background, with small pictographs of trees, in green, consisting of vertical trunks and horizontal branches/foliage to either side. The patriotic red, white, and blue roadway becomes muted as it nears the pale yellow "H" of the masthead, creating a subtle tension between the surface and depth. In the table of contents, *Holiday* included a brief hint of the content of the next issue along with an instructive explanation of the current issue's cover.

For July, 1952 the description reads in part:

FIGURE 4.2 (and color plate) *Robert Geissman, "Travel in the USA," cover,* Holiday, *July 1952, Drexel University, Hagerty Library*

Our July cover symbolizes Travel, USA. The red-white-and-blue road represents the highways of the land; its lightning-like zigs are speed; its diminishing perspective is distance, and the little evergreens are the green American landscape. Artist Robert Geissman says that as a tourist, himself, he is forever halting the family car "with a screaming of brakes" to admire this landscape. Maybe that zigzag road is really a symbol of a typical Geissman family outing.

By interjecting Geissman himself and his family's vacations into the narrative description, the editors suggests that the artist, just like the reader, is just another tourist at heart. Geissman's "symbolic" cover was inherently "graphic," but his condensed approach to cover design was intermittent at *Holiday* and did not represent a radical shift in art direction: landscape photography and illustration, as well as traditional portrait photography continued to appear on *Holiday* covers during the first half of the 1950s (Figures 4.3 and 4.4), though more graphic covers were generally those singled out for recognition in the *Annual of Advertising and Editorial Art*.

Holiday, July 1952: Advertisements and Audience

Following the table of contents and until p. 33, advertisements dominated the pages of the July 1952 *Holiday* issue. In fact, leafing through the pages of *Holiday* today, the features sometimes seem like an interruption to the steady if somewhat uneven rhythm of ads, with some pages

FIGURE 4.3 *"July in Michigan," cover,* Holiday, *July 1951, Drexel University, Hagerty Library*

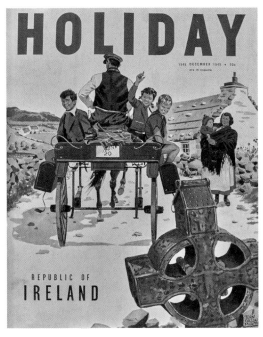

FIGURE 4.4 *"Republic of Ireland," cover,* Holiday, *December 1949, Drexel University, Hagerty Library*

divided into four columns of twelve rectangular units-per-column; where single columns of text appear toward the end of each issue, they seemed to be drowned out by the "noise" of advertisements (Figure 4.5; might the same be said of network television today, sometimes employing a split screen with ad on one side and programming on the other?).

There was no discernible template or design parameters for advertisements: unsurprisingly all bore some relationship to travel, whether directly (and prominently) to promote means of transportation and destinations, or indirectly through a rich array of travel accessories. The larger ads, full-page or even double-page and in color, most often promoted larger companies such as automobile brands, airplane manufacturers (e.g. Douglas, Lockheed, Figure 4.6), airline carriers (e.g. American Airlines, TWA), resorts, as well as increasing numbers of ads sponsored by local governments promoting tourism in their states, and brandy (*Holiday* broke rank with Curtis's editorial policy for its other journals that did *not* permit advertisements for alcoholic beverages, strengthening an association between alcohol consumption and enjoyable leisure activities).

Throughout the 1950s, illustration was more prevalent than photography in *Holiday* advertisements, and many ads continued to include testimonials from celebrities and other standard types of narrative copy familiar in mass-circulation magazines. For July 1952 there were few, if any, traces of the bolder and more immediate, visual, and pared-down "New Advertising" (see also chapter 5 on Levy's rye bread, pp. 143 ff.). When the newer approach appears, it is most often found in ads for fashion or fashion accessories (e.g. cosmetics), with color photographs of models or products contrasting against the white ground of the blank page, as in an advertisement for Dana cologne/Charles of the Ritz and perfume (Figure 4.7).

Generally the page layout followed the approach in Curtis Publishing's other mass-circulation magazines, maximizing advertising space with a tight four-column grid, small point sizes for copy, the use of color, and a wide variety of display typefaces to direct viewer attention toward products or brands. Similar approaches to advertising layout are found in the pages of *Ladies Home Journal*, in which one finds crowded layouts on the features pages as well. While advertising revenue was essential to the success of *Holiday*, the magazine's advertisements generally lacked white space, humor, or the use of simplified drawing or color contrast associated with modern graphic design, adhering to traditional formulas for selling products using idealized illustrations depicting attractive models and crowding as much copy as possible into the available space. An example may be found on the inside cover for the July 1952 issue for Ray-Ban sunglasses (Figure 4.8), showing a handsome couple illustrated against a sandy beach with ocean and a sky interrupted by a pair of oversized sunglasses with copy extolling the distinctive features of the glasses, and five *more* illustrated vignettes at the bottom with individual user testimonials.

The advertising pages in *Holiday* attest to the unprecedented growth and promotion of the travel and tourism industries in the United States. Industry statistics show a four-fold increase in expenditures for recreation among American families between 1945 and 1965; advertisements also demonstrate tourism's broader economic impact, not just in relation to automobile and tire manufacturer sales, or commercial airlines, but the countless businesses and initiatives that benefited from increased travel or that stimulated travel, from luggage to binoculars, casual shoes, portable radios, 35-millimeter cameras and movie cameras, preparation for careers in the hospitality industry, hotels, pet carriers, tennis racquet strings, hotels, liquor, portable radios, clothing, lightweight footwear, sun tan lotion and sunglasses, state and local tourist bureaus, as well as the US government authorization for the construction of a network of interstate highways and turnpikes (Federal Aid Highway Act, 1956 and after). Not only was travel easier than ever before, but products and services (e.g. binoculars, cameras) enhanced travelers' experience as well as helping to overcome lingering doubts and uncertainties (flat tires, sunburn, affordable

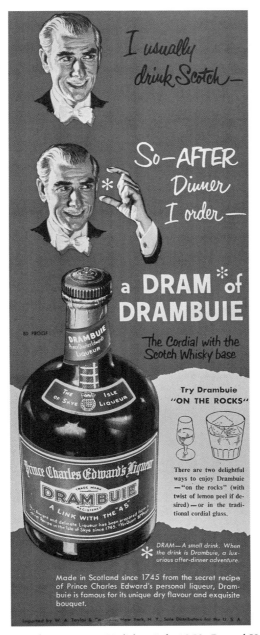

FIGURE 4.5 *Drambuie liquor advertisement*, Holiday, *July 1952, Drexel University, Hagerty Library*

and convenient lodging and restaurants), along with editorial tips ranging from calendars of seasonal events to suggestions for packing. United States Census Bureau statistics reveal a steady rise in median incomes, from an average of $3,011 in 1947 to $5,620 in 1965 (although average incomes for African American families were roughly *half* of that for white families), the presence of more women (wives) in paid labor, and airline ridership doubling during the same time

FIGURE 4.6 *Douglas Aircraft advertisement*, Holiday, *July 1952, Drexel University, Hagerty Library*

FIGURE 4.7 *Dana Cologne for Charles of the Ritz advertisement, Holiday, March, 1956, Drexel University Libraries*

FIGURE 4.8 *Ray-Ban Sunglasses advertisement*, Holiday, *July 1952, Drexel University, Hagerty Library*

period. Equally if not more important than income was the widespread provision for employer-paid vacations for salaried middle-class and wage-earning working-class labor. With paid leave, workers received the benefit of leisure *time*, along with disposable income with which to fill that time. Travel was one of many options available to consumers, one that was productive in generating new products, sales, and jobs for scores of travel-related businesses; but in order for that income and time to be *spent on travel*, it had to be *sold*. The printing trade journal *Printers Ink* documented increases in travel industry advertising, including a 7 percent increase from 1952 to 1953, stating "today travel is one of the largest industries in the world," exceeding 1.3 billion dollars (1953), with New York City the top destination for foreign travelers and Europe

PLATE 1.1 *Josef Müller-Brockmann, © ARS, NY. Poster, schützt das Kind! [Protect the Child!], 1953. Offset lithograph on wove paper, lined, 1275 × 905 mm (50 3/16 × 35 5/8 in.) Museum purchase from General Acquisitions Endowment Fund. 1999-46- Photo Credit: Cooper Hewitt, Smithsonian Design Museum/Art Resource, NY. Photo: Matt Flynn © Smithsonian Institution, Cooper Hewitt, Smithsonian Design Museum, New York, NY, USA Artists Rights Society*

PLATE 1.7 *Hans Thöni, "Vorsicht—Kinder!" (Watch out—Children!), poster, chromolithography, 1955, 128 × 90.5 cm, Plakatsammlung SfG Basel*

PLATE 1.11 *Herbert Matter, © Copyright. Poster: Engelberg, Trübsee/Switzerland. Switzerland, 1936. Offset lithograph on white wove paper. 1019 × 637 mm (40 1/8 × 25 1/16 in.). Museum purchase from General Acquisitions Endowment Fund, 2006-15-1. Photo: Matt Flynn, Cooper Hewitt, Smithsonian Design Museum. Photo Credit: Cooper Hewitt, Smithsonian Design Museum/Art Resource, NY; Artists Rights Society*

PLATE 2.1 *Ettore Sottsass, "Yellow Cabinet" (Mobile Giallo), Burled maple, briar, ebonized oak veneer, gilded wood knobs, 57 ½ × 51 7/8 × 18 1/8 in., 1988–9, Bridgeman, Artists Rights Society*

PLATE 2.3 *Moser, Koloman (Kolo) (1868–1918). Ver Sacrum, XIII, Poster for the 13th Secession exhibition. 1902. Lithograph, 73 3/16 × 25 3/16 in. (185.9 × 64 cm). Printer: Lith. Anst. A. Berger, Wien. Gift of Joseph H. Heil, by exchange. The Museum of Modern Art. Digital Image © The Museum of Modern Art/Licensed by SCALA/Art Resource, NY*

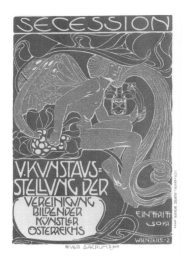

PLATE 2.4 *Koloman Moser, Fifth Secession Exhibition Poster, 98.4 × 66.7 cm, chromolithography, 1899, MAK–Österreichisches Museum für angewandte Kunst/Gegenwartskunst*

PLATE 2.9 *Kolomon Moser, "Richardsquelle" Mineral Water advertising poster, c. 1897, chromolithograph, 56.8 × 68.58 cm, Albertina Museum, Vienna*

PLATE 2.10 *Carl Müller, "Street in Vienna", 1903, 27.3 × 37.7 cm, watercolor and chalk, Vienna Museum. Karlsplatz, Bridgeman*

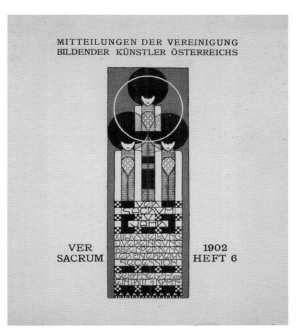

PLATE 2.13 *Koloman Moser, title page, Ver Sacrum, Jahr V, no. 6, 1902. Courtesy of Marquand Library of Art and Archaeology, Princeton University. Photographer: John Blazejewski*

PLATE 2.27 *Alois Hans Schram, Poster for Thirty-Fifth Kunstlerhaus Exhbition, Vienna, 1902, Albertina, Vienna, reproduced in Ottokar Mascha, Österreichische Plakatkunst, Vienna, J. Löwy, 1915, color plate 4, New York Public Library*

PLATE 2.39 *Alfred Roller, Exhibition Poster (Max Slevogt), chromolithograph, 47.9 × 49.3 cm, Vienna, 1897, MAK–Österreichisches Museum für angewandte Kunst/Gegenwartskunst*

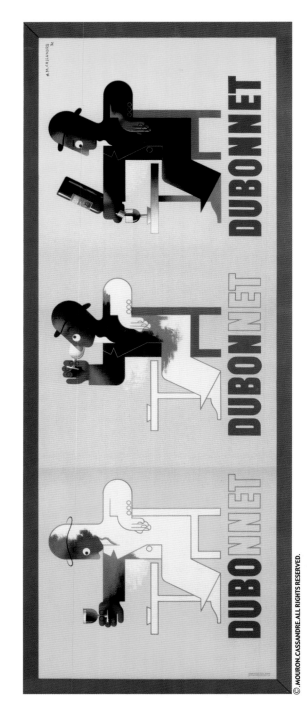

PLATE 3.1 A. M. Cassandre, "Dubo-Dubon-Dubonnet," 1932, chromolithograph, 120 × 160 cm and 240 × 320 cm, Alliance Graphique, TM & © Mouron. Cassandre License no. 2019-20-08-02 www.cassandre.fr

PLATE 3.4 *Jules Chéret, "Quinquina Dubonnet, Apéritif, Dans tous les Cafés." 1895. Lithograph, 124.6 × 87.1 cm, Printer: Imp. Chaix (Ateliers Chéret), Paris. Given anonymously. The Museum of Modern Art, New York, NY, USA. Digital Image © The Museum of Modern Art/Licensed by SCALA/Art Resource, NY*

PLATE 3.5 *Leonetto Cappiello, "Absinthe extra-supérieure J. Edouard Pernot", lithograph, 152 × 105 cm, Bibliothèque nationale de France*

PLATE 3.9 *A. M. Cassandre, "Sools" poster for men's hat shop, chromolithograph, 160 × 240 cm, chromolithograph, 1929, TM & © Mouron. Cassandre License no. 2019-20-08-02 www.cassandre.fr*

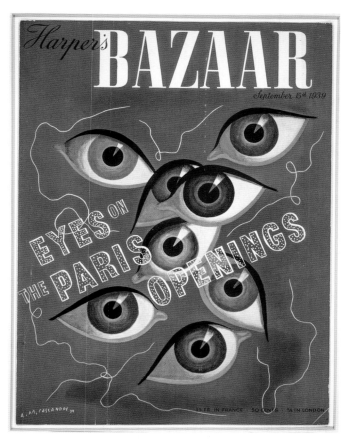

PLATE 3.15 *A.M. Cassandre, cover from* Harper's Bazaar, *September (or October), 1938, TM &*
© Mouron. Cassandre License no. 2019-20-08-02 www.cassandre.fr

PLATE 3.16 *A. M. Cassandre, "Watch the Fords Go By," billboard advertisement, offset lithograph,*
264 × 594 cm, 1937, N. W. Ayer & Sons, TM & © Mouron. Cassandre License no. 2019-20-08-02
www.cassandre.fr

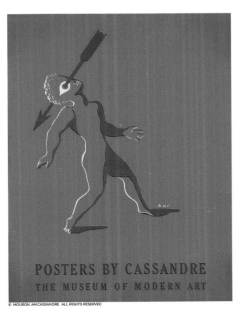

PLATE 3.27 *A. M. Cassandre, Exhibition catalogue for "Posters by Cassandre" January 14-February 16, 1936 (cover). Publisher: The Museum of Modern Art, New York, NY, USA. TM. & © MOURON. CASSANDRE. Lic 2019-20-08-02 www.cassandre.fr*

PLATE 4.2 *Robert Geissman, "Travel in the USA," cover,* Holiday, *July 1952, Drexel University Libraries*

PLATE 4.17 *"America's own Fashions," feature from* Holiday, *July 1952, Drexel University Libraries*

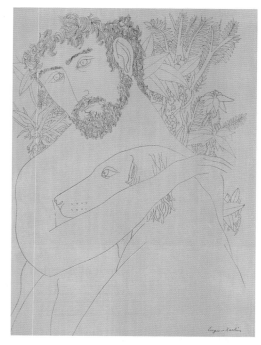

PLATE 4.20 *Eugene Karlin, illustration for the "Man who saw the Garden of Eden," December 1957, Drexel University Libraries*

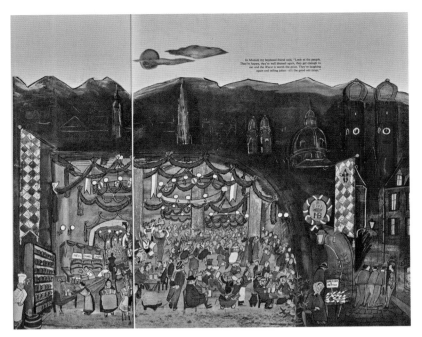

PLATE 4.22 *Ludwig Bemelmans, illustration of Munich Beer Hall,* Holiday, *January 1954, Drexel University Libraries, courtesy Barbara Bemelmans*

PLATE 4.23 *George Giusti, "Europe 1954," cover,* Holiday, *January 1954, RIT Cary Graphic Arts Collection*

PLATE 4.25 *Paul Rand, "Tenth Anniversary," cover,* Holiday, *March 1956, courtesy Paul Rand Foundation*

PLATE 4.30 *Three-page spread of Grand Canyon from Michener article,* Holiday, *March 1956, Drexel University Libraries*

PLATE 4.31 *Henry Wolf, art director, "The Americanization of Paris," cover,* Esquire, *July, 1958*

PLATE 4.41 *George Giusti, "Africa," cover,* Holiday, *April, 1959, RIT Cary Graphic Arts Collection*

PLATE 5.2 *Levy's rye bread posters, 45" × 29 ½," offset lithography, Judy Protas, writer; William Taubin, art director; Howard Zieff, photographer; Doyle Dane Bernbach Advertising Agency, New York, c. 1963, Library of Congress, DDB Worldwide*

PLATE 5.6 *Levy's rye bread posters,*
45" × 29 ½," offset lithography, Judy Protas,
writer; William Taubin, art director; Howard
Zieff, photographer; Doyle Dane Bernbach
Advertising Agency, New York, c. 1963–70,
Library of Congress, DDB Worldwide

PLATE 5.7 *Levy's rye bread posters, 45" × 29 ½,"*
offset lithography, Judy Protas, writer; William
Taubin, art director; Howard Zieff, photographer;
Doyle Dane Bernbach Advertising Agency, New
York, c. 1963–70, New York Transit Museum,
photo: Rebecca Haggerty

PLATE 6.9 *Jean-Léon Gérôme, "Ave Caesar Imperator, morituri ad salutant," oil on canvas,*
92.6 × 145.3 cm, 1859, courtesy Yale University Art Museum

PLATE 7.3 *Sir Christopher Wren, Sheldonian Theatre, Oxford, 1664–9, photo: author*

PLATE 7.9 *Philippe de Champaigne, "Moses Presenting the Tables of the Law", oil on canvas, 99 × 76.2 cm, Milwaukee Museum of Art*

the major destination for American travelers, followed by Latin America and the Near East, Mexico, and the Bahamas. Air-conditioning allowed for longer travel periods to warm-weather locations such as Florida, and *Printers Ink* acknowledged that "vacations with pay are now standard." The journal also analyzed where travel dollars were being spent, with equal parts for transportation and lodging, slightly higher percentages for meals and combined shopping and entertainment. And vacation travel, along with the growing interstate highway system, helps to explain a preponderance of automobile advertising in the pages of *Holiday*.

Print magazines were certainly the major vehicle for the promotion of travel after World War II, but the magazine industry was highly competitive and expenditures were closely monitored, balancing the cost of staff and steadily rising production expenses (including postage and paper) against newsstand sales, subscriptions, and advertising revenues. Generally magazine revenues were on the rise, but attracting newsstand buyers, subscribers, and advertisers required intensive marketing efforts, gauging consumers' lifestyle choices in the face of competition from television and newspapers. Graphic design was one of the "investments" that publishing companies made to their editorial staffs in order to attract and shape the desires of an audience who increasingly possessed the means to devote time and money to leisure travel. While we celebrate the art director's decisions and creative freedom in the choice of photographs or illustrations, types and type sizes, text blocks, and the overall disposition on the page, the investment itself, that is, the basis for the designer's creative freedom, depended upon intensive quantitative and qualitative

FIGURE 4.9 *Russell Lynes, "Hi-brow, Middle-brow, Low-brow," chart by Tom Funk from* Life *magazine, April 11, 1949, Drexel University, Hagerty Library*

market research, including reader surveys and interviews, undertaken with an eye toward differentiating between active consumers and passive "bleacherites," that is, distinguishing readers whose interest in travel was less likely to result in the purchase of goods and services from those who were more motivated to take to the highways, railways, and airways, and to *spend*. This kind of data enabled publishers to refine the form as well as the content of their journals, communicating with text and image a mood or "lifestyle" that included the use of precious leisure time for the varied enjoyments of travel. From the standpoint of marketing, the purpose of, or justification for, art direction was to attract and maintain the reader's attention as long as possible in order to guarantee or increase the likelihood that advertisements would be noticed. To borrow from the vocabulary of a popularly advertised leisure activity, art direction was that combination of art and marketing science that produced the bait that in turn attracted a particular type of fish.

Holiday occupied a unique place within the magazine publishing industry. Critics have compared it to the fashion-focused *Vogue* and *Harper's Bazaar*, and its fifty-cent newsstand price was the same as both of those journals. But comparisons of this sort don't take into consideration the differences between fashion and travel and their roles in the lives of readers. As circulation statistics and the discussion of content below will demonstrate, *Holiday*'s readership was initially more broadly based than that of its fashion counterparts at rival publishers Hearst and Condé Nast. The mass-circulation magazines of the time, such as the weekly *Saturday Evening Post* or monthly *Ladies Home Journal*, cost ten cents (three dollars per year), and *Life* (also weekly) was twenty cents at the newsstand. But circulation figures for the early 1950s show that while *Holiday* lagged considerably behind Curtis's or Henry Luce's mass-market magazines (*Life* magazine's circulation was over five million in 1954, and *Ladies Home Journal* was more than four-and-a-half million), its readership was close to double that of either *Vogue* or *Harper's Bazaar*: in the second half of 1960 circulation for *Holiday* was reported at 921,000, while neither *Vogue* nor *Harper's Bazaar* broke 500,000 during the same period of time. Between 1953 and 1960, *Holiday*'s circulation had more than doubled—the magazine's figures for the second half of 1960 exceeded those of the whole of 1953. In the same year advertising linage in *Holiday* increased more than 13 percent over 1959, in comparison with an industry-wide increase of 5 percent.

As Russell Lynes observed in his entertaining 1949 essay titled "Highbrow, Middlebrow, Lowbrow," first published in *Harper's* and later reproduced with an accompanying illustrated chart in *Life* magazine (Figure 4.9), American society could be divided into three broad social and cultural groupings (high-brow, middle-brow, low-brow), each identified not by wealth or family background, but by lifestyle and consumer behavior, that is, the goods and services they chose to purchase, the clothing they wore, the furniture with which they decorated their homes, and the magazines they read.

Lynes's categories have become part of the general twentieth-century cultural discourse, but the categories are not as clear-cut or rigid as they may first appear: according to Lynes, the three categories of taste in post-World War II America were neither monolithic nor entirely distinct: each could be divided into sub-groupings, and there were areas of overlap and fluidity among them. Looking through the issues of post-World War II *Holiday*, I would posit that the editorial team of the magazine represented Lynes's upper middle brow grouping, while the intended readership was more socially diverse, corresponding to Lynes's lower middle-brow group. For Lynes, the upper middle-brow are the "purveyors of hi-brow ideas" while lower middle-brow are the group most exploited by advertisers. Such a characterization fits well with the emphasis and findings of market research through the early 1950s, before a shift took place during the later 1950s, targeting higher income readers whose potential as consumers was greater (even if magazine circulation declined as a result). Publishers belong to the upper middle-brow group, balancing a refined taste for literature, classical music, jazz, modern art, and the kind of furniture that was "not available in department stores," with the business model at Curtis and the less exclusive desires of a broader popular taste that encompassed both male and female readers through the early 1950s, when demographic analysis supported a wider, more inclusive net.

During the later 1950s *Holiday* increasingly targeted a more sophisticated readership. One might compare the shift to the trajectory of post-World War II modern design more generally. As historian Jeffrey Meikle has pointed out, modern design in the United States became more elitist during the later 1950s, less concerned with appealing to or with shaping middle-brow taste; when University of Pennsylvania sociologist Herbert Gans was asked to characterize modern design in the postwar period for an exhibition held in 1982 at the Philadelphia Museum of Art, he called the exhibition a "treasure trove of progressive upper middle-class culture" (Meikle, 2005; Gans, 1982). While consumer spending continued to rise in the later 1960s and increased unabated through the remainder of the century, the fate of magazines such as *Holiday* was less rosy. With advertising dollars gravitating to the newer medium of television, the large format art-directed magazines and their publishers faced challenges. When *Holiday* folded in 1977 circulation had to dropped to under 400,000 per year; while print advertising continued to support the fashion industry through magazines such as *Vogue*, the tourism industry had turned elsewhere to communicate with audiences. A glance at television today with its ubiquitous automobile manufacturer and airline commercials is proof enough of a shift in the means and media of visual communication for travel and tourism. The undifferentiated mass audience was better served, more economically served, by television advertising rather than print media. As television sales increased and viewing audiences grew, advertisers chose a new medium that reached millions of homes. Even if a smaller percentage of viewers became buyers, the sheer size of the television audience made it a wise advertising investment to reach the mass market. Magazines, by contrast, needed to become more targeted, more homogenous, in order to define their market and attract and retain advertising dollars. At *Holiday*, market research in the early 1950s had shown that income levels of vacationers were well above the national average, that 60 percent of subscribers were college-educated, that 70 percent worked in professional or managerial positions, with a slightly higher percentage of urban versus rural readers. These findings led to more sophisticated fashion features in *Holiday*, more literary rather than practical or informational content, all aimed at appealing to a better educated, more affluent high-brow reader (*Printers Ink*, April 26, 1954).

Holiday, July 1952: Features and Photographs

The features in *Holiday* during the 1950s usually combined informative editorial essays on vacation destinations accompanied by photographs and captions introduced with bold titles and short introductions in larger type. After the opening spread, editorial essays generally proceeded to a three-column format in slighter larger type but continued on single columns on a four-column grid in the back of the magazine, a space-saving but not necessarily reader-friendly practice borrowed from other Curtis publications such as *Ladies Home Journal* and the *Saturday Evening Post*. There the text also shared space (and competed for attention) with advertising in the other columns. The typeface used for *Holiday* was Caslon, at 10 point for general body type and 16 or 18 point for larger text blocks at the beginning of feature articles and photo-essays. Clearly readers' attention was first drawn to the larger and bolder introductory paragraphs and photography rather than the closely spaced columns of unmarked continued text hidden in narrower columns toward the back of the magazine.

The July 1952 "Travel in the USA" issue included four photographic essays: "Americans on the Move," "Land of Plenty" [devoted to food], "The Pursuit of Happiness," and a feature on summer fashions. For all, color photography dominated the magazine's large 10 3/4" × 13 1/2" pages. Each essay promoted travel as an inherent, intrinsic, and natural aspect of the *American* experience, balancing traditional values that emphasized and prized a strict work ethic, independence, sacrifice, savings, and religious respect for self-restraint and self-denial, along with fears of the excesses of rampant materialism and hedonism and the lack of self-control they implied.

The introductory "Americans on the Move" essay begins with a short editorial in large type in two columns with ample white space at the top on p. 33. Editor Ted Patrick connected mobility with the history of the United States as a nation created by people who escaped persecution or tyranny by *traveling* in search of a new home. Today (i.e. in 1952), as Patrick explained, Americans continue to travel, but for pleasure and adventure, taking advantage of modern roads and expanding means of transportation, exploring a country enriched both by captivating natural as well as man-made destinations ripe for vacations. In other words, travel was an innate part of the American character. The brief editorial is followed by twelve pages of color photography, beginning with an atmospheric shot of the Manhattan skyline dominated by the Empire State Building against a hazy blue-grey sky, followed by the Grand Canyon, Golden Gate Bridge, Old Faithful Geyser at Yellowstone Park, the modest eighteenth-century brick Independence Hall in the Old City section of Philadelphia, Crater Lake (Oregon), New Orleans' French Quarter viewed from a wrought iron balcony, Niagara Falls, The Capitol building in Washington, DC at night against an orange background framed by trees, the Columbia River Gorge, Redwood Forest in northern California, and a quaint white colonial-era village church in Massachusetts, alternating minimally framed with full-bleed photos, all displayed without labels or explanatory captions. High-quality photography, increasingly in color, was a hallmark of *Holiday* under Zachary's art direction. Satisfying the desire for timely information during the World War II years that were a feature of *Life* magazine, *Holiday* turned to photography to encourage tourism and promote a variety of incentives for Americans to travel as the war ended (Figure 4.10).

Many of the photographs aim for awe-inspiring majesty and monumentality through scale and color, while others are decidedly humble and quaint, most noticeably in the brick and wood Independence Hall, or a local church in rural New England (Figure 4.11).

The combination of colonial charm, natural majesty, along with man-made grandeur and national pride is typical of *Holiday*'s inclusive editorial approach to its subject. The editorial voice was instructive but not overly prescriptive, and seems to have been aimed to reach as many sub-groups of readers as possible, from youth (there were occasional features devoted to campus life at particular colleges and universities), young couples, families, the affluent middle-aged, and retirees. Some content as well as advertisements were more gender-specific, for instance, fishing (usually depicted in ads or photographs with men) or swimwear (directed toward women, often suggestive rather than openly erotic). In 1952 *Holiday*'s editors appear to have understood that the expansion of the travel industry meant appealing to a wider variety of tastes that included middle- as well as high-brow. This is evident not only in the selection of photographs

FIGURE 4.10 *Old Faithful*, Holiday, *July 1952, Drexel University, Hagerty Library*

FIGURE 4.11 *New England Church,* Holiday, *July 1952, Drexel University, Hagerty Library*

for "Americans on the Move" but also in the range of advertisements that emphasize thrift and "do-it-yourself" products as well as luxury goods. For instance, the July 1952 issue of *Holiday* includes advertisements for family camping trailers and station wagons along with full-page illustrations of elegant Chrysler Imperials and sporty Oldsmobile coupes (Figures 4.12 and 4.13). Absent, however, are the mass-entertainment venues of the first half of the twentieth century, for instance, Coney Island, associated with arcades and side shows for day trippers rather than longer family vacations.

Following the expansive photo spread for "Americans on the Move" appears a lengthier essay by assistant editor (later executive editor) Carl Biemiller entitled "Our Wonderful Restlessness," with the opening title and lead paragraph of the text in large italic facing a striking aerial photograph of a modern six-lane limited access highway (Figure 4.14). Reinforcing the theme of the previous photographic essay ("Americans on the Move"), Biemiller presents travel as something intrinsically "American." Below the introductory spread are five smaller color photographs or illustrations of various modes of transportation: the commercial airplane, steamboat, bus, yacht, and diesel locomotive. Again there is ample white space at the top of the introductory page, and the arrangement of bold sans serif title, italic opening paragraph, column of continuing text at the right (three-column), series of photo/illustration below, is asymmetrical and designed to interrupt expected left-right and top-down reading habits, moving the viewer's eye more actively from title, to image, and to text. In the essay Biemiller demonstrates statistically that vacations have become more commonplace than at any previous time in American history, and he provides several reasons for the growth of the travel industry, for instance, improvements in transportation (communicated visually with photographs), the productive value of tourism

FIGURE 4.12 *Vagabond Camping Trailer advertisement*, Holiday, *July 1952, Drexel University, Hagerty Library*

FIGURE 4.13 *Chrysler Imperial advertisement*, Holiday, *July 1952, Drexel University, Hagerty Library*

FIGURE 4.14 *"Our Wonderful Restlessness," feature for* Holiday, *July 1952, Drexel University, Hagerty Library*

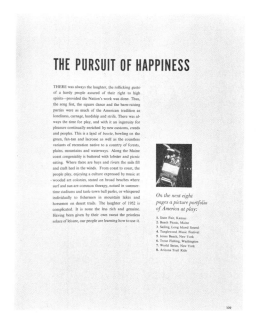

FIGURE 4.15 *Essay introducing "The Pursuit of Happiness,"* Holiday, *July 1952, 109, Drexel University, Hagerty Library*

(seven to ten billion dollars annually at the time) and paid vacations for middle- and working-class Americans. Biemiller connects tourism with technological improvement and economic growth, resulting in social progress with leisure as the benefit of a higher standard of living in a democratic society. He examines growth and change within the travel industry, from the increasing importance of airplane travel, to travel agents and "package tours" that make vacations more standardized but affordable, and the rise of the motel (a new form of lodging at the time, geared to the automobile), accompanied by photographs of a motel swimming pool and a family on vacation riding in a convertible against the backdrop of a mountain range.

Yet not everything about America's "restlessness" was wonderful; Biemiller also offered a more complex, troubling interpretation of his subject, one that equated restlessness with immaturity and aimlessness rather than an adventurous, pioneering spirit, even suggesting that travelers may be taking a "last fling" in the face of global tensions and fears of the atom bomb. Such equivocation demonstrated a need for the *guidance*, the authorial voice, offered by Holiday's editors and authors, not only suggesting *what* travelers should see but *how* to see and appreciate it. A recurring editorial feature of *Holiday*, essays such as Biemiller's "America's Restlessness" balanced optimism and the projected promises of advertising with some of the uncertainties of the post-World War II era, from the atom bomb, to the horrors and destruction wrought by World War II, to Cold War fears and an ongoing Korean Conflict, and postwar colonial tensions in Africa and India (see p. 138). *Holiday* was more than a sunny travel brochure: in promoting travel, its editors chronicled some of the cultural complexities that accompanied increased tourism, while its photographs encouraged readers to relax and think that *now*, rather than *later*, was the best time to travel.

A third photo essay in the July 1952 issue of the magazine accompanied an editorial titled "The Pursuit of Happiness" (Figure 4.15). One key to Holiday's success following the lukewarm reception of its early issues, was the magazine's ability not just to promote tourism, but to a *justify* tourism and frame it in a broader cultural context. *Holiday* was not unique in exploring the meaning, and the *value*, of leisure in America. In July 1948, *Life* magazine published a feature article (with photographs) reporting on a "roundtable" (sponsored by the magazine) that took place in Rye, New York devoted to the "Pursuit of Happiness," one of the three unalienable "Rights" enshrined in the United States Declaration of Independence along with "Life" and "Liberty." There a group of respected figures in the fields of business, philosophy, and education debated the current meaning of the "The Third Right" and the relationship between happiness and leisure for Americans. During a weekend of dialogue the group rejected equations between happiness and pleasure or between happiness and material progress. If higher incomes were a barometer of "happiness" they argued, why were divorce rates and juvenile delinquency statistically on the rise in the United States? The consensus among the group was that happiness was the result of both internal (inner) and external (outer) factors—and they concluded, along humanist lines, that an individual's happiness depends to some degree upon the happiness (real or hopeful) of the society at large. The experts also agreed that leisure was an ingredient in the attainment, or potential attainment of happiness. And when it came to the nature of leisure in post-World War II America, the experts suggested that by and large Americans "don't use leisure to full advantage," that often leisure is a distraction rather than making "full use of [one's] faculties." While "escape," in the form of radio and mainstream Hollywood movies, was acknowledged as one aspect of leisure, the arts constituted a more rewarding form of recreation, certainly a nod to Russell Lynes's high-brow taste category (today's film critics no longer seem to endorse such qualitative or hierarchical distinctions between Hollywood motion pictures and "high art"—magazines such as the *New Yorker* regularly review both genres in the same section).

The experts assembled at the *Life* magazine roundtable did not mention travel as a form of leisure (or shopping for that matter), and *Holiday*'s approach to the subject was decidedly more middle-brow. The range of activities featured in the accompanying photo-essay in *Holiday* is again striking for the diversity of tastes it represents: excited kids riding a roller-coaster at the annual Kansas State Fair, a family picnic along the Maine coast, a young woman practicing the flute at the Tanglewood Music Festival in western Massachusetts, an Arizona trail ride, an aerial view of the vast expanse of seashore at Jones Beach on Long Island, and a baseball game in immense Yankee Stadium in the Bronx—all forms of recreation representing common urban as well as rural pastimes, group as well as individual activities, and geographic as well as topographic variety (Figure 4.16).

Editor Ted Patrick reminded his readers that play has always been part of the American experience (after work that is!), liberally flowing from the varied backgrounds of a nation of immigrants:

> THERE was always the laughter, the rollicking gusto of a hardy people assured of their right to high spirits—provided the Nation's work was done. Thus, the song fest, the square dance and the arm-raising parties were as much of the American tradition as loneliness, carnage, hardship, and strife. There was always time for play, and with it an ingenuity for pleasure continually enriched by new customs, creeds, and peoples. (*Holiday*, July 1952, page 109)

FIGURE 4.16 *Photograph of Yankee Stadium*, Holiday, *July 1952, Drexel University, Hagerty Library*

Leisure is presented as the well-deserved *reward* for hard work rather than an end in itself, a common, unifying feature of a socially, ethnically, and racially diverse nation. Unlike the landscapes of "Americans on the Move," the human figure is a more active and integral part of the selection of photographs illustrating "The Pursuit of Happiness." When *Holiday* next treated the subject in depth, in the tenth anniversary issue of March, 1956, the copy had more in common with the views expressed at the *Life* roundtable, reminding the reader that material and technological progress did not translate directly into the satisfying use of leisure time (see p. 127 ff.).

A final photographic essay was devoted to fashion, focusing upon *casual* rather than formal or business attire. Entitled "America's Own Fashions," the six-page spread was written by *Holiday* fashion editor Toni Robin, the only woman listed as an "Associate Editor" in the magazine's table of contents (see p. 132 ff.). The text is light and breezy, identifying an "American look" with the notion of "play clothes." Robin quotes from French couturier Edward Molyneux (1891–1974), who commented that it is "incontestable that America leads the world in the creation of bright modern clothes for play and leisure." Photographed by Arnold Newman, the clothed female figure dominates the layouts, with strong contrast provided by ample blue background space and varied column widths for the two double-page spreads (Figure 4.17 and color plate). The larger photographs, both in color and black and white, feature asymmetrical compositions and a variety of casually posed female models on a boardwalk, whose bodies create distinct shapes against a deep azure backdrop.

FIGURE 4.17 (and color plate) *"America's own Fashions," feature from* Holiday, *July 1952, Drexel University, Hagerty Library*

FIGURE 4.18 *Map of USA with monuments for each state*, Holiday, *July 1952, Drexel University, Hagerty Library*

Taking a cue from the more heavily art-directed fashion magazines such as *Harper's Bazaar* or *Vogue*, asymmetrical layouts, contrast, and large amounts of "air" or empty surrounding space appeared more frequently in the pages of *Holiday* as the decade wore on. The arrangement of areas of text and image on the page or double-page spread created carefully orchestrated relationships among shapes to unify the composition, providing a combination of visual order, immediacy, and a more active viewing experience that either complimented or "was" the story, especially for the display of fashion. These larger carefully constructed images are balanced by smaller images of men as well as women engaged in a variety of leisure activities from fishing, to bicycling, and picnicking.

As noted above, an element of *Holiday's* content during the early 1950s was practical travel advice, ranging from educational "places to see" to being task-oriented (e.g. "Living in a Trailer," and a listing of art, science, and Americana museums throughout the country; pp. 127–30). Gradually the old-fashioned maps of geographical areas "peopled" (or cluttered) with tiny images of familiar monuments and activities (Figure 4.18) gave way to the photographic essay and the collage, but both approaches co-existed in the early 1950s.

Earlier issues provided tips on packing efficiently, but such useful content became less frequent in the later 1950s and early 1960s, yielding to photographic presentations of the enjoyment of leisure with reduced emphasis upon pragmatic travel advice. A case in point is found in the March 1956 tenth anniversary issue of *Holiday*, about which we'll have more to say below. Here photographs of open-plan modern interiors are accompanied with text by designer and critic George Nelson, titled "Down with Housekeeping," commenting upon how design and technology in the home have helped to create a new, modern lifestyle that reduces time spent on household chores, resulting in increased time for leisure (Figure 4.19). The text is displayed in two columns and interspersed with full-bleed photographs of the "jet set" relaxing in homes with swimming pools, patios, and terraces.

FIGURE 4.19 *"Down with Housekeeping,"* Holiday, *March 1956, Drexel University, Hagerty Library*

It's difficult to overstate the role high-quality photography played in the commercial success and critical appreciation of *Holiday*. Photographs, shot from provocative angles, unframed and often bleeding off the page, whether carefully staged or seemingly candid, printed in rich colors or with subtle atmospheric gradations in black and white, projected not only a viewer's "eye" and first-hand experience of a particular tourist destination, but also communicated or distilled the "essence" of a place, that is, a mood, memory, or value that could be recognized and shared with the reader and realized through his or her own first-hand travel. Perhaps this is what Zachary meant when he wrote that "photographs create illusions, not facts" (see also the discussion of photography in chapter 1, p. 19, 23 ff.), or when he stated that he was less interested in capturing a "tiger" than the animal's "tiger-ishness," It was the responsibility of the art director and his team of art editors to assemble headings, text boxes, and photographs as a collage within the ample space of a single or double-page spread, as well as to coordinate the flow between successive pages, to create visual excitement that intensified and stimulated reader interest, triggering associations, and desire.

Illustration

While photography came to dominate art direction in *Holiday*, illustration, a mainstay of other Curtis publications such as *Ladies Home Journal*, also remained. Zachary employed a stable of artists whose illustrations accompanied many of the magazine's features. Rather than the idealized masculine and feminine stereotypes found in advertisements and other contemporary mass-circulation magazines, Zachary preferred lightly drawn, and often light-hearted, sketch-like approaches to illustration, whether in line art or tinted drawing against richly saturated colored backgrounds. An example was a delicate line-drawn illustration against a striking avocado-green background, accompanying a feature article entitled "The man who saw the Garden of Eden," written by Aubrey Menen and illustrated by artist Eugene Karlin (Figure 4.20 and color plate).

Tonally the drawing was consistent with the typography and ample use of white space in layouts generally, providing an even texture and unity between printed and unprinted areas of the opening double-page spread, and the drawing was reproduced in the 1958 *Annual of Advertising and Editorial Art*. The accompanying text, recounting a strange folklore tale told to the essay's author, was only tangentially related to travel, suggestive of the shift toward a more generalized definition of leisure that included reading as well as travel beginning in the later 1950s.

Other illustrators appeared frequently throughout the monthly issues of *Holiday*: among the most favored was European-born Ludwig Bemelmans (1898–1962), creator the *Madeline* series of

FIGURE 4.20 (and color plate) *Eugene Karlin, illustration for the "Man who saw the Garden of Eden," December 1957, Drexel University, Hagerty Library*

FIGURE 4.21 *Ronald Searle, "American Summer," cover,* Holiday, *July 1959, Drexel University, Hagerty Library*

children's books, as well as cartoonist Saul Steinberg (1914–99), Al Hirschfield (1903–2003), and the English illustrator Ronald Searle (1920–2011). Searle's illustrations, for instance, on the July, 1959 cover and announcing an essay by Alex Atkinson on indigenous culture in the American west, were more agitated than delicate, and most often humorous, including an element of satire. In our Figure 4.21, Searle depicted a Native American Indian chief dressed in elaborate costume standing atop a precipice overlooking a vast expanse of western American landscape, peering with one eye through the viewfinder of a camera, playing the *tourist* rather the object of tourism.

Bemelmans was a "go-to" illustrator in Zachary's *Holiday*, especially for issues that featured cosmopolitan cities such as Paris, London, or New York. The artist, who was born in Italy and grew up in Germany, immigrated to the United States during World War I and lived there for most of his career. His use of bold colors for backgrounds and abbreviated drawing style call to mind the work of French painter Raoul Dufy (1877–1953) and communicated an accessible, modern sensibility toward leisure, mobility, and casual sophistication that seemed appropriate to his mostly urban subjects. A clever example can be seen in an issue devoted to Europe as a tourist destination in 1954 (see directly below). Bemelmans created his impressions of contemporary European cities as he experienced and remembered them before as well as after World War II. Spread across two facing pages (61–2) is the city of Munich in southern Germany (Figure 4.22 and color plate), where against a dark background with lightly traced outlines of historic domed buildings, towers, and side streets with pedestrians and a peddler (selling soft pretzels and fresh radishes), Bemelmans sketched a light-filled festive beer hall, with a band, well-fed customers, and servers communicating a postwar return to the charm of the city's everyday leisure activities enjoyed by residents and tourists alike.

It's not difficult to understand Zachary's affinity for this kind of modern illustration. Figurative, accessible, with clever asides that smacked of first-hand experience (pretzels and radishes!), Bemelmans' illustrations possessed the immediacy of an everyday encounter along with a generalized meaning associated with typical, pleasurable pastimes in particular locations (e.g. beer halls in Germany, double-decker bus rides in London) familiar to the would-be tourist.

FIGURE 4.22 (and color plate) *Ludwig Bemelmans, illustration of Munich Beer Hall,* Holiday, *January 1954, Drexel University, Hagerty Library, courtesy Barbara Bemelmans*

Europe, Eurocentrism, and American "Identity"

The photograph of Zachary at the cathedral of Notre Dame in Paris (Figure 4.1), the Bemelmans drawings of European cities, the entire January 1954 issue of *Holiday* titled "Europe" and January issues annually between 1956 and 1959 along with others during the 1950s and early 1960s devoted to Rome, Paris, France, Spain, Portugal, and Italy suggest an attraction to Europe as a tourist destination among the magazine's editors that has not been lost on other writers—in his 2013 *Vanity Fair* article Michael Callahan referred to *Holiday's* "continental inflection." Artist George Giusti's cover for January 1954 (Figure 4.23) was a modern collage, using areas of red and blue color and rough, heavy black line to symbolize the pieces of a stained glass window, alternating with fragments of engravings of well-known European monuments including the Coliseum, the Hellenistic Laocöon group (Vatican Museums, Rome) and Venus de Milo (the Louvre, Paris), and elevations and facades of Gothic cathedrals.

Oddly, perhaps, the cover image was a modern and more freely handled variation, or reinterpretation, of the more traditional graphic map with tiny drawings of monuments of sites and activities used frequently to represent familiar attractions associated with particular geographical areas (e.g. Figure 4.18). And interestingly, all of the images, unified by being incorporated into a leaded stained-glass window, reference monuments from the "past," rather than the present. A photo essay by Henri Cartier-Bresson (1908–2004) captured a series of "moments," suggesting the persistence of a remembered past still active in the present, some with children at play or taking part in ceremonies and festivals, or figures posed against medieval and other time-worn

FIGURE 4.23 (and color plate) *George Giusti, "Europe 1954," cover,* Holiday, *January 1954, RIT Cary Graphic Arts Collection*

monuments. For *Holiday's* April 1955 issue, the focus was Italy. Here the country's Etruscan, Roman, and Renaissance past played a role in the selection of photographs accompanying several feature articles, but with an entire issue devoted to its subject, writer Sean O'Faolin emphasized regional difference, Italy's reputation for respected traditions of fine craftsmanship (for instance, in leather, with a photograph of a Florentine shoemaker who once worked for Ferragamo, still part of Italy's national design identity today), along with the country's modern film industry, its architecture, shopping, and the "joy of total relaxation, sunshine and balm, brilliant colors, constant, pleasantly distracting to and fro of Italy's idlest hours" In other words, Italy was painted as the perfect place for a vacation, illustrated with photographs of contemporary Italians at work and at play, blending the nostalgic tone of Cartier-Bresson's photo essay in the previous year's Europe issue with images (many in color) that suggest youth and the excitement of a modern and vibrant lifestyle.

The Italy issue of *Holiday* and the essays in the January 1954 "Europe" issue reveal a particularly "American" attitude toward Europe, one that suggests the United States' continuity with Western civilization but sounding a note of American difference, independence, and energy characterized by informality, a desire for spontaneity, a more self-conscious "modernity," and at times seized with an insatiable need for constant stimulation. This "American" character is found in a tongue-in-cheek essay by Ruth McKenney, poking fun at the French reputation in literature for "affairs" during her and her husband's experience of living in Brussels, noting (with

FIGURE 4.24 *Henri Cartier Bresson, Breton Women in front of the Royal Portal, Chartres Cathedral, photograph,* Holiday, *January, 1954, Drexel University Libraries. Courtesy Magnum Photos London*

some disappointment) how conventional and devoted she found a particular French couple she met during her stay. One can also note a similar attitude in Al Hine's review of films for the same issue, which praises the 1953 film "Roman Holiday," whose plot concerns an old-world princess (Audrey Hepburn) who meets an American reporter (Gregory Peck) on assignment in Rome and with whom she enjoys the more carefree and fun-loving lifestyle she secretly desires.

In the issue's lead essay, "The Meaning of Europe," historian and journalist Alan Nevins acknowledges a natural affinity between Europe and America in the connections of a shared history and ethnic ties, while at the same time remarking that American travelers today are drawn as well to adventure and the more rugged experience of the frontier. Nevins provides examples of Europe's cultural legacy in music, literature, art, law, and "ideas," encouraging readers to experience such a legacy "first-hand," that is, through travel. Almost as an afterthought he encourages readers to "have fun." Essentially the other feature articles in the issue provide a visual counterpart to such first-hand encounters, primarily through photography. Nevins's essay is followed by Cartier-Bresson's extensive photo-essay, with its juxtapositions of past and present (Figure 4.24).

Destination Europe: Tourism and Politics

There was a political, foreign policy dimension at work in *Holiday's* repeated features on European travel. Still within a decade of the end of World War II, preserving the "image" of Europe in *Holiday* was a way of supporting the United States' investment in the economic recovery of European nations through tourism and the far-reaching stimulus program known as the Marshall Plan (aka Economic Recovery Plan or ERP), begun in 1948, bolstering private enterprise to foster capitalist economic development as a bulwark against the spread of communism along with the military alliance known as the North American Treaty Organization

(NATO, 1949). It's interesting to note that aside from the review of "Roman Holiday" with its memorable scene of co-stars Audrey Hepburn and Gregory Peck riding a Vespa motor scooter through the streets of the city, there's nary a mention or image of present-day Europe in the January 1954 issue of *Holiday*: the focus is on the past, that is, the familiar "image" of Europe's history rather than its present or future; a little more than a year later, the editorial tone is more fun-loving and progressive. By that time gross domestic product among the nations of Europe had exceeded prewar levels, employment levels had risen, and safeguards and protections for the unemployed and needy were put in place as a safeguard against social unrest. Tourism contributed to balancing trade deficits with the United States, strengthened the value of national currencies, and was part of flow of goods and services resulting from cooperation that the Marshall Plan supported in the interests of free trade and open markets; as a result, present and future complemented nostalgia for the past. With a US Congress initially wary of contributing to alleviate widespread destruction during the conflict, displacement, and despair in World War II's aftermath, the Marshall Plan envisioned aid as a form of investment and influence rather than a gesture of charity (Ellwood, 1992). *Holiday*'s editorial voice was a private rather than governmental form of economic stimulus, in which American tourism contributed to a host of broader concerns for the economic and political stability of Europe. The content of *Holiday* issues during the early 1950s demonstrates the dovetailing of tourism with the United States' global strategic political and economic interests with increasing emphasis upon "modern" as well as "historic" Europe: the magazine devoted eleven articles to France in 1953 and twelve to Belgium and England. The entire January 1954 issue featured Europe in addition to another eight illustrated articles that year on France, thirteen articles on France in 1955, and an additional fifteen devoted to England and other European nations. Joint US—European Associations such as the Organization of European Economic Cooperation (OEEC, founded 1949) promoted economic cooperation and free trade, a prelude to the establishment of the European Union and common euro currency (EU, 1993, euro introduced 1999). Tourism was a building block in restoring and *constructing* European identity and confidence—Italian author and journalist Guido Piovene (1907–74) published his *Viaggio in Italia* in 1957 (translated into English the following year), a photo-essay that celebrated the natural beauty of the country along with signs of the modernization that was reducing the economic disparity between Italy's industrial northern and agricultural southern regions.

A New Era of Leisure—*Holiday*'s Tenth Anniversary

In March 1956 *Holiday* celebrated its tenth year of publication with a special anniversary issue. The festive, colorful cover was designed by Paul Rand (Figure 4.25).

Against a banded background of red, white, and yellow, the flames of ten lit candles atop a layered birthday cake pointed toward the masthead, whose letters appeared in white, pink, green, and blue. Two areas of text against yellow backgrounds proclaimed the spirit of a "new leisure," "the biggest change of our time," enabling readers to "live more fully" and "enjoy personal rewards."

Aside from a few exceptions (for fashion accessories: Dana perfume and Charles of the Ritz lipstick to name two; for an example, see Figure 4.7), the advertisements remained decidedly old-fashioned. Even those that used photography were frequently narrative, or consisted of symmetrical sequences of square images that tried to squeeze as much visual and textual information as possible into the available space (Figure 4.26).

FIGURE 4.25 (and color plate) *Paul Rand, "Tenth Anniversary," cover,* Holiday, *March 1956, courtesy Paul Rand Foundation*

FIGURE 4.26 *Western Pacific Railroad advertisement,* Holiday, *March 1956, Drexel University Libraries, permission Western Pacific Railroad Museum, Portola, California*

THE NEW LEISURE

FIGURE 4.27 *Opening page of "The New Leisure" essay,* Holiday, *March 1956, Drexel University, Hagerty Library*

Editorially, the lead essay appeared on p. 34 with the words "THE NEW LEISURE" in bold mono-weight upper case sans serif centered against an entirely empty background.

The contrast with the preceding and cramped pages of advertisements couldn't have been greater (Figure 4.27)—and it's clear that the visual presentation was as important as the copy, with the article title boldly proclaiming the subject's importance, leaving the viewer wondering what exactly was "new" about leisure in 1956. The facing one-page essay asserted that leisure was the "blessing" of American technological and economic progress, constituting an increasing and significant amount of time during the day and throughout the year.

But echoing some of the caution noted above in the July 1952 issue (pp. 116–17), *spending* that time in a rewarding way was challenging, and frequently led to disappointment—Americans do not seem to know *how* to appreciate or make the best use of their hard-earned and well-deserved leisure time. The author explains the impediments to rewarding leisure: a traditional morality that condemned "idleness," and a misguided devotion to a single leisure pursuit such as golf or fishing that quickly becomes either a routine (or obsession), depriving individuals of the enjoyment of leisure and rendering it less satisfying than it might be or *should* be. With a mildly didactic tone, the author encouraged readers to "learn the secret of *constructive* leisure," that is, using leisure to nurture body, mind, and spirit. Leisure is now a "given" in modern life rather than a goal—the question is no longer an apology for leisure time, but a strategy for the optimal use of that time. In the next article, titled "Heavy, Heavy, What Hangs Over," a clever cartoon by Saul Steinberg (Figure 4.28) depicts a male figure suspended precariously in the air between two trees (as if in a hammock but without the hammock!) reading a book, with the caption: "The average American is uneasy even when he tries to relax. The qualities that were indispensable in creating our standard of living become a formidable handicap when he seeks to earn his hard-won leisure."

Steinberg's humor betrays a degree of sophisticated and effacing self-awareness, not unlike the strategies of the "New Advertising" that acknowledged and depended for their persuasiveness upon a media-savvy reader, a viewer accustomed, in this case, to more familiar representations

FIGURE 4.28 Holiday, *March 1956, drawing by Saul Steinberg*, Untitled, c. *1947, ink on paper, 11 × 14 in., courtesy Spiesshofer Collection*

of Americans at play. The article sounds a similar, if more serious note in its italic introduction: "It's leisure, rarest of treasures, but to many of us a burden, a fraud, and a crushing bore. Why do we make every pleasure trip a race against time, every sport a battle for supremacy?"

While the editors continued in 1956 to defend leisure in the face of a traditional American work ethic (as they did in July 1952, see p. 113), the problem now was less with a justification *for* leisure, than with *how* to use leisure in satisfying ways. Drawing upon familiar advertising strategies, editors presented a problem, and marshaled their editors, writers, and photographers to craft a solution. What followed in the anniversary essay were not the more usual informed travelogues found in most issues of the magazine but sections devoted to leisure pastimes and hobbies such as music, photography, collecting, and entertaining, along with an essay by author James Michener on the pleasures of travel (titled "This Great Big Wonderful World"), with photographs taking up the majority of each of the essay's nine pages, combining majestic high-viewpoint landscapes in color alternating with scenes of local interest (Shinto Priests in the court of the Meiji Temple by Werner Bischof [1918–2003; Figure 4.29]; an Egyptian resting in the shadow of his camel against the bleached background of the Stepped Pyramid of Saqqara), often stretching across the gutter and limiting text to one or two columns per double-page spread, concluding with a foldout of Arizona's Grand Canyon (Figure 4.30 and color plate), increasing the total width to twenty-seven inches across three pages, and all serving as specific visual counterparts to the bold title and the words "big" and "wonderful."

Michener's illustrated travelogue touted the enjoyment of "active" travel, immersing oneself in a different *culture* through its monuments, its food, an understanding or at least an awareness of its religion, habits, and language, and a particular kind of curiosity about *difference*, distinct from superficiality and an impatient desire to see and do as much as possible in a brief and frenetic tour, as if travel was a competition to do more and see more than one's neighbor. It is also contemporary with other expressions of ambivalence and concern about American affluence as a measure of progress, or of "happiness," including David M. Potter's *People of Plenty: Economic Abundance and the American Character* (1954) or John Kenneth

FIGURE 4.29 Holiday, *March 1956, Japanese Monks, accompanying an article by James Michener. Photograph: Werner Bischof, courtesy Magnum Photos London*

FIGURE 4.30 (and color plate) *Three-page spread of Grand Canyon from Michener article,* Holiday, *March 1956, Drexel University Libraries*

Galbraith's *The Affluent Society* (1958), or even David Riesman's *The Lonely Crowd* (1960) that distinguished between "inner"- and "outer"-directed human action, the latter dependent upon conformity to the opinions of others.

The particular association of leisure with instant gratification as a form of American "difference" taps into a theme found elsewhere in the tenth anniversary issue of *Holiday*, as it does in a well-known cover for *Esquire* magazine designed by Henry Wolf in July, 1958 (Figure 4.31 and color plate): the tagline reads "The Americanization of Paris," juxtaposing a

FIGURE 4.31 (and color plate) *Henry Wolf, art director, "The Americanization of Paris," cover,* Esquire, *March 1958*

wine glass with a paper packet of "instant wine," a reference to immediate reward in contrast to the pleasure of enjoying idle time (see also chapter 3 on Cassandre's Monsieur Dubo posters, p. 82). A similar contrast is found in post-World War II European resistance to the long-term effects of American economic intervention through the Marshall Plan, including the fears, or cultural "costs" to national identity and autonomy (Ellwood, 1992). As noted above, illustrated feature articles in *Holiday* on European travel steered a middle ground between a time-honored national history and character and a more fun-loving, youthful, and active present.

The Women of *Holiday*

Aside from fashion editor Toni Robin (replaced later by Ruth Massey) and art editor Gertrude Gordon, men occupied the top editorial and administrative positions at *Holiday*. Women's names appear in the credits on the table of contents page, but they rarely rose above the level of "assistant." Women's representation in the magazine, however, as well as the role of women authors, are both significant aspects of post-World War II *Holiday*, providing much material for viewers today to consider in relation to gender roles and stereotypes at the time. And the reasons are not hard to find.

FIGURE 4.32 *Advertisement for Parliament Cigarettes*, Holiday, *March 1956, Drexel University, Hagerty Library*

FIGURE 4.33 *Emily Jay and Ruth Orkin, "When You Travel Alone," feature from* Cosmopolitan, *vol. 133, no. 3, September 1952, Orkin/Engel Film and Photo Archive, NY*

Russel Lynes's essay on post-World War II American taste, discussed above, noted that women in the "lower middle-brow" category of taste were the principal consumers of goods and services, including of course, products related to travel such as luggage, casual clothing, cosmetics and perfumes, and souvenirs, as well as a voice in the choice of vacation destinations; not surprisingly, women were the target for numerous advertisements in *Holiday*. The "women" Lynes was referring to were generally married; in the world of leisure advertisements, independent women hardly seem to exist. In the ads for *Holiday*, women do not travel on their own, and aside from fashion (see below) are represented outside the home almost *exclusively* with husbands or children, whether in the car, by the pool or beach, or in a cigarette advertisement depicting a couple on safari (March 1956, p. 2; Figure 4.32).

An exception is to be found not in *Holiday* but in a series of photographs by photojournalist Ruth Orkin (1921–85) that appeared in an article in *Cosmopolitan* in September, 1952 titled "When You Travel Alone." Here the photographs featured an adventurous young American woman (Ninalee Allen Craig, then known as "Jinx" Allen, 1927–2018) who met and befriended Orkin in Florence while the photographer was on assignment. The article contained practical travel information for young women planning a trip in Europe, minimizing their fears or reservations, while the photographs illustrate a series of everyday experiences including asking for directions, dealing with foreign currency, and being leered at by men (Figure 4.33). The caption to Orkin's photograph reads: "Public admiration in Florence shouldn't fluster you. Ogling the ladies is a popular, harmless, and flattering pastime you'll run into in many foreign countries. The gentlemen are usually louder and more demonstrative than American men but they mean no harm."

As decision makers for consumer goods, women are as interested as their husbands in the comfort as well as the practicality (for family vacations) of automobiles or even the tapered contour of an outboard motor (March 1956, p. 4); they enjoy the informality and ease of movement in casual clothes, delight in looking and smelling good with perfumes and other cosmetics when they travel, and help to select travel locations where they can sunbathe while their husbands fish, or even fish themselves (see below, Figure 4.37)! In other words, they are man's ideal partner: trim and attractive, fun-loving, practical, responsible, at times even adventurous.

Perhaps not all women readers of *Holiday* in the mid-1950s fit the restrictive middle-class mold of housewife and traveling companion. Editorial features occasionally appealed to women readers' independence and activities *outside* of the home, particularly in a series of three articles written by Roger Angell (b. 1920) and illustrated with photographs, celebrating individual achievements of remarkable woman. Titled "World of Women," the features appeared monthly from December 1955 through February 1956. Unlike advertisements, feature articles on destinations, and fashion spreads, "World of Women" was not directly related to travel, but its female subjects communicated worldliness through their diverse races and ethnicities and the location of the *work* in which they were engaged. Varied in age all were active professionally in fields ranging from medicine to diplomacy, and Angell presented examples of accomplishment that challenged gender stereotypes that focused upon domesticity, appearance, and playing the perfect partner. The series also paralleled the contributions of women as *Holiday* authors, in particular the in-depth articles written by well-traveled author Santha Rama Rau (1923–2009), who contributed feature stories on the nations of Asia.

Women also figure prominently in fashion spreads from issue to issue, almost always in casual fashion (sports- or active-wear rather than formal attire), appearing youthful and in comfortable, relaxed poses. In this world the lines between editorial and advertisement blur, as photo-essays devoted to fashion often include the names of designers, manufacturers, and even

FIGURE 4.34 *"The Lovely Shape of Summer,"* Holiday, *June 1954, p. 104ff, Drexel University Libraries*

FIGURE 4.35 *"The Bathing Suit," featuring Mara Lane, cover,* Holiday, *June 1954, Drexel University, Hagerty Library*

retail outlets and prices. The June, 1954 cover of *Holiday* featured Mara Lane, identified as the "English Marilyn Monroe" wearing a strapless one-piece striped swimsuit, her hourglass figure lying diagonally across the page next to a swimming pool (Figure 4.34).

The issue featured a six-page spread on swimwear. The captions not only include the names of designers but also the names of the models, the majority of whom are married. Married women also appear in features about travel, fashion, and resort destinations.

And an illustrated story from August, 1952 focused upon Bucks County, Pennsylvania, showing celebrity couples enjoying bucolic surroundings, escaping from their apartments in nearby Manhattan. Entitled "Easy Life, Easy Clothes," the black and white photographs (Figure 4.35) include a combination of mostly high-brow and upper middle-brow vacationers, mingling with the "locals," fitting in rather than standing out. The photos include writers, painters, playwrights, producers, and retired businessmen, "real" people in the company of their wives. The feature not only illustrates one of the most common conventions for representing women in *Holiday*, but also the fluid character of social groupings that *Holiday* editors seem to have mastered, where new forms of leisure reduce rather than reinforce social distinctions. Following this theme, in the June 1954 issue there is an illustrated story titled "The Decline of East Coast Resorts." Here the theme also relates directly to issues of taste, focusing upon older forms of relaxation as defined for a "leisure class" associated with the east coast and with lifestyles of those who pursue leisure as a full-time occupation, that is, those who don't have to work, and who "cultivate with and distinguish themselves by their manners." But "the leisure class" and many of its pursuits and venues, is on the wane, described by the author as a "by-gone era," and the "new leisure" is neither so exclusive nor stodgy, and is less a full-time occupation of the privileged than the well-deserved reward for productive work.

To return to women and their representation in *Holiday*, in addition to appearing in advertisements and fashion features, the photography in the magazine occasionally strikes a note of eroticism. A photo essay from January 1947, before Zachary was hired as an associate editor, featured a "monthly guide" in this issue with photos of "starlet" Mae Grubb wearing bathing suits (Figure 4.36), akin to, if not as revealing, as today's *Sports Illustrated* annual Swimsuit Issue.

Early on, such features seem to have raised a few eyebrows about propriety. In the "Letters to the Editor" page for May, 1952 issue of *Holiday*, a reader chastised the editors for a feature in the previous March issue on the state of Louisiana that included a "lewd" photograph of an exotic dancer. The editor defended the photograph, suggesting in effect that the pursuit of happiness, the theme of that issue (see p. 113 ff.), included a healthy appreciation for the nude female body, hinting that the appreciation was aesthetic rather than lustful. An illustrated bathing beauty appeared in an American Airlines ad in July 1952 (on a double-page spread opposite a couple fishing, Figure 4.37), and increasingly the exotic "tropical paradise," whether the island of Ibiza in March 1952, Bali in July 1955, were featured both in photo-essays and in advertisements with the growth of international air travel, and included photographs of the female nude in her "natural" surroundings (Figure 4.38).

The nude female figure is also the subject of a photograph of artist Angelo de Benedetto (1913–92) painting a female model posed against a tree *en plein air* in a destination feature on the state of Colorado (September 1952, Figure 4.39), and an essay about changing ideals of female beauty in art by Irish-Indian writer Aubrey Menen (tenth-anniversary issue, March, 1956) with a photograph of a female nude lying on her front looking toward an arrangement of photographs of female figures from the Western canon (Figure 4.40), including Renoir's "After

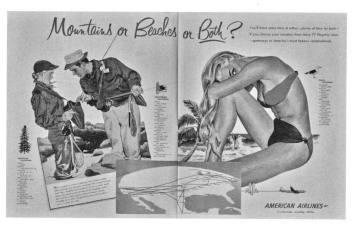

FIGURE 4.36 *Illustrated spread featuring "Mae Grubb,"* Holiday, *January 1947, Drexel University, Hagerty Library*

FIGURE 4.37 *American Airlines advertisement*, Holiday, *July 1952, Drexel University, Hagerty Library*

FIGURE 4.38 *Feature on Bali,* Holiday *July 1955, Drexel University, Hagerty Library*

FIGURE 4.39 *Artist Angelo DiBenedetto painting a nude, feature illustrated story on Colorado,* Holiday, *September, 1952, Drexel University Libraries*

FIGURE 4.40 *Aubrey Menen, "Changing Ideals of Female Beauty,"* Holiday *March 1956, Drexel University, Hagerty Library*

the Bath," The "Venus de Milo," Picasso's "La Paix," and Lucas Cranach's "Venus" (wearing a fashionable hat), each reflecting attitudes toward the human body, what Menen calls "the thinking of the time." What raised an eyebrow in a 1952 letter to the editor was presumably acceptable, if not liberating, only a few years later.

Holiday and the World at Large

Holiday's mission was to actively promote leisure travel through a combination of text and image, advertisement, editorial, and feature, a variety of places to go, how to get there, where to stay, what to wear, as well as what to see and how one might best enjoy one's time. But as with the subject of taste noted in Russell Lynes' "purveyors of high-brow culture to the Lower-Middle-Brow," *Holiday's* editors and writers, in their selection of material and its presentation, trod a middle ground between exclusivity and inclusion, between prescription and suggestion, between a well-meaning, gentle paternalism and an ability to have fun without passing judgment. This included an awareness of sensitive topics. While there was little evidence, beyond Roger Angell's "World of Women" articles mentioned above, (p. 134) of proto-feminist concerns in *Holiday*, along with the magazine's hiring of women writers with first-hand experience of living abroad, it's not hard to be struck today by the occasional

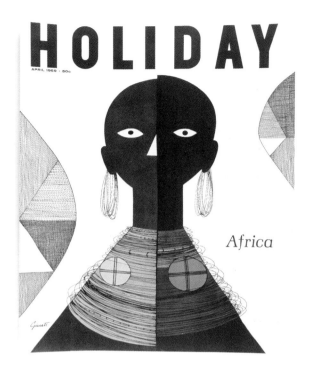

FIGURE 4.41 (and color plate) Holiday, *July 1959, George Giusti, "Africa" cover, RIT Cary Graphic Arts Collection*

intrusion of controversial topics, from Cold War fears to Apartheid in South Africa, as well as more complex "insider" rather than touristic views of remote areas, for instance Santha Rama Rau's "World of Asia" series mentioned above, or even the July 1959 feature on the American Indian, in which *Holiday's* upper-middle-brow "experts" included the well-traveled and well-published author John Gunther, essayist Clifton Fadiman, and novelists James Michener and William Faulkner. These were among yesteryear's "talking heads," public intellectuals whose credibility rested on their published work for a well-read audience but who somewhat effortlessly entered the world of mass communication through broadcast radio and the emerging medium of network television in post-World War II America, as well as through monthlies such as *Holiday*. More accessible than academics, they inhabited a space in which intellectuals mingled somewhat comfortably with a public more trusting of their informed opinions, creating the possibility of a common cultural discourse rather than a clash of cultures, suspicion toward an educated elite, or a more antagonistic identity politics. The role of "experts" in *Holiday* reminds me of Clive James's characterization of the café society of early twentieth-century Vienna, describing the intellectual community of the city, home to writers, artists, and scholars, as well as businessmen, publishers, and editors from the varied parts of the Austro-Hungarian empire, mingling in its coffee houses and sharing a space and a dialogue without any group imposing its will upon the other (see page 68 ff.). While one might dispute the degree to which the Vienna Secession stood in the center or at the fringes of James's idea of Viennese café society, such a discourse appears plausible, during

Holiday's heyday in the 1950s, at least under Ted Patrick's editorship and Frank Zachary's art direction.

For example, the July 1959 *Holiday* was a destination issue devoted to the African continent, with essays ranging from history, to contemporary politics, to fashion. George Giusti's cover of a Masai warrior (Figure 4.41) was graphic, part African mask, part modernist distortion and appropriation of an instinctive, "primitive" tribal art. Remembering that the journal's purpose was to advertise and promote travel as an attractive use of Americans' increasing leisure time, it is somewhat surprising to encounter Johannesburg resident Nadine Gordimer's article describing the harshness of strict segregation and discrimination as sanctioned by white government policy. The opening spread of "Africa: Ordeal by Color—APARTHEID" was a double-page spread with a single centered photograph of a white resident seated in a rickshaw carried by a black laborer dressed in Zulu costume. Gordimer detailed the dominant reality of racism, segregation, and the absence of communication or possibility of advancement for blacks in South Africa, her account made more human and empathetic by personal experience of thwarted efforts to communicate with black friends and the hollow official justifications of the Apartheid policy (see the comment of James Baldwin, quoted p. 179). In this issue the editorial team seems to have gone to great lengths to present a complex rather than superficial or homogenous image or identity for Africa, certainly one that goes beyond Giusti's reductive cover, including photographs of urban life, contemporary Western dress (Figure 4.42), cultural exchange and interaction, postcolonial African independence, religious diversity (including Muslim North Africa), along with images of magical landscapes and big game reserves. Here *Holiday*'s selection of authors, subjects, and photographs communicate a more varied picture of the traveler's world in which tourism played a part, based upon encouraging a productive use of leisure and combining safety, security, and free enterprise, along with an awareness, or at least a hint, of the tensions that might threaten the continued expansion of the travel industry.

Another sensitive subject was the Cold War, and again, *Holiday* did not shy away from visiting nations behind the Iron Curtain or commenting upon the threat of the atomic bomb.

FIGURE 4.42 *Photo from feature on Africa with photograph of Africans in Western dress,* Holiday, *July 1959, Drexel University, Hagerty Library*

Here the editors tended toward the upbeat while acknowledging the destructive threat of the atom, as when associate editor Carl Biemiller noted the benefits of atomic energy from August 1952 as they pertained to leisure. After attending a "contained" atomic test in the New Mexico desert with other members of the press, Biemiller balanced the lingering memory of the bomb's devastating power with optimism about the atom's peaceful applications, as fuel that would power transportation and benefit tourism. Along with features on Japan's economic recovery (August, 1952), *Holiday* surveyed the international landscape politically as a part of an informed approach to modern leisure rather than one exclusively focused upon escape.

As early as l947, *Holiday* featured several related stories and photos of Soviet Russia through the eyes of John Gunther (1901–70), who had established a reputation as an educated world traveler with the publication of his series of "Inside" books such as *Inside Europe* (1936) and others. The feature was hopeful regarding travel in Russia but also realistic in noting the physical and bureaucratic hardships that were impediments to would-be tourists who might more easily venture elsewhere.

When Zachary left *Holiday* following Ted Patrick's death in 1964, he found work in public relations and advertising, where he'd cut his teeth earlier as an underling to promoter Grover Whelan for the 1939 New York World's Fair (interestingly, William Bernbach, see chapter 5, also worked for Whelan in the same capacity). It's not clear how that experience translated into his role as associate editor, graphics editor, and finally art director at *Holiday*, but the planning of the fair also entailed visualizing on a grand scale a popular and uplifting combination of technological and social progress for a mass audience, combining entertainment and fantasy in a world threatened by fascism and war escalating war in Europe. In a 1964 piece for *New Yorker*, Zachary humorously recounted his work for the 1939 World's Fair and its failure as a privately funded commercial venture, despite having attracted close to 45 million visitors. But while the 1939 World's Fair purposely avoided areas of conflict or unease, *Holiday*'s editorial voices usually presented an upbeat, confident, but not entirely escapist world view ignorant of the challenges, complexities, and uncertainties the post-World War II era and the United States' role in facing those challenges, both in terms of possibilities as well as limitations and even resistance (not always of course; while Japan is featured as a tourist destination in the early 1950s in relation to post-World War reconstruction, the editors avoided mentioning the Korean conflict in those same years, 1950–3). The combination of celebration, information, and insight was enhanced by the collaboration of editor and art director, a team effort involving layout, photography, illustration, copy, and market research, attracting and holding reader interest, communicating the essentials of the narrative directly and effectively, distinguished from the often more predictable, crowded, bland, repetitive advertisements. Perhaps this is one reason why historians of graphic design might more carefully consider the work of the art director in magazine publication within the framework of the entire journal, its contributors, its editors, its readers, not only examining individual pages or spreads that received awards in professional journals, but thinking about the magazine as a whole, as the sum, or even something greater than the sum of its constituent parts; removing an image or single layout, spread, or sequence from this broader context of reading and readership undervalues meaning by separating form from content.

Zachary returned briefly to *Holiday* in 1969, but came too late to help the failing Curtis magazine, which folded in 1977. In 1972 he became managing editor of the magazine *Town and Country*, and is generally credited with making the moribund journal successful, though that success lies beyond the purview of this chapter. When the Art Director's Club inducted him into its Hall of Fame in 1990, Zachary was still managing editor at *Town and Country* at the age of seventy-six. He retired in 1991. Happily, his contributions began to be recognized while he was still alive, not only by the Art Director's Club, but by the American Institute of Graphic Arts (AIGA) and in print for *New Yorker* and elsewhere, followed by features in *Print, Vanity Fair*, and the *Paris Review* as he reached his nineties and in obituaries that followed upon his death in 2015. These appreciations often note that Zachary's place in the history of graphic design had something to do with his background as a writer—the visual skills that made him an art director came later, most likely from his working relationship with Alexey Brodovitch on the short-lived *Portfolio* magazine (1950–1) and the assimilation of Brodovitch's keen understanding of photography and illustration in the design of modern magazines (see also chapter 5 on Levy's rye bread and the Doyle Dane Bernbach art editors Robert Gage, Helmut Krone, and Williams Taubin who also came under the tutelage of Brodovitch, pp. 157; 162). The combination of his skills, both literary and visual, still elicits our admiration in the large pages and spreads of *Holiday*, where reading and seeing combine to celebrate and enhance our understanding of the rich phenomenon of modern worldwide travel and leisure.

What Happened to *Holiday*?

A concluding note for this chapter concerns the demise of *Holiday* and decline overall of mass-circulation magazines. Just as cable television expanded but fragmented television's viewing audience, the mass market for the print magazine gave way to the niche market, offering entrepreneurial opportunity for publishers and editors but geared to target audiences with a common interest or identity rather than to the consensus-shared content of magazines such as *Saturday Evening Post*. While *Holiday's* editors seem to have recognized the potential of women readers as consumers in their decisions about content, they seemed at the same time oblivious to African Americans as a potential market. *Holiday* is a decidedly "white" magazine in terms of content as well as advertising, making the inclusion of blacks in mass advertising for Levy's rye bread in our next chapter all the more striking.

Even graphic design and art direction were not enough to save *Holiday* or Curtis's *Saturday Evening Post*: Herb Lubalin redesigned the masthead for *SEP* in 1961 (compare Figures 4.43 and 4.44) but circulation continued to decline and the magazine folded in 1969—graphic design alone was not sufficient to rescue a sinking ship.

Life became a monthly rather than weekly magazine in 1978, and relinquished its large format in 1993. With advertising dollars dispersed among the numerous available communication outlets such as television and the Internet available on home and portable computers, in miniature and on-the-go via mobile phones, it indeed seems justified to speak of a "golden age" of magazine publication in the years in which *Holiday* thrived under Patrick, Zachary, and so many others who shared and contributed to constructing a vision of travel and leisure that might be captured and promoted in print during a period of unprecedented economic growth and American political expansion and influence abroad. The special position of art director at *Holiday* emerges in an essay that appeared in the *Annual of Advertising and Editorial Art* for 1939 entitled "What is an Art Director?" The article, written by an art director for an advertising agency, defines art direction as selling with pictures—the element of advertising, of commerce, is not suppressed but directly proclaimed. Whether selling products or distilling the character of a destination, art directors stimulated desire through an understanding of consumers and of the power of word and image in print.

FIGURE 4.43 *Norman Rockwell, "It's Income Tax Time Again," cover,* Saturday Evening Post, *March 1945, Norman Rockwell Foundation*

FIGURE 4.44 *Herb Lubalin and redesign for* Saturday Evening Post, *September 16, 1961, Norman Rockwell Foundation*

Chapter 5

Food, Race, and the "New Advertising": The Levy's Jewish Rye Bread Campaign 1963–1969

Advertising owes its existence to the capacity of human beings to respond to ideas clothed in beauty, sincerity, and originality.

—PRINTERS INK, JULY 22, 1960

Introduction

Each February, the annual National Football League's championship game (the "Super Bowl"—the first Super Bowl took place in 1967) attracts the largest television audience of the year, reaching more than 111 million worldwide viewers in 2017 and achieving a Nielson rating of 45.3, meaning that almost one-half of all households watching television during that time were tuned into the game. For this reason the pre-Super Bowl hype, game day warm-up, the game itself and its half-time extravaganza command the most expensive advertising spots, with thirty seconds of air time costing companies as much as five million dollars not including the production costs of the advertisements themselves; indeed, according to a report by the Prosper Insights and Analytics Company, advertisements (rather than the drama or outcome of the game) constitute the most important part of the event for 17.7 percent of the viewing audience.

In the days following the live broadcast, consumer analytics newspapers and websites such as *Adweek*, *AdAge*, and *Adblitz* publish surveys of viewers' favorite Super Bowl commercials, based in part upon tracking the number of "views" of Super Bowl ads that are posted on the website YouTube. Judgment of the game's "best" ads, then, is based upon their ability to amuse and sustain the attention of viewers, with some combination of humor, surprise, nostalgia, and originality. An early example of attention-grabbing Super Bowl advertising is a Xerox commercial (Super Bowl XI, 1977, with subsequent print advertising) featuring "Brother Dominic," a pudgy tonsured scribe dressed in a medieval monk's cowl (Figure 5.1), whose

FIGURE 5.1 *Brother Dominic and the Abbot, still from Super Bowl television advertisement, 1977,* © *Xerox Corporation*

superior demands 500 copies of a multi-page document poor Dominic has just finished copying painstakingly by hand. Worried, Dominic hurries to the local copy center to enlist the help of a new Xerox brand copy machine (that not only copies but collates); the result: a miracle, as Dominic and his superior raise their eyes to heaven! (Figure 5.1)

This annual Super Bowl ritual celebrates the blurring of entertainment and advertising that we may trace to a century-old debate in the advertising industry centered upon the effectiveness of "soft" versus "hard" advertising, of entertainment (or "art") *versus* stronger techniques of visual and verbal persuasion, though individual ads may not fit wholly into one or the other of these two camps. The more recent roots of this advertising industry debate, especially in the United States, date to the 1950s and to the strategy generally known as the "New Advertising" or "advertising's creative revolution." Critics and historians have celebrated the "New Advertising" for its resourcefulness, originality, irreverence, and the courage its designers and copywriters displayed in challenging conventional industry practice, and for engaging controversial subjects such as race and gender. In questioning authority, the protagonists of "New Advertising" not only contested the inherited wisdom of their industry peers in the 1950s and 1960s; their non-conformity has also appeared to some writers as symptomatic of the subjectivity and individualism associated with the disruptive social and political movements of the later 1960s youth counterculture and its attack on mainstream values (Drucker/McVarish, 2013). In trade journal articles of the time, pioneers of the New Advertising referred to themselves, and were referred *to*, as "young Turks," a reference to a combination of aggressiveness with non-conformity to accepted industry practice.

Elements of the "New Advertising" include the preference for photography over illustration, short copy combined with catchy slogans that suggest a clever "double-entendre" or self-conscious ambiguity that spurs "active" engagement with the viewer, and an enjoyment akin to solving a riddle or puzzle. Other features involve a more casual, friendly relationship between the "voice" of an advertisement and the viewer rather than endorsements from "authorities," and a team-based approach to the advertising process itself that places copy and image on equal footing rather than in a top-down hierarchy that privileges copy-writing over image and layout.

Many of these characteristics apply to the memorable "You don't have to be Jewish to love Levy's *real* Jewish rye" poster campaign developed by the Doyle Dane Bernbach advertising agency in New York beginning in 1963 and continuing through the decade. Exploring the history and context of this campaign permits a more precise understanding of advertising's "golden age" and questions some of the myths it has engendered, including the ways in which it relates to the theme of "rebellion," subversion, protest, and the 1960s counterculture, as well as the campaign's particular engagement with contemporary and controversial issues of racial and ethnic stereotypes in advertising and photojournalism in the United States. In doing so we trace the history of Levy's breads with the Doyle Dane Bernbach advertising agency from its inception in the late 1940s through the "You don't have to be Jewish" campaign of the early 1960s, examining the efforts of a talented series of art directors, photographers, and copywriters.

The Levy's rye bread poster campaign has garnered media and some recent scholarly attention. The tagline served as the title of a popular comedy record album released in 1965 ("You Don't Have to Be Jewish," see Figure 5.28) and art historian Kerri Steinberg analyzed the campaign in her lively and informative *Jewish Mad Men: Advertising and the Design of the American Jewish Experience* (2015) in relation to Jewish-American identity in the twentieth century. Most graphic design surveys illustrate posters from the campaign with a focus upon William Bernbach's role as the most prominent pioneer and champion of the "New Advertising," an image Mr. Bernbach cultivated (or marketed) himself in speeches and published interviews mostly conducted by associates along with recollections by colleagues published beginning in the early 1980s (Mr. Bernbach died in October, 1982; Levenson, 1987). Bernbach also contributed articles to *Advertising Age* and other trade as well as news magazines, though sadly agency records from the period of the Levy's campaign no longer exist. With an expanding list of clients, offices, revenues, and professional recognition throughout the 1950s and 1960s, Doyle Dane Bernbach became a publicly traded company in 1965, merging with another large advertising agency in 1986. Since 1996 the company has been known as DDB Worldwide, billing over ten billion dollars annually and with hundreds of offices throughout the world. While a mainstay of the canon of graphic design history, the Levy's 1960s poster campaign barely figures today in DDB's own company history.

The Levy's Real Jewish Rye Bread Ad Campaign 1961–1975

The Levy's "You don't have to be Jewish (to love Levy's Jewish Rye)" ad campaign (1961–c. 1975) consisted of a series of posters featuring its now-famous tagline framing above and below over-life-size bust-length frontal photographs of individual figures, each differentiated by age, race, or occupation (less often by gender—all but one of the posters featured men or male children). The posters appeared on the tiled subway station walls of the vast New York Metropolitan Transit Authority (MTA) system (Figures 5.2 through 5.10; see Figure 5.7 illustrating an example as posted on a subway station wall).

Each poster measures 45" by 29 ½", printed in color on a glossy plain white background. The undated photograph illustrated in Figure 5.7 shows a slightly worn example of the series in situ in the Court Street station in Brooklyn and now in the New York City Transit Museum. The poster campaign is credited to Judy Protas (writer, 1922–2014), William Taubin (art director, 1919–2000, see also p. 162 ff.), and Howard Zieff (photographer, 1927–2009). It appears that other photographers were also involved in the campaign's development: the 1965

FIGURE 5.2 (and color plate) *Levy's rye bread posters, 45" x 29 ½," offset lithography, Judy Protas, writer; William Taubin, art director; Howard Zieff, photographer; Doyle Dane Bernbach Advertising Agency, New York, c. 1963, Library of Congress*

FIGURE 5.3 *Levy's rye bread posters, 45" x 29 ½," offset lithography, Judy Protas, writer; William Taubin, art director; Howard Zieff, photographer; Doyle Dane Bernbach Advertising Agency, New York, c. 1963, Library of Congress*

FIGURE 5.4 *Levy's rye bread posters, 45" x 29 ½," offset lithography, Judy Protas, writer; William Taubin, art director; Howard Zieff, photographer; Doyle Dane Bernbach Advertising Agency, New York, c. 1963–70, Library of Congress*

FIGURE 5.5 *Levy's rye bread posters, 45" x 29 ½," offset lithography, Judy Protas, writer; William Taubin, art director; Howard Zieff, photographer; Doyle Dane Bernbach Advertising Agency, New York, c. 1963–70, Library of Congress*

FIGURE 5.6 (and color plate) *Levy's rye bread posters, 45" x 29 ½," offset lithography, Judy Protas, writer; William Taubin, art director; Howard Zieff, photographer; Doyle Dane Bernbach Advertising Agency, New York, c. 1963–70, Library of Congress*

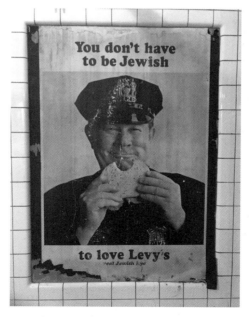

FIGURE 5.7 (and color plate) *Levy's rye bread posters, 45" x 29 ½," offset lithography, Judy Protas, writer; William Taubin, art director; Howard Zieff, photographer; Doyle Dane Bernbach Advertising Agency, New York, c. 1963–70, Library of Congress*

FIGURE 5.8 *Levy's rye bread posters, 45" x 29 ½," offset lithography, Judy Protas, writer; William Taubin, art director; Howard Zieff, photographer; Doyle Dane Bernbach Advertising Agency, New York, c. 1963–70, Library of Congress*

FIGURE 5.9 *Levy's rye bread posters, 45" x 29 ½," offset lithography, Judy Protas, writer; William Taubin, art director; Howard Zieff, photographer; Doyle Dane Bernbach Advertising Agency, New York, c. 1963–70, Library of Congress*

FIGURE 5.10 *Levy's rye bread posters, 45" x 29 ½," offset lithography, Judy Protas, writer; William Taubin, art director; Howard Zieff, photographer; Doyle Dane Bernbach Advertising Agency, New York, c. 1963–70, Library of Congress*

FIGURE 5.11 *Kent Wakeford, photograph, 1964–5, reproduced in* Art Directors Club Annual, *1965, no. 546, Distinctive Merit Award*

Art Directors Club Annual included a photograph of a Native American by Kent Wakeford (b. 1928); the same individual appeared in the advertising poster series but featuring one of Mr. Zieff's photographs (Mr. Zieff claimed that he found the model "on the street" and that he was an engineer for the New York Central Railroad) that earned a "distinctive merit award" in the photography category from the Art Directors Club (compare Figures 5.6 and 5.11). The *Art Directors Club Annual* credits Doyle Dane Bernbach as the advertising agency, William Taubin as art director, and Levy's rye bread as client. The poster series was produced by the Elliot-Unger-Elliot company in New York, who also produced television commercials for Doyle Dane Bernbach.

Certainly novel for its time in mass advertising campaigns, two of the figures (a child and adult, the New York-based popular actor and comedian Godfrey Cambridge, 1933–76) are African-American (Figures 5.2 and color plate, and 5.3), two (again a child and an adult) are Asian (Figures 5.4. and 5.5, one is a Native American (Figure 5.6), another a uniformed New York City policeman (Figure 5.7), and yet another a white Christian choirboy, identified by a loose-fitting white shirt and large red bow (Figure 5.8). Another (and probably later) poster in the series features a middle-aged white woman with grayish hair tied in a bun, wearing a blouse and apron, standing behind a table with a salami on a red striped, faintly checkered tablecloth (Figure 5.9). Also among the final and more consciously staged examples in the series is a young Asian man wearing a Karate-gi uniform and holding a packaged loaf of the rye bread (not illustrated here). In addition to Godfrey Cambridge, another identifiable or "celebrity" figure (see pp. 169–170) is the ageing white deadpan silent screen comedian Buster Keaton (1895–1966), who alone (and characteristically) frowns rather than smiles (Figure 5.10).

William Taubin's layouts for the Levy's posters were strikingly simple and direct. The typeface is a heavy old style display font called Cooper Black (designed by Oswald Bruce Cooper in 1922 for the Barnhart Brothers & Spindler foundry, since 1911 part of American Type Founders), distinguished by the extreme angled shading of the strokes and counters, for instance, in the letter "O" and the slightly rounded (rather than straight horizontal) serifs. The photographs of the addressing figures themselves fill the frame: only the aproned woman in Figure 5.9 is posed behind a table in three-quarter length view (as well as the full-length Karate man), further from the viewer and accompanied by "accessories" (salami, red-and-white checkered tablecloth) that are absent (save for the bread) from the other examples in the series. The compositions are centered, and the copy is divided into two parts by the photograph to create not just a tagline, but a *punch* line—there is little else to distract the pedestrian viewer from "taking in" the posters' three elements (two lines of text plus close-up bust-length photograph) fully and immediately. I'm unable to provide a chronology for the series, but offer a tentative one at the conclusion of the chapter, based upon dated photographs and reproductions of individual examples in the *Art Directors Club Annual*. The photographs feature, in almost all cases, frontal half-length or bust-length standing or seated figures facing the viewer and holding a slice of rye bread or a sandwich in one or both hands. In some cases a bite has been taken out of the sandwich; in all cases (aside from the straight-faced silent screen actor Buster Keaton, Figure 5.10) the figures are smiling and their mouths are closed.

The Posters as Series

Despite the similarities that accrue from the consistent layout, typeface, sandwich, and the figures' contented grin among this group of ads, there are subtle differences that merit renewed attention and avoid exact repetition: how the bread is held, whether eyes are open or closed, whether figures are standing or seated, whether a bite has, or hasn't been taken out of the rye bread slice or sandwich, or whether the figures are adults or children. As a series they work together to attract and to maintain viewer attention through a deft combination of familiarity and difference. Industry professionals at the time recognized the effectiveness of such strategies to trigger viewers' memory but avoid indifference or boredom. In one of a regular series of short articles in the advertising trade journal *Printers Ink*, veteran copywriter and contributor Hal Stebbins remarked upon a series of full-page newspaper ads (1964) for the Heinz foods corporation (now Kraft Heinz), also created by Doyle Dane Bernbach, that combined repetition with novelty through a compositional formula featuring a collage of photographs of fresh vegetables against a plain background accompanied by a series of different short first-person quotations from company founder Henry J. Heinz (1844–1919) that called attention to the freshness of the company's canned soups (Figure 5.12).

Another regular feature of *Printers Ink* were weekly comparisons between two or more ads, most often for the same product and even developed by the same agency, comparing reader interest as measured by the well-established market research company Daniel Starch and Staff, titled "Which ad pulled best?" An installment from 1965 compared four subway cards (placed end-on-end horizontally on the curved upper walls of subway cars) for Del Monte canned food products (sauces and fruit), three of which were similar in layout and a fourth that differed from the other three by using a different typeface and a layout with photographs against a colored background rather than contrasted more strongly with white space. The Starch survey found that subway riders, and in particular women, remembered and responded more favorably to the series of related posters than to the example that differed from the rest. In this case the advertising agency wasn't Doyle Dane Bernbach, but the larger New York firm McCann Erickson (Figure 5.13).

FIGURE 5.12 *Heinz soups advertisement, Doyle Dane Bernbach, reproduced in* Art Directors Club Annual, *1965, no. 25 (Bert Steinhauser, Art Director; Donald Mack, Photographer; Fran Wexler, Copywriter),* Drexel University Libraries

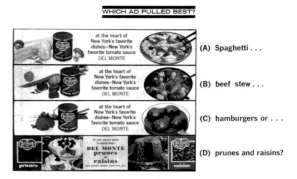

FIGURE 5.13 *"Which ad pulled best,"* Printers Ink, *January 22, 1965, Courtesy Paley Library, Temple University*

Levy's Baking Company

The 1960s "You don't have to be Jewish" poster campaign marked the culmination of a decade-long partnership between the Levy's Baking Company and the Doyle Dane Bernbach Advertising Agency. Henry S. Levy was a Russian Jewish immigrant whose Brooklyn bakery (founded 1888) served a mostly local orthodox Jewish clientele. The family-owned bakery sold a variety of breads, including rye, pumpernickel, and "cheese bread," all known for their flavor and thick, chewy, crust (later termed "oven krust" in Levy's advertising).

When Henry Levy died in 1943 his son Abraham took over the company and expanded and industrialized the bakery's production to include packaged breads for distribution in delicatessens and supermarkets in the larger New York metropolitan area. Abraham's decision to enlarge the family business was not unusual given the increasing secularization and assimilation of American Jews into mainstream society, and the migration of Jewish families to the suburbs after World War II (Steinberg, 2015): nationally branded and commercially manufactured ethnic Jewish foods, ranging from Manischewitz Passover matzos to the company's sweet wine and soups, appealed to Jewish homemakers eager to assimilate into American consumer culture while maintaining ties to ethnic Jewish culture and religious traditions. The Joseph Jacobs advertising agency in New York, founded in 1919, actively pursued the potential commercial advantages of promoting products for this expanding market, creating the "K" symbol that signified compliance with kosher dietary laws for clients such as Manischewitz, and creating campaigns to advertise other generic nationally branded products such as Quaker Oats, JELL-O, and Maxwell House Coffee in Jewish (Yiddish language) daily newspapers (Steinberg, 2015).

Initially, however, Abraham Levy's entrepreneurial efforts for the company's breads were not successful; Levy's declared bankruptcy in 1949 and hired businessman Samuel ("Whitey") Rubin as company president, appointed to return the baking company to solvency. Part of Rubin's business plan included an investment in advertising to increase the visibility and stimulate sales of Levy's packaged breads. Rubin, familiar with Doyle Dane Bernbach's novel campaign for the Jewish-owned New York department store Ohrbach's (see p. 157), chose the fledgling Madison Avenue agency to manage Levy's advertising. Rubin's decision was auspicious—rather than focus upon the Jewish market for their breads, William Bernbach recommended targeting the mass market in New York; that decision determined the creative direction of the agency's advertising campaigns for Levy's over the next two decades, aimed to attract the attention of a diverse audience and persuade them to choose Levy's breads over competitors' products; in time, the agency settled upon the company's rye bread's "Jewishness."

In 1950 bread advertisements in newspapers and magazines were rare. Supermarket ads featured fresh produce, brand-named packaged foods such as Royal Gelatin desserts or Bird's Eye frozen vegetables, meats, poultry, and fish, and either skipped bread entirely or included white bread grouped with nationally or regionally branded crackers, cupcakes, and doughnuts. By 1951 and 1952, grocery stores were offering and advertising wheat, rye, and pumpernickel breads as alternatives to white bread, increasing variety as well as competition and creating a need for product differentiation through advertising.

The original contract between Levy's and Doyle Dane Bernbach in 1950 was for $35,000, a small budget for an advertising campaign at the time. With agency yield calculated at 15 percent this amounts to a profit of only $5,250. But in 1950 Doyle Dane Bernbach (founded June 1949) was a newcomer to Madison Avenue, with few clients and a staff of thirteen employees. By 1960 the agency's annual billing had reached more than forty million dollars, still medium sized by the standards of Madison Avenue (J. Walter Thompson was billing 250 million); in the meantime the Levy's advertising budget had also grown, with an annual investment of $250,000. In 1965 Doyle Dane Bernbach boasted more than one thousand employees, operated ten branch offices worldwide, with billings close to 150 million dollars (Loring, 1988).

Advertising Levy's Bread: USP
(Unique Selling Proposition)

As a smaller agency and prior to the "You don't have to be Jewish" poster campaign in 1961, Doyle Dane Bernbach struggled to find a unique selling proposition (USP) for Levy's packaged breads. In the advertising industry, USP was the cornerstone of a successful advertising campaign: consumers need to focus upon a single overriding reason to choose one brand over another in an increasingly competitive and expanding marketplace of often similar products. In taking the account, Bernbach remarked that there was nothing particularly distinguishing about the flavor or texture of Levy's packaged breads, certainly not in comparison with fresh-baked goods, and it seemed unlikely that Jews in New York would abandon their local bakeries for the convenience of ordinary packaged bread purchased in the aisles of supermarkets. (Steinberg even suggests that local orthodox Jews resented the loss of exclusivity and religious identity that were sacrificed by the company's expanded marketing strategy.) Doyle Dane Bernbach's earliest print ads in newspapers made no mention of the brand's "Jewishness," nor did the ads focus upon rye bread: in fact, like other bread advertisements at the time, a series of Levy's newspaper ads from the early 1950s focused upon nutrition. Some brands touted that their breads were enriched with vitamins or had earned the "Good Housekeeping Seal of Approval." Looking through the food advertising pages in New York newspapers of the time (they regularly appeared in the Thursday edition), branded bread advertisements or grocery store attention to breads were somewhat rare in comparison with canned vegetables, packaged cakes, or other dessert foods—perhaps Bernbach's comments about Levy's rye bread being quite ordinary was generally true of packaged breads in comparison with their local bakery counterparts. Like competitors such as Arnold or Tip-Top, Levy's compared their own "oven-krust bread" with other packaged breads, featuring low-cost line art with copy that touted the bread's nutritional benefits (Figure 5.14) and freshness. Bernbach also recommended taking advertising space in the city's *New York World Telegram* and *Journal American*, both known for their broad readership in suburban Long Island (and supermarkets rather than bakeries or delicatessens), rather than the *New York Times* (by 1954 Levy's was also advertising in the *Times*). The advertising strategy accords with the recommendation of psychologist and marketing consultant Ernest Dichter (1907–91), who wrote that consumers reacted positively to bread that was "home-baked" with both nutritional as well as emotional associations; Dichter stated that the feeling a bread was baked by a "real" baker trumped its hygienic perfection and any perceived association between softness and freshness. This may be seen, for instance, in a comparison between two advertisements illustrated in Figures 5.14 and 5.15, the first for Levy's "oven krust" white bread and the second, touting Arnold bread's "uniform tenderness of its texture." (Dichter, 1964).

This example of a "reason why" approach was standard practice for advertising copy writers (along with other strategies such as "before and after" testimonials). A more visual example of a comparative "reason why" campaign from the Doyle Dane Bernbach agency in the mid-1960s is a photograph of Heinz Ketchup next to a competing brand that was watery while Heinz remained thick as proof of its added flavor (Figure 5.16).

FIGURE 5.14 *Levy's "oven krust" white bread print advertisement,* c. 1950, *Doyle Dane Bernbach, Bimbo Bakeries, Horsham, PA*

FIGURE 5.15 *Arnold' bread advertisement*, New York Journal American, *April 3, 1952*

FIGURE 5.16 *Heinz Ketchup advertisement, Doyle Dane Bernbach, 1964*, Art Directors Club Annual, *1965, Drexel University Libraries*

1952: Robert Gage and the New Advertising

The 1960s Levy's rye bread poster series did not emerge *ex nihilo*, and tracing the trajectory of Levy's advertising throughout the 1950s is instructive, beginning with product-oriented full-page print and poster advertisements featuring stronger visual impact adapted from European interwar graphic design, supplanted in 1954 by a "people-oriented" campaign featuring candid

FIGURE 5.17 *"New York is eating it up," magazine advertisements for Levy's Real Jewish Rye, Judy Protas, writer; Bob Gage, art director, 1952,* Art Directors Club Annual, *Drexel University Libraries*

close-up photography by Howard Zieff. Both of these campaigns were art-directed by Robert Gage (1921–2000), Doyle Dane Bernbach's first art director; the 1952 ads featured three large slices of bread (white "oven krust," not rye) arranged vertically in the center of the page or poster, the first with a bite removed, the second with four bites removed, and the final image showing only a piece of crust overlaid with text in a condensed sans serif font reading from top to bottom "NEW YORK—IS EATING—IT UP!" (Figure 5.17)

A related newspaper ad for Levy's rye bread featured three identical slices of bread with the tagline "ONE SLICE—LEADS TO—ANOTHER" and adds the word "real" at the bottom of the page. The simple concept for these advertisements combines the verbal reference to eating with the disappearing slice of bread, and proceeds as a unified sequence from top to bottom both in terms of reading and viewing. The tagline addresses (all) "New York," a clear reference to a mass rather than segmented (targeted) market; but there is at this point still no hint of Levy's breads being "Jewish."

The 1952 campaign offers an example of the connection between the history of twentieth-century graphic design and the emergence of the "New Advertising." As his biographers have noted, William Bernbach was a veteran ad man, having worked early on in public relations and as a copy writer for other advertising agencies in New York. Prior to leaving the Grey advertising agency to form his own agency in 1949, Bernbach wrote advertising copy for the (William H.) Weintraub Agency, where he became friendly with graphic designer Paul Rand (born Peretz Rosenbaum, 1914–96), head of art direction at Weintraub. During their time together at Weintraub, Bernbach and Rand met frequently to discuss advertising; Rand was a strong advocate of the pared-down European tradition of the object poster ("Sachplakat") with minimal copy, a straightforward, simplified presentation of product together with company name, often featuring light-hearted drawings and occasional stock photography rather than the then-conventional narrative illustration. Rand committed his views on advertising to print in 1947 with the publication of a small book titled *Thoughts on Design*. The following passage from the book articulates the kind of design thinking that Bernbach discussed with his colleague and brought to his new agency:

> In advertising, the contemporary approach to art is based on a simple concept, a concept of the advertisement as an organic and functional unit, each element of which is integrally related to the others, in harmony with the whole, and essential to the execution of the idea. From this standpoint, copy, art, and typography are indissoluble ... Such an evolution logically precludes extraneous trimmings and "streamlined" affectations. (Rand, 1947)

Examples of Rand's advertising work, distinguished by reduction, contrast, clever visual and verbal metaphors, collage, and minimal copy, include campaigns for Kaufmann's department store in Pittsburgh, Pennsylvania, Ohrbach's department store in Manhattan's Union Square (the Ohrbach's account was with the Grey advertising agency—Bernbach left Weintraub to work at Grey, and subcontracted Rand to work on the early Ohrbach ads), and magazine advertising of mainstream national brands such El Producto cigars, Coronet brandy, along with US distribution for the French aperitif Dubonnet, borrowing the mascot "Monsieur Dubo" from A. M. Cassandre's 1932 French posters for the same company (see Figures 3.2 and 3.33).

Robert Gage studied art and design with Alexey Brodovitch at the design "laboratories" he conducted in New York (*Art Directors Club Annual*, 1971), championing the use of photography, surprise, abstraction, and simplified collage-like layouts in art direction and advertising: Gage's work demonstrates an appreciation for the impact created by a closer relationship between word and image, visual metaphor, and a commitment to reduce or eliminate added copy or detail. Recognizing the excitement that comes with surprise and encountering the unexpected, Gage directed a successful advertising strategy for Ohrbach's Department Store in the early 1950s with a regular series of newspaper advertisements striking for the clarity of their selling point (high fashion at bargain prices), use of photo-montage, and their humorous play on words and clever visual puns. An example is an Ohrbach's advertisement that was reproduced in the 1951 *Art Directors Annual*, juxtaposing, with a cut-and-paste method, centered photographs of a draped table below a well-dressed horizontal female figure with ample white space between them and carefully right-margin-placed tagline, copy, and company name whose asymmetry creates eye movement and a hierarchy of information (Figure 5.18). In addition to the ample white space, the key to the layout's power is the juxtaposition of the word "magic" with the levitating female figure (a similar horizontal cut-out female figure was used in another Ohrbach's advertisement with the tagline "Liberal Trade-In") that in turn transforms an ordinary draped piece of furniture into a magician's table, and "magic" now refers to Ohrbach's combination of "high fashion at low prices" as explained in the body copy at the left—a clever sleight of hand indeed! The Ohrbachs campaign featured full-page ads in *The New York Times* once or twice a month in the early 1950s. For all their novelty, looking at these ads in the context of the daily newspaper itself reveals the attention and expenditure devoted to fashion advertising at the time. Ohrbach's was but one of several competing New York department stores advertising women's clothing in the *Times* in the early 1950s. B. Altman, Macy's, Bonwit Teller, Russeks, Saks Fifth Avenue, McGreery's, Bloomingdales, along with Lord & Taylor, all advertised regularly, often on a daily basis, and all used photographs or sketch-like fashion illustrations of models wearing the latest fitted "New Look" suits and dresses. Gage did not so much *deviate* from the expectation of the well-dressed model in the traditional fashion ad, as use the text and a manipulation of the model to shift the focus of the advertisement from the addressing figure (the model) to the addressee, that is, to the viewer who connects high fashion with affordable prices, distinguishing

FIGURE 5.18 *Ohrbach's Department Store, newspaper advertisement, New York, 1950, art director Robert Gage; artist Joe De Casseres,* Art Directors Club Annual, *1951, Drexel University Libraries*

Ohrbach's store from its competitors in the retail fashion market. In addition to its aesthetic sophistication, the strategy introduces a new kind of engagement or agency with its audience, not simply the desire for emulation and the role clothing assumes in communicating personal and social identity, but adding, or substituting an element of individual *choice* as to how such a transformation may be achieved.

Given Gage's visual and verbal intelligence, it's hardly surprising that the "NEW YORK—IS EATING—IT UP?" campaign of 1952 incorporates the element of time, recalling the successive stages of pouring, drinking, and finishing a glass of wine in A. M. Cassandre's celebrated 1932 poster campaign for Dubonnet (again, see chapter 3 and Figure 3.2). Cassandre reinforced the sequence of related images verbally as well with the letters DUBO-DUBON-DUBONNET to suggest the progression of a satisfying eating (or drinking) experience. Cassandre visited and worked in the United States from 1936 to 1938 and was the subject of the Museum of Modern Art's first one-person exhibition of advertising posters in 1936; examples of his poster designs were published in color in the business magazine *Fortune* (March, 1937) and he created advertisements for the Ford Corporation and the Container Corporation of America. Gage used the repeated sequence of word and image in several ads for Levy's, and seems to have recognized its applicability to the growing medium of television advertising: it appears in a 1955 television spot with the word "Levy's" behind the slice of bread, appearing only *after* the bread was "eaten" (*Art Directors Club Annual*, 1956).

The integration of bold tagline with a clever visual metaphor combined directness, novelty, and brevity, in forging a new direction in American advertising. In an essay that appeared in the *Art Directors Annual* in 1955, Gage criticized conservatism in the advertising industry, stating that "safety is an obstacle to vitality and originality; it must break through the prison of convention." But the questioning of standard industry practice was hardly limited to Doyle Dane Bernbach: other agencies were also experimenting with ads that presented visual puzzles that actively engaged and entertained the viewer, offering them the enjoyment of "getting it" as in a joke or cartoon; for example, in March, 1954, *Printers Ink* featured an advertisement designed for, and *by*, the Young

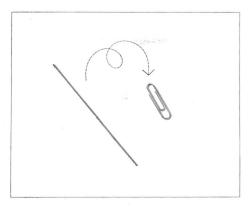

All it takes is the right twist

An ingenious twist turns a piece of wire into
a highly useful object.

And an ingenious twist can often turn an ordinary advertising campaign into one that pro-
duces extraordinary sales results. IF you know
how to make the twist . . . and *when.*

YOUNG & RUBICAM, INC.
Advertising • New York   Chicago   Detroit   San Francisco   Los Angeles
Hollywood   Montreal   Toronto   Mexico City   London

PRINTERS' INK

FIGURE 5.19 *"All it takes is the right twist," advertisement in* Printers Ink, *March 12, 1954, for and by Young & Rubicam, Inc., Courtesy Paley Library, Temple University*

& Rubicam advertising agency, with the transformation of a piece of wire into a paper clip and the tag line "All it takes is the right twist" to tout the agency's ingenuity (Figure 5.19).

As with Gage's fashion advertisements for Ohrbach's, aspects of the Levy campaign's approach to food advertising in the early 1950s played upon familiar elements of industry practice, putting a new spin on time-honored strategies, in particular the ways in which advertising agencies generally approached the promotion of packaged and canned food products. National brands for cake mixes, frozen foods, and other industrially manufactured foods used high-quality color photography to generate appeal for their products, not by picturing them as they were seen in standard-sized cans or packages on the grocery store shelf, but as they were served on a table for a meal, often by a housewife/mother, and featuring a fancy casserole or dessert. Examples abound: Figure 5.20 from *Ladie's Home Journal* magazine (1948) advertises Del Monte brand canned corn with a photograph of a "Star Corn" casserole topped with tomatoes and garnished with parsley, including a recipe for homemakers to cut out and file in their kitchens, intended to make viewers hungry (and housewives or hosts feel "creative"), much like the ads on late-night television for snacks and fast-food restaurants function today.

It's hardly surprising that manufacturers of packaged mass-produced food products sought to present their products as being "home-made," as fresh as the fruits and vegetables found in grocery stores, farmers' markets, or harvested from the consumer's backyard garden. And while advertisers sought to use color photography to un-do the uniformity and standardization of their clients' packaged food products in the 1950s, American artist Andy Warhol (1928–87), who worked early in his career as an advertising illustrator in New York, *celebrated* those very qualities, along with abundance, in his series of silk-screened Campbell Soup cans (1962 and after).

FIGURE 5.20 *Del Monte canned corn advertisement,* Ladies Home Journal, *June, 1948, Hagerty Library, Drexel University*

1954: Howard Zieff and Targeting the Mass Market

In 1954 Gage teamed with photographer Howard Zieff for a new series of Levy's magazine ads with close-up views of white children and working-class New Yorkers (a transit worker and construction worker) eating Levy's rye bread and casually turning toward the viewer (as if on a lunch-break) with the tagline "Mouth-Watering" (Figure 5.21).

For the first time, the campaign focused upon the baking campaign's rye bread and openly acknowledged the product's "Jewishness" ("*real* Jewish rye"). Unlike the 1952 "EAT IT UP" campaign, the 1954 advertisements employ an addressing figure rather than the product to communicate with the viewer. Once again the appeal of the short tagline "Mouth Watering" is to flavor, directed to a typical or average consumer, employing a white child and working-class laborers to erase barriers of budget or class between product and consumer.

Other examples in the 1954 series of ads introduce Levy's bread's "Jewishness," with one photograph staged in a kosher butcher shop with a demanding (even threatening, though fashionably dressed) housewife arguing with the butcher about getting her Levy's rye bread before the store's supply runs out. In one example, she holds a string of kosher hot dogs around the frightened butcher's neck (like a noose) with jars of Manischewitz products lined up on the counter (Figure 5.23). The images of children that appear in the 1960s poster series repeat the 1954 advertising strategy and are employed frequently in traditional advertising for food products (Figure 5.22), while the photographs of workers suggest a hearty and well-deserved lunch break during a day of hard work.

Gage's use of Zieff's candid photographs (here with a casual camera angle) and ordinary models rather than celebrities or authorities also carried over to the "You don't have to be Jewish" poster campaign in 1963 with William Taubin (who joined Doyle Dane Bernbach in

FIGURE 5.21 *"Mouth-Watering,"* *Levy's real Jewish rye, print advertisements, Howard Zieff, photographer; Judy Protas, copywriter; Robert Gage, art director; Doyle Dane Bernbach, 1954,* Art Directors Club Annual, *Drexel University Libraries*

FIGURE 5.22 *"Mouth-Watering" (with child), print advertisement for Levy's real Jewish rye,* New York Times, *March 1, 1954, Howard Zieff, photographer; Judy Protas, copy writer; Robert Gage, art director; Doyle Dane Bernbach, 1954*

FIGURE 5.23 *"All Right Already ..." print advertisement for Levy's real Jewish rye,* New York Times, *September 30, 1954, Howard Zieff, photographer; Judy Protas, copy writer; Robert Gage, art director; Doyle Dane Bernbach*

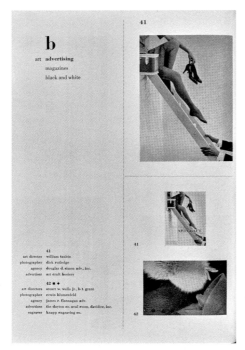

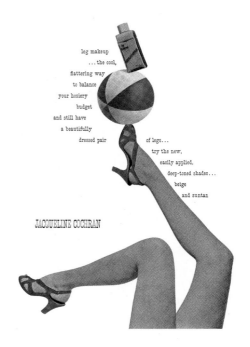

FIGURE 5.24 *ARTCRAFT Hosiery, magazine advertisement, art director William Taubin; photographer Dick Routledge, 1954,* Art Directors Club Annual, *1955, Drexel University Libraries*

FIGURE 5.25 *Paul Rand, advertisement for Jacqueline Cochran Hosiery, 1946,* Art Directors Club Annual, *1946, Courtesy Paul Rand Foundation*

1955) as art director, and Zieff retained as photographer. As we'll see, the new campaign was striking for its use of (mostly) non-white and recognizably non-Jewish models, but the figures themselves are more formally posed than their 1950s precursors and differ from the majority of Zieff's previous advertising work.

William Taubin

In order to meet the demands of Doyle Dane Bernbach's growing client list in the 1950s, Gage hired William Taubin and Helmut Krone (1925–96) as art directors in 1955; it was Krone who would art-direct the agency's celebrated Volkswagen advertising campaign beginning in 1959. Like Gage, both Taubin and Krone had attended Russian-born designer Alexey Brodovitch's (1898–1971) design laboratories at the New School for Social Research in New York. Brodovitch served as art director at the fashion magazine *Harper's Bazaar* from 1934 to 1958. In his design laboratories Brodovitch introduced students to examples from European magazines such as *art et métiers graphiques* (see chapter 3, e.g. p. 96) to encourage experimentation with photography, collage, and asymmetrical layouts for magazine features and print advertising (Purcell, 2002).

FIGURE 5.26 *Barton's Candy magazine advertisement, art director Helmut Krone; photographer Tony Ficatora, 1955,* Art Directors Club Annual, *1956, Drexel University Libraries*

Taubin championed the use of striking photography for advertising and embraced the integration of text and image in aesthetically constructed compositions. Fashion was the most common subject for such creative effects, explored with great success by Brodovitch, working with photographers Irving Penn, Richard Avedon, and other artists who found a receptive readership for their art-directed work in large format fashion magazines that included *Harper's Bazaar* and *Vogue*. Fashion spreads with full-bleed photography were regularly reproduced and celebrated in the *Art Directors Club Annual* during the 1950s, and fashion magazines were among the largest recipients of advertising linage, pages, and expenditures. *Printers Ink* reported in 1960 (August 19) that magazine advertising had grown 15 percent in comparison with the previous year, with fashion magazines (*Vogue, Harper's Bazaar, Glamour*) garnering the highest increases in advertising linage among those magazines surveyed.

While working at the Douglas Simon Agency in New York (prior to being hired at Doyle Dane Bernbach), Taubin art-directed an advertisement for ARTCRAFT hosiery with a cut-off view of a woman's legs appearing out of a window (along with a suitcase) at the upper left of the page stepping onto a ladder that leads diagonally to the bottom right where the name ARTCRAFT appears (Figure 5.24).

Dramatically reductive and suggestive (the waiting arms of the man holding the ladder evoke a secret elopement while preserving a sense of high fashion!), the ad demonstrates the power of photography and innuendo, in this case a pair of shapely legs against a white background in a carefully crafted cut-and-paste composition. Perhaps it's neither surprise nor coincidence that a similar cut-off pair of legs and collage-like composition appear in a 1946 hosiery advertisement art-directed by Paul Rand for the Jacqueline Cochran (Hosiery) Company, with the pair of disembodied legs balancing a beach ball like a trained seal in a water park or circus act and unjustified text framing the beach ball and the model's shin (Figure 5.25).

Taubin, along with Gage and Krone, excelled at the juxtaposition of pared-down copy with photography that communicated immediately and economically, and eliminated distracting detail and background wherever possible. This "copy-light" strategy, increasingly noted in advertising trade publications of the time, is also seen in a Krone art-directed full-page magazine ad for Barton's chocolates in 1955, a Doyle Dane Bernbach client since 1950, also (like Levy's breads) with Jewish ownership. As with the Levy's 1952 "NEW YORK IS—EATING IT UP!" campaign, Krone juxtaposes a box full of chocolates above with a half-eaten box below, separated by parts of the lower-case phrase "delicious ... wasn't it?" balanced at the bottom with the product name, a humorous, updated variation of the copy-writer's "before-and-after" advertising strategy used commonly for weight loss products or cosmetics (Figure 5.26).

Although well-versed in both "product" and "people" approaches to food advertising, and with both strategies having been employed by Doyle Dane Bernbach in its advertisements for Levy's breads, Taubin adopted Zieff's "man in the street" photography for the 1963 "You don't have to be Jewish" poster campaign, opting to target a diverse market of subway commuters rather than the more sophisticated readership of fashion magazines. In addition to being the United States' largest and most concentrated city with a population of close to eight million in its five boroughs, New York was also the nation's most diverse city, with 20 percent of its population listing themselves as being foreign-born (more than double the national average), and 13 percent identifying as black. The Asian population remained relatively small, but doubled between 1960 and 1970 according to the United States Census, reaching 1.2 percent (the 2010 Census reports the Asian population at roughly 5.5 percent of the total population).

1963: "You don't have to be Jewish"

As briefly noted above, Zieff's photographs for the Levy's 1963 subway posters are more formally posed than those of the workers in the 1954 "Mouth-Watering" campaign, perhaps a decision based upon the difference between a print campaign and a poster campaign where a frontal view commands attention more immediately than three-quarter views with heads of the addressers turned more casually toward the viewer. Also, the use of frontally posed addressing figures seems to follow industry practice: in a "Which ad pulled best?" feature from *Printers Ink*, two advertisements for brassieres appearing in *Seventeen* were compared (1965), one showing a half-length photograph of a woman viewed with her head turned away from the viewer, the other showing a different model smiling and looking at the viewer. The Starch and Staff Company reader analysis recorded a more favorable rating for the ad with the model facing maintaining eye contact with the viewer.

As to the use of more "ordinary" addressing figures, in a *New York Times* article from 2002, writer Bernard Weintraub quoted from his interview with Zieff:

"We wanted normal-looking people, not blond, perfectly proportioned models," Mr. Zieff recalled. The advertisements, for Levy's rye bread, featured an American Indian, a Chinese man and a black child. " I saw the Indian on the street; he was an engineer for the New York Central," Mr. Zieff said. "The Chinese guy worked in a restaurant near my Midtown Manhattan office. And the kid we found in Harlem. They all had great faces, interesting faces, expressive faces" (*New York Times*, February 21, 2002).

Rye, Jewishness, and Diversity

Doyle Dane Bernbach's focus upon rye bread and its connection to "Jewishness" were key components of the 1960s poster campaign. For the purposes of our study these decisions raise two related issues: how did rye bread come to be "Jewish," and why (how) would Jewish rye bread appeal to non-Jewish consumers?

In developing the 1954 and 1960s Levy's advertising campaigns, Robert Gage and William Taubin appropriated a popular, if debatable connection between the Eastern European immigrant Jewish community in New York and rye bread. The connection was certainly more generically "ethnic" than exclusively "Jewish": Jews in the diaspora adopted local recipes wherever they settled in conformity with local culture; like Henry S. Levy, they brought those recipes with them when they emigrated to the United States to settle and earn a living as laborers and small local business owners during the third wave of Jewish immigration that began in the 1880s and brought as many as two million Jewish families to North America, the majority from Eastern Europe.

That fresh neighborhood rye bread had a reputation for quality and an association with Jewish bakeries may be gleaned from Betty Smith's popular 1943 novel *A Tree Grows in Brooklyn* recounting the narrator Francie's upbringing as the thoughtful and resourceful daughter of a poor working-class German/Irish couple in Brooklyn in the period before World War I. With extra pennies earned selling tin foil from chewing-gum wrappers and other sorts of "junk" collected by neighborhood children on the street, Francie's mother tells her to walk

FIGURE 5.27 *Molly Goldberg, her children Rosalie and Sammy, and Uncle David, film still from "The Goldbergs," television series, c. 1953, Getty Images*

to the nearby Jewish neighborhood ("Jew town") to buy "sour rye bread fresh from the oven": "[W]ith its crisp yet tender crust and floury bottom, it was easily the most wonderful bread in the world, she thought, when it was fresh" (Smith, 1943).

Mass media, through print advertising and commercial radio, reinforced the *popular* association between Eastern European foods such as rye bread or sour pickles and a traditional ethnic Jewish identity. As argued by Kerri Steinberg, the Joseph Jacobs advertising agency in New York built their successful food marketing strategy around reconciling the desire of immigrants to conform to the habits of modern American secular life while preserving elements of religious tradition and ethnic cultural identity such as weekly Sabbath candle-lighting, family dinners, the festive Passover meal (Seder), and other holiday meals throughout the religious year.

Radio and television programming forged popular associations between ethnic Jewish culture and broadly based traditional family values as the social and economic pressures to assimilate and conform to a modern secular consumer society tested those values. The popular weekly radio series "The Goldbergs," written by Gertrude Berg (1899–1966) beginning in 1929 (to 1946) and re-emerging as a television series in 1949 (until 1956), featured the lead character Molly Goldberg, the matriarch of an immigrant Jewish family living in the Bronx. With a heavy Yiddish accent and array of malapropisms betraying her old-world background ("My head is trumpets [thumping]," Molly laments to her family, waking up with a headache), Molly and her family spent much of their time (on camera) in the kitchen. As popular culture historian Joyce Antler noted, Molly described herself as a "woman of yesterday, … growing up in one world but coming from another," willing to adjust to modern demands of heightened individualism and materialism without abandoning the value of having empathy for others, including, of course, caring for her family (Kugelmass, 2003). It was through Molly's role as homemaker, including the preparation of meals, that she communicated that empathy in daily, ordinary interactions.

In one television episode Molly appears as a contestant on a televised quiz show and selects "Gastronomics" as the category of questions for which she is most knowledgeable and best prepared. This identification between a Jewish ethnic tradition, family, and food gained momentum in advertising and entertainment in the 1960s, for instance, in the 1967 Broadway musical mentioned above ("How to be a Jewish Mother"), or even earlier in 1964 with the long-running Broadway musical "Fiddler on the Roof" and its signature song "Tradition." Such popular associations, loosely based on instances of fact, constructed and reinforced through marketing and advertising, lie at the root of the successful Levy's rye bread poster campaign that began in 1963; in emphasizing Levy's "real Jewish" rye Doyle Dane Bernbach tapped into an already familiar association between Jewishness and the maintenance of ethnic traditions that resonated with Jew and non-Jew alike. While an association between food, tradition, and empathy may have been a part of the Jewish immigrant experience, it was also not "exclusively" Jewish; indeed it was a value that could be easily shared with the larger non-Jewish mainstream, in particular with other ethnic and racial minorities.

While earlier Levy's advertising campaigns touted the bread's flavor and nutrition, and appealed to the enjoyment of eating tasty foods, Taubin's poster campaign in 1963 linked these selling points more directly to Levy's rye bread's "Jewishness." The shift signified a change in attitudes about ethnic and racial identity, not only for the Jewish community, but in acknowledging racial and ethnic diversity within American society more generally. Jews in the United States experienced anti-Semitism in the first half of the twentieth century through various forms of prejudice that included discrimination in access to higher education and employment opportunities. The price of assimilation was the suppression of difference; a case in point is graphic designer Paul Rand, who changed his birth name (Peretz Rosenbaum) at least in part to avoid possible anti-Semitic bias. As Jews gradually gained acceptance into mainstream

FIGURE 5.28 *"You Don't Have to be Jewish," record album cover, Kapp Records, 1965*

American society after World War II, they became less self-conscious, less secretive about their religious and ethnic heritage and identity; as historian Eric Goldstein noted, Jews could "afford to be different" (Goldstein, 2006). The shift was most apparent in the 1960s. In 1965, the Levy's tagline was used for the title of a popular comedy album "You don't have to be Jewish," released by Kapp Records and featuring a series of skits with Yiddish words and self-deprecating Jewish humor poking fun at stereotypical Jewish mothers, common associations of Jews with stinginess, status, and guilt (Figure 5.28 – the "voices" on the album cover wear a variety of ethnic costumes).

Jews may have been less anxious about expressing their discrete religious identity, but they also embraced being part of a broader more inclusive American society. As Kerri Steinberg put it, American Jews were "having it both ways," as "insiders" and "outsiders." Indeed, the "message" of the Levy's rye bread tagline and campaign worked on two levels, suggesting that ethnic identity was something of which Jews and other minorities might be proud, *and* that despite differences of race, religion, or ethnicity, a diverse America could share the enjoyment of one another's distinct heritage. One even wonders whether the "Italian" woman in one of the Levy's posters (Figure 5.9) might just as well be a "Jewish Mother" minus the salami and checkered tablecloth! The broader food industry was an area in which manufacturers and restaurateurs found difference an acceptable and enjoyable form of multiculturalism. As Bernard Manischewitz explained in a talk delivered at a symposium held at Hunter College in New York in 1956 (entitled "Jewish Life as Reflected in Jewish Foods"), "More and more, with the characteristic American predilection for absorbing the best in many cultures, a growing number of non-Jews are adopting many of the traditional Jewish dishes in their homes, just as they have taken to the foods of many other peoples and lands."

In the Levy's subway posters the word "Jewish" appears twice in the tagline, both above and below the photograph of the addressing figure. And the brand "Levy's" reinforces the point: as the campaign developed, Bill Bernbach himself had remarked to an associate, "For God's sake, your name is Levy's. They are not going to mistake you for a high Episcopalian" (Levenson,

1987). The posters juxtapose the word "Jewish" with a careful selection of easily recognizable *non*-Jewish addressing figures; as with the 1950s "Mouth-Watering" ads, the newer campaign targets the broader New York market, but here references minority ethnic identities rather than diversity in social class. While this shift serves as another example of creative risk taking on the part of Doyle Dane Bernbach by rejecting the predictable "whiteness" that characterized mass advertising at the time, the posters acknowledge emerging identity-based movements in the 1960s and a reduction in the pressure or burden on the part of minorities to conform or assimilate to a single or dominant universal white American identity.

The "voice" of the tagline is that of the figure in the photograph, boldly declaring in effect, "See, I'm NOT Jewish, but ... 'You don't *have* to be Jewish to love Levy's *real* Jewish rye.'" The speaker announces, and presumes, that it is common knowledge that "real" rye bread is Jewish, *and* that Levy's makes it widely available to Asians, African Americans, Native Americans, Irish Americans, or Italian Americans, that is, to a "plural" America (or plural "New York") rather than to an exclusively "white" America. The posters make no distinction between ethnicities and races—both exemplify diversity and undermine the identification of "average" or "typical" with whiteness. And it is a healthy rather than divisive pluralism that is at work here: instead of being cast as outsiders or "the other," minority ethnicities *and* races participate in a shared, tolerant, universalizing culture of ethnic foods, and a reassuring, cohesive *national* identity constructed through American patterns of consumption. While recognizing difference and pluralism, the Levy's advertising posters suggest that food, or *taste*, provides the basis for common ground, breaking down barriers of self-containment and isolation, and the economic and social marginalization that often characterizes narrow ethnic or racial difference.

As we've seen throughout this chapter, Doyle Dane Bernbach often updated or re-cast elements of traditional advertising practice in developing their selling points: here the association between authenticity in food products and ethnic origins of various kinds was hardly uncommon in advertising at the time, particularly for nationally or regionally branded packaged food products. In the Levy's advertising posters, "*real* Jewish Rye" (with the word "real" in italics) communicates this authenticity in the copy. In an age of industrially manufactured, artificial, standardized and packaged products, authenticity becomes a marketable quality of a brand, compensating for the impersonality of supermarket shopping and shelves filled with lookalike, packaged products from the assembly line. As Ernest Dichter explained, consumers prefer bread with "homemade connotations"; "a bread that imparted the feeling that it was baked by a real baker" (Dichter, 1964). In a 1958 *Life* magazine advertisement for Chef BOY-AR-DEE spaghetti and meat sauce, for instance, the copy states that the sauce is made from an "old Italian recipe" (Figure 5.29, and a magazine advertisement reproduced in the 1958 *Art Directors Annual* for Franco-American spaghetti sauce includes the tagline "Here's spaghetti sauce with meat, the way Italians make it.") The Chef BOY-AR-DEE ads vacillate between and yet reconcile being "modern" *and* "traditional," touting the time-saving convenience of preparing a lunch or dinner in a hurry but not sacrificing the emotional appeal of a homemade meal.

It is ironic that while the Levy's campaign was premised upon the bread's authenticity, the actual product was a diluted version of Henry Levy's original rye bread recipe. Like most packaged breads, it contained preservatives and used wheat as well as rye grain; even Bernbach admitted that the packaged version of Levy's rye bread didn't taste the same as the bakery version (Sax, 2009; Levenson, 1987). As a result, the bread was a shadow of its former bakery shop self. While industrialization and the promise of increased sales *eroded* the rye bread's authenticity (in terms of ingredients and baking methods), and by extension its ethnicity, advertising constructed and supplied in suggestion what the product may have lacked in substance: an Eastern European ethnic "Jewishness" became *the* marketable quality, the "unique selling proposition" (USP)—

Tasty idea for tonight... real Italian-style
CHEF BOY-AR-DEE® Spaghetti and Meat Balls

Enjoy tender, firm spaghetti...plump beef meat balls...rich red sauce—
just as served in Venice. Yours for the heating. You'll notice youngsters need
no coaxing when *this* good-for-'em dish is on the menu! It costs
about 14¢ a portion. Look for the 2-serving can or economical 5-serving size.

FIGURE 5.29 *Advertisement for Chef BOY-AR-DEE Spaghetti and Meat Balls,* Life, *February 3, 1958, p. 80, Drexel University Libraries*

something to be shared generously with the broader population and a celebration of the diverse urban experience and identity of New York City.

Another irony of the campaign is the virtual absence of women in the ads; while we might presume that women did the majority of grocery shopping for their families, the Levy's ads depicted male adults and children, with the exception of the Italian woman in the act of preparing a sandwich in the kitchen. One can only speculate on Doyle Dane Bernbach's reasoning: whereas female subjects would appeal mainly to women, men would identify more easily with male addressing figures while women would see happy faces enjoying Levy's rye bread, a result of discerning homemakers' choice of the most "authentic" foods for their husbands and children.

Celebrity

In addition to Godfrey Cambridge, another identifiable or "celebrity" figure is the ageing deadpan silent screen comedian Buster Keaton (1895–1966), who alone (and characteristically) frowns rather than smiles (Figure 5.10). In selecting Buster Keaton and Godfrey Cambridge, the Doyle Dane Bernbach creative team banked on a reversal of audience expectations of celebrity endorsers for products, who more commonly were not only white, but also attractive, sophisticated media stars and starlets recommending products in print or on television, such as film star Tony Curtis (Figure 5.30).

Doyle Dane Bernbach was not the only agency to use surprise to undermine viewer expectations of celebrity advertising—a series of Smirnoff vodka magazine advertisements from 1966 feature comedian, actor, and director Woody Allen (b. 1935) together with actress and model Monique van Vooren (b. 1929) riding a hobby "mule" rather than horse with a recipe for making a "Moscow Mule" cocktail (Figure 5.31).

FIGURE 5.30 *Van Heusen magazine advertisement with Tony Curtis, c. 1958,* ©*Van Heusen*

FIGURE 5.31 *Smirnoff Vodka magazine advertisement, with Woody Allen and Monique von Vooren, c. 1965,* Art Directors Club Annual, *1965, Drexel University Libraries*

Allen, like Cambridge or Keaton, was an unlikely endorser—diminutive in stature, insecure and self-deprecating, often hapless or anxious in relationships with the opposite sex and generally awkward on screen; his presence, dressed in a tuxedo in the company of an attractive model is incongruous, a play on this genre of advertising itself and one of the humorous techniques associated with the "New Advertising."

There may also be an added and local reason behind both recognized celebrities in the Levy's poster ads: Godfrey Cambridge was the co-star in a Broadway play titled "How to be a Jewish Mother" with actress Molly Pecon in 1967 based upon a book of the same title written by Dan Greenburg, and Keaton, who continued to appear in television variety shows at the time, was also featured in an illustrated *Life* magazine article for the week of August 14, 1964 while acting in a film being shot on location in New York. (*Life,* as listed above; the film was titled "Film," and released in 1965, based upon a story by Samuel Beckett.)

Results

A market research publication prepared for the Joseph Jacobs advertising agency in New York ("The Pulse") for the years 1960–75 confirmed that while Jewish consumers still preferred fresh rye bread from local bakeries to packaged rye bread from the supermarket, non-Jewish buyers were just as likely to purchase Levy's packaged varieties of rye bread as fresh bakery products;

and among Jews who *did* buy packaged rye bread, Pulse surveys reported that Levy's doubled the sales of its closest competitor (Grossinger's) and was the largest selling baker of rye bread in the New York metropolitan area (Steinberg, 2015). The market research establishes that the Levy's campaign was successful for Jewish and non-Jewish consumers alike (though Levenson claimed that Levy's was not a big money-maker for DDB). The campaign certainly helped to keep the Henry S. Levy Baking Company profitable and Levy's remained a Doyle Dane Bernbach client until 1979. In that year the baking company, with 150 employees in three Brooklyn locations, was sold to the national brand Arnold's Bakers (based in Greenwich, Connecticut) and shuttered its Brooklyn manufacturing operation (it remained a "brand" but ceased to be an independent baking company). In 2009 Bimbo Bakeries USA (headquartered in Horsham, PA but part of a large Mexican-controlled multinational food products corporation) acquired Arnold's brands. One can easily find the brand in today's New York local and chain grocery stores.

Stereotypes and Advertising

In representing ethnic and racial minorities, the Levy's poster campaign also contributes to the history of the use of stereotypes in advertising. When represented *at all* in American advertising, minorities, in particular African Americans, generally appear as "the other," that is, outsiders to mainstream white Anglo-American culture. Bias is obvious, for instance, in ads for food products such as "Aunt Jemima's" pancake mix or "Uncle Ben's," ads that include blacks in the American experience in the role of cooks or servants who perform their duties for their white employers (or slave owners), a convenient foil for southern hospitality. Moreover, any casual perusal of mass-circulation magazines such as *Life*, *Look*, *Holiday* (the subject of chapter 4 see pp. 103 ff.), or the *National Geographic* in the later 1950s and early 1960s demonstrates that while articles and photo features may have aroused or responded to growing curiosity about non-Western cultures, postcolonial politics in Africa, Southeast Asia, or even reported occasionally on tense race relations, civil rights, and an emerging, rebellious youth culture in the United States, advertisements avoided unpleasant feelings that might be aroused by representing racial diversity and remained almost exclusively "white," with white children and adults as addressing figures, presumed to be typical and generally ignoring diverse ethnic or racial identity (Figure 5.32).

This disconnect is not all that surprising: the advertising industry itself was almost exclusively white (though women were employed in the industry in editorial positions in part because of the role they played in advertising for fashion and home magazines), as stories and photographs accompanying news of personnel moves and hiring in trade publications such as *Advertising Age* attest. A well-known exception is Georg Olden (1920–75), who worked as a graphic designer and art director for the Columbia Broadcast System (CBS) as well holding positions at major New York and national advertising agencies such as McCann Erickson. Even in this case, however, Olden's entry into the advertising profession was due to the personal relationship he forged during World War II as a graphic designer in the Office of Strategic Services (OSS) with Colonel Lawrence Lowman, who became vice president of CBS's television division after the war (Lasky, 2007).

Articles in business journals from the later 1960s called attention to the growing "negro market" in terms of increasing numbers of consumers and their spending power (23 million consumers spending $30 billion in 1968) in comparison with the dearth of African Americans appearing in advertising (less than 1 percent), as revealed in industry surveys of consumers and

FIGURE 5.32 *Jane Parker white enriched bread advertisement,* Woman's Day, *June 1, 1958, p. 23*

their reaction to the representation of blacks in advertisements. Such surveys reported that black readers/viewers, *as well as* whites, preferred integrated ads to "white-only" ads, discrediting a widely held industry presumption that integrated ads would offend or threaten southern whites. At the same time, organizations such as the NAACP (National Association for the Advancement of Colored People) lobbied to increase the representation of blacks in national advertising. Though slow to change, openness to diversity in mass advertising emerged not only as a means to acknowledge if not substantially address racial inequality, but also as a pragmatic business strategy to attract and profit from a growing market of consumers who responded favorably to seeing themselves represented in commercials. By the later 1960s, the *Art Directors Club* regularly reproduced African Americans (and more generally people of color) in advertisements and art-directed features in its annual publication and awards for professional excellence.

While Zieff's photographs were remarkable for representing (capturing) ordinary people rather than models or attractive celebrities, they nonetheless rely upon generalization, association, and careful selection (see Zieff's comments above, p. 164): each addressing figure is unique and individual, yet at the same time "typecast" as an easily recognized member of a particular race or ethnicity based upon skin color as well as associations the viewer has with clothing, props, uniforms, such as an identification between New York policemen and Irish Americans. The advertiser is making certain "assumptions," banking on the viewers' immediate recognition and acceptance of their truth: African Americans, Asians, and Native Americans are not Jewish, policemen are Irish, checkered table cloths are Italian, and rosy-cheeked choirboys with wide ribbon ties sing in churches rather than in synagogues.

Stereotypes and graphic design, of course, are joined at the hip; stereotypes use simplification and abbreviation to immediately and clearly identify and typecast their subjects; in chapter 6 of this book, we'll see that Thomas Nast exaggerated the heft of William "Boss" Tweed in cartoons for *Harper's Weekly* (see, e.g. Figure 6.6) to signify Tweed's gluttony and greed. Are all overweight people greedy? Surely not, but Nast takes advantage of our tendency to categorize, to generalize, to judge and "typecast" people rather than see them as unique and individual:

"a stereotype is an oversimplified expression which imposes uniformity on a group without consideration of individual differences" (*Ethnic Images in Advertising*, 1984).

The Levy's rye bread campaign makes use of generalized assumptions, ignoring differences within races, ethnicities, and religions, for instance, African Americans who are Jewish, Jewish police officers, Asian communities of Jews, or Native American converts to Judaism. As noted above, in the Levy's poster series, stereotyping is achieved primarily by skin color, but where that proves inconclusive, clothing, most often communicated through hats (and uniforms for policemen), does the job, for instance with the broad-brimmed hat of the Native American, or the choir boy's white shirt and red bow (Figures 5.6, 5.7, and 5.8).

While in speeches and interviews William Bernbach criticized market research as a hindrance to creativity in advertising, intuition and risk were at times balanced by testing, especially if there was a possibility of negative stereotyping. The Levy's "You don't have to be Jewish" poster campaign offers a good example: art director William Taubin noted that the agency only decided to use the photograph of a choirboy in the Levy's poster campaign (Figure 5.8) "after hundreds of men and women were interviewed as to whether they were offended by this ethnic treatment."

Creativity in Advertising

The less authoritative tone of the addressers in the Levy's posters was a hallmark of Bill Bernbach's approach to advertising; using Howard Zieff's diverse and more ordinary addressers (or less conventional celebrities), advertisements such as the Levy's rye bread posters created a more casual relationship between advertiser and viewer (addresser and addressee); it recalled and at the same time *challenged* viewer expectations of traditional advertising strategies for food products. Bernbach reasoned that conventional approaches were not necessarily "wrong," but resulted in conformity and eventual boredom for the viewer, so that novelty and surprise had the advantage of freshness and an ability to more easily capture attention and stand out in comparison with competitors' ads. A feature article for *Advertising Age* (March 31, 1958) entitled "The art does it" acknowledged a "new school" of advertising photography whose proponents used more "human and natural" rather than idealized images of addressers and whose opinions carried increasing weight in agency decision making. Bernbach often touted his skepticism towards rules of thumb and relished being an "outsider" within the advertising industry; *Advertising Age* labeled Bernbach and his team at Doyle Dane Bernbach "young Turks." The outsider status was a marketing bonanza! It gained attention for the agency and attracted clients such as Levy's.

That creativity lay at the heart of Doyle Dane Bernbach's advertising approach was a clear selling point for the agency: William Bernbach touted intuition over research, explaining in *Advertising Age* (1961) that creativity could "lift your claims out of the swamp of sameness," resulting in an economical (presumably meaning less reliance upon the costs of statistical research and added bureaucracy in decision making) and effective stimulus to increased sales. At the same time Bernbach qualified what he meant by "creativity"—he didn't condone unrestrained freedom of imagination but rather was an advocate for the "harnessing" of imagination through discipline (attention to selling point), a combination that resulted in more vivid, believable, memorable, and persuasive ads. In Bernbach's view this could never be achieved by following "rules"; indeed "art" was better than "science" as a way of achieving success in advertising. In fact, Bernbach was fond in his speeches to groups of advertisers of quoting the physicist Albert Einstein who rated "intuition" more important than "logic" in discovering the laws that govern the cosmos.

"Honesty and Promotion: The Politics of the New Advertising"

There was an additional, political agenda at work in the "New Advertising" in the United States. Casual camera angles and "ordinary" models were strategies that worked to restore "honesty" in advertising. Through photographs of addressing figures with whom viewers might identify more casually and naturally, copywriters and agencies sought to combat mounting consumer distrust stemming from exaggerated claims for products and charges of manipulation by manufacturers and agencies who played upon consumer fears and frailties (e.g. products that compensated for embarrassing social situations such as bad breath, perspiration, or conditions such as acne and dandruff). While advertising expenditures by businesses grew annually during the 1950s (especially with increases in television advertising), the editors of trade publications voiced their fear of government interference by the Federal Trade Commission (FTC). The FTC had been established by the United States Congress in 1914 to monitor fair trade practices among companies but in the 1950s the agency began to turn its attention to *consumer* protection, motivated in part by grassroots consumer advocacy groups and activists. The tobacco industry was one of the targets of consumer groups, eventually leading to mandated warning labels that were signed into federal law in 1965 and to the banning of cigarette advertising on television and radio by 1971. Editors urged self-reform of the advertising industry rather than government intervention and worried about the threat of taxes imposed upon advertising or the elimination of tax deductions for business advertising. Neither of those initiatives became law, but the advertising industry was wary, encouraging internal reform through greater honesty, believability, and sophistication as tactics to combat charges of self-interest and consumer manipulation. In 1960 *Printers Ink* reported that companies as well as advertising agencies bore responsibility for "truth and taste" to combat the backlash against the advertising industry, and that organizations such as the American Association of Advertising Agencies and the Association of National Advertisers were taking steps to (re)build trust between consumers and products. The same article noted that the McCann Ericson advertising agency had appointed one of its executives to a newly created position of "Arbitrator of Good Taste." Critics and agencies alike were most concerned about the growth of the television industry, where advertisers sponsored shows and exercised control of their content as well as using commercials to promote their products. In the climate of the Cold War, industry defenders were critical of increasing government control of business, likening it to the kind of centralization and nationalization associated with communism, and painting regulation efforts as an infringement of free will and individual rights.

The advertising industry marshaled originality and creativity as strategies to combat public mistrust, arguing, in effect, that advertising was an expression of creative freedom and individual talent. During the 1950s, creativity became a buzzword in the industry, the subject of articles in *Printers Ink* that lamented the lack of creative talent in the field and complained that universities were not encouraging their brightest students to enter the profession. In one article an industrial psychologist claimed he could profile job applicants for prospective employers to discern the level of creativity each might contribute to an agency. Creativity aligned with the "New Advertising," that is, the non-conformity recommended by Bernbach in *Advertising Age* and elsewhere, addressing concerns of industry critics while at the same time serving the objectives of product promotion to attract attention and stimulate sales. Business historian Helen Warlaumont labeled this phenomenon "turncoat" advertising, that is, fending off criticism by appearing to take the side of the consumer/critic, communicating with them in more familiar and less authoritarian ways, even sharing their skepticism of the industry itself with humor and irony (Warlaumont, 2001).

But while the creativity of the "New Advertising" may have challenged aspects of traditional American advertising industry practice, the "soft sell" still aimed to sell. Although Doyle Dane Bernbach capitalized on its "outsider" status and may have shared with the counterculture in the 1960s a general mistrust towards authority, the "creative revolution" in advertising was exactly that: creative rather than radical or subversive, an outgrowth of the 1950s rather than the 1960s. As early as 1954, *Printers Ink* published a series of humorous European poster ads under the rubric "European Posters—Selling Softly," contemporary with the "New Advertising" and as a response to advertising industry concerns with misleading, manipulative ads and consumer backlash.

The outsider status of the "New Advertising" appears to have little in common with anti-war protests, civil rights demonstrations, or the anti-materialist rhetoric of hippy communes. Nor did it share the ethical sentiments and high ground of British graphic designers Ken Garland's 1964 "First Things First" manifesto, signed by and addressed to members of the graphic design profession and offering, in critic Rick Poyner's words, "a plea for a shift in designers' priorities away from the 'high-pitched scream of consumer selling' into worthier forms of activity" (*Looking Closer 3*, 1999).

Neither did the "New Advertising" adopt the ethical restraint of post-World War II Swiss and other European designers who, in their advertising work, felt a responsibility to "inform" rather than to persuade (on this issue, see above, chapter 1, pp. 16–17), or sympathize with the general skepticism towards the advertising profession acknowledged by graphic and industrial designer Gui Bonsiepe (b. 1934) in a 1965 essay that contains the following words: "That the interests of business do not always coincide with the interests of society is a recognition nobody can avoid who works with the communication industry" (*Looking Closer 3*, 1999). Indeed, while the "New Advertising" may have borrowed some of the visual and verbal economy pioneered in European graphic design in the interwar period, Doyle Dane Bernbach and other Madison Avenue advertising agencies do not appear to have questioned that their primary job was persuasion, and that success was to be judged by sales and their clients' satisfaction. Bernbach conceded as much when, as noted above, he insisted that creative freedom in advertising required "discipline," that is, a clear focus upon selling point in order to be effective.

"Active" Advertising

In addition to honesty, proponents of the "New Advertising" also endorsed an active rather than passive approach toward the viewer as an advertising strategy. One might interpret the term "active" in a variety of ways: for instance, an "active" viewer would appreciate being presented with facts rather than (passively) accepting an exaggerated claim, and would appreciate being talked "to" rather than talked "at" as a sign of respect. It might also mean that a viewer would enjoy making connections between words and images that required the recognition of a metaphor or supplying the missing part of an incomplete image that substitutes for the whole; or that in place of testimonials or endorsements, an "active" viewer would respond well to advertisements that masked persuasion under the guise of a clever, humorous play on words or an unexpected juxtaposition, for instance, the surprise of juxtaposing a Jewish rye bread with an Asian or African American face. Indeed, for the celebrated 1960 Volkswagen campaign, the selling point was "honesty" expressed visually through minimal design and an emphasis upon "small;" its effectiveness also depended upon viewer familiarity with traditional automobile advertising: the Beetle was inexpensive, admittedly "ugly" in relation to the Detroit styling of the time, as well as unpretentious in an age of annual model changes, associations with luxury, powerful engines, and jet-age tailfins, appealing to independent thinkers unconcerned with or skeptical toward the outward material signs of status linked to automobile ownership and "keeping up with the Joneses." But whereas the Volkswagen campaign was "low-key" in its minimal design and its placement in *New Yorker* suggested a target audience of sophisticated consumers (rather than a mass-circulation magazine such as *Life* or *Saturday Evening Post*), the Levy's campaign, equally clever in its visual and verbal sophistication, was an example of mass rather than segmented advertising. Perhaps for this reason, the posters maintain a connection with familiar as well as "creative" elements: despite the novelty of their racial diversity, the smiling, well-dressed African American and Asian children appeal to a recognized tradition in marketing packaged food brands using contented (white) kids.

The United States in the World: Advertising and Beyond

The Levy's "You don't have to be Jewish" poster campaign paralleled other contemporary efforts to acknowledge racial and ethnic pluralism after World War II. In six consecutive issues beginning in July 1948 the monthly mass circulation magazine *Ladies Home Journal* (Curtis Publications, based in Philadelphia) featured a series of photo-essays under the title "People are People the World Over," focusing upon twelve families from different parts of the world engaging in common activities that included education, worship, bathing, play, and (relevant to the present chapter) eating. For the purposes of comparison globally, the families selected were all rural. The series emphasized the commonality of family life all over the world; but critics have noted a distinct bias toward the United States, most visible in the role of technology in the American home, in modern appliances, suggesting American families were more "advanced" than their third world counterparts or in a Western Europe recovering from the extreme hardships suffered during and in the immediate aftermath of World War II. There is an implied, if unspoken, assertion not only of American prosperity, but also of global leadership, of bringing "our" way of life to the rest of the world (see also chapter 4 on *Holiday* magazine, pp. 124–6).

In the 1950s, one of the best known and well-publicized efforts to celebrate diversity was Edward Steichen's "The Family of Man," an exhibition of photographs that premiered at the Museum of Modern Art in 1955 and toured thirty-seven cities worldwide over the next decade, viewed by an estimated nine million people and reaching an even broader audience through the show's published catalog that appeared in multiple printings (Figure 5.33 and 5.34).

The exhibition and its critical reception have been the subject of numerous scholarly studies, and only a brief introduction is offered here. Steichen (1879–1973) was an internationally acclaimed photographer who also served as curator of photography at MoMA; he and his curatorial team selected the photographs for the well-publicized exhibition from a combination of responses to an open invitation for submissions along with combing the rich photographic archives of *Life* magazine (from 1936); Steichen and his assistant, Wayne Miller, surveyed more than two million images and negatives which they condensed to ten thousand, and then reduced to the final number of 503. The photographs were displayed as asymmetrical ensembles, printed in different sizes, and grouped by theme on wall panels; like the *Ladies Home Journal's* "People are People" photo-essays, the themes centered around family life, birth and childhood, work (agricultural and industrial), love (heterosexual), entertainment, play, religious observance, and community. A sub-category of the themes, connected with work as well as family, was devoted to food and labeled as such in the exhibition's master inventory list. Under this rubric an anonymous mural-size photograph of a wheat field was inset with two images of women holding loaves of

FIGURE 5.33 *Installation view of the exhibition, "The Family of Man." January 24, 1955 through May 8, 1955. The Museum of Modern Art, New York. Photographic Archive. The Museum of Modern Art Archives, New York. Photographer: Rolf Petersen, The Museum of Modern Art. Digital Image © The Museum of Modern Art/Licensed by SCALA/Art Resource, NY*

FIGURE 5.34 *Installation view of the exhibition, "The Family of Man." January 24, 1955 through May 8, 1955. The Museum of Modern Art, New York. Photographic Archive. The Museum of Modern Art Archives, New York. Photographer: Rolf Petersen, The Museum of Modern Art. Digital Image © The Museum of Modern Art/Licensed by SCALA/Art Resource, NY*

bread, one taken by Steichen himself with his mother as the subject. A cursive caption, based on a Russian proverb, accompanied the wall arrangement and emphasized the equation between bread and a common, elemental humanity: "Eat bread and salt and tell the truth" (Figure 5.34).

Partially funded by the United Nations Educational, Scientific and Cultural Organization (UNESCO, founded 1945), "The Family of Man" did not promote a commercial product, but both the exhibition and the Levy's rye bread poster advertising campaign represent racial diversity in the service of a healthy pluralism that seeks to unite rather than divide people and nations. And both exhibition and ad campaign represent *food* as a means through which difference is both acknowledged *and* transcended by universal human experience and authentic expression, whether in the service of global understanding and peace, or in the mass marketing of a New York baking company's rye bread. Both exhibition and advertising campaign offered an encouraging picture of human relations, emphasizing the ties that bind rather than the disparities and differences that identify and divide nations, races, and ethnicities, suggesting harmony rather than discord or discrimination and a hopeful rather than troubling message. For "The Family of Man" a large panel with a photograph of a mushroom cloud served as a reminder of the atomic bomb, the Cold War build-up of nuclear weapons, and well-founded fears of the existential threat they posed to a striving humankind still mindful of the destruction wrought by the atomic bombs dropped in Japan in August 1945 and fearful of conflict between nations with catastrophic consequences.

"The Family of Man" and its accompanying catalog were a popular and critical success. *Life* magazine wrote admiringly of the exhibition, and reproduced a sampling of photographs with short text which reads in part "pictures by photographers from all over the world portraying the emotions which all members of the human family share, no matter in what country or at what stage of civilization they live." *Life* organized the images around phrases such as "Ties of Family," "Harmony in Work and Play," "Loneliness, even among many," and even "Tensions turned to dread and hate." Photographer Barbara Morgan, whose images were among those included in the exhibition, wrote in the journal *Aperture* that "Empathy with these hundreds of human beings truly expands our sense of values."

But while the experience of two world wars and contemporary fears of nuclear holocaust motivated Steichen's "Family of Man" project, one critic characterized "The Family of Man" as a "timeless realm of sentiment" while yet another wrote that the exhibition was an "anthology" of middle-class taste and the expression of a Western liberal ideology that gave overwhelming weight to white races, ignoring hunger and other problematic global disparities stemming from a systemic unequal distribution of wealth and resources throughout the world. Critical reaction was shaped in part by resentment toward American involvement in Western European politics and economics through the Marshall Plan (see also, p. 132), seen as a threat to traditional national identity and autonomy. When the exhibition was staged in France, the French cultural critic Roland Barthes wrote that "every family looks like a western family." American writer and critic Susan Sontag remarked that "Steichen's choice of photographs assumes a human condition or a human nature shared by everybody. By purporting to show that individuals are born, work, laugh, and die everywhere in the same way, 'The Family of Man' denies the determining weight of history—of genuine and historically embedded differences, injustices, and conflicts." All of these criticisms indicate that despite Steichen's best intentions and efforts through selection and display to construct an optimistic narrative of comforting multiculturalism, he and his team were unable to control the meaning(s) of the images they selected and assembled for "The Family of Man," images that masked more complex, troubling social realities and political tensions revolving around the position of the United States in the postwar world (Sandeen, 1995).

Race in America

If some viewers felt a disparity between Steichen's common humanity as portrayed in "The Family of Man" and social and political reality globally in the 1950s, a similar gap might also be expected between William Taubin's art direction of the inclusive Levy's rye bread posters in the 1960s and race relations in the United States. While Jews and African Americans were both minorities, the pace of their acceptance into the American mainstream differed. Jews may have been "having it both ways" (see p. 167), but a growing impatience with the progress of the nation's civil rights movement led to disillusion and the emergence of black identity-based, sometimes militant, movements, presenting a more radical, potentially violent alternative to the belief in racial integration, assimilation, and a shared culture.

The disparity in opportunity that separated ethnic from racial identity, between mainstream white America and its black "other," may be gauged in the 1964 photo-essay book *Nothing Personal*, a collaboration between photographer Richard Avedon (1923–2004; a contributor to "The Family of Man") and African-American writer and social critic James Baldwin (1924–87). Baldwin, who had lived for years in Paris, remarked upon his return on the "whiteness" of the entertainment industry through television programming and advertising, either excluding or offering "sanitized" images of minorities, and deplored the violence he witnessed and experienced in American cities (he had been arrested with a white friend in Manhattan, a victim of racial profiling). Baldwin's essay in *Nothing Personal* was accompanied by Avedon's full-bleed black and white photographs presenting a cross-section of American life, of affluent whites, blacks, couples, the elderly, youth, the mentally and physically disabled, and well-known white and black political and cultural figures on all sides of the political spectrum (Figures 5.35 and 5.36).

Despite the author's weary despair, however, the photo-essay was neither militant nor nihilistic; Baldwin's faith in the future appears shaken but not broken, as when he remarked that "[b]ut if a society permits one portion of its citizenry to be menaced or destroyed, then, very soon, no one in that society is safe." *Nothing Personal* retains a note of empathy, stemming at least in part from the universality of human experience; Baldwin refers in his text to a "fearful hope," captured in *Nothing Personal*'s final image of a civil rights march in Atlanta Georgia (Figure 5.36) and in the book's coda:

> This is why one must say YES to life and embrace it wherever it is found … For nothing is fixed, forever and forever and forever, it is not fixed … The sea rises, the light falls, lovers cling to each other, and children cling to us. The moment we cease to hold each other, the moment we break faith with one another, the sea engulfs us and the light goes out.

Print media and television reported on the civil rights movement and grappled with representing it; the complexity surrounding these efforts appears in the photographs of Gordon Parks for *Life* ("How does it feel to be Black," August 16, 1963) as well as a public television documentary produced by Henry Morganthau in 1963 entitled "The Negro and the American Promise," where African American psychologist and educator Kenneth Bancroft Clark conducted interviews with Martin Luther King, Malcolm X, and James Baldwin.

The "You don't have to be Jewish" campaign for Levy's rye bread's use of racial and ethnic stereotypes appealed to rather than troubled or distanced viewers. It's worth noting that when Doyle Dane Bernbach's creative team selected photographs of African Americans for the Levy's rye bread posters, they chose a young, well-dressed child and a nightclub and television

FIGURE 5.35 *Richard Avedon, Wedding of Mr. and Mrs. Richard Dinielli, City Hall, New York, June 3, 1961, The Wedding of Mr. and Mrs. Mario Niles, City Hall, New York, June 3, 1961, The Wedding of Mr. and Mrs. William Munoz, City Hall, New York City, 1961, from* Northing Personal, *New York, Atheneum, 1964 37 × 30.8 cm, Avedon Foundation*

FIGURE 5.36 *Richard Avedon, Julian Bond and members of the Student Nonviolent Coordinating Committee, Atlanta, Georgia, March 23, 1963, from* Northing Personal, *New York, Atheneum, 1964 37 × 30.8 cm, Avedon Foundation*

comedian familiar to white and black audiences alike rather than a black "man in the street" or student activist, reducing the possibility of an alternative, threatening reading of African-American presence that might communicate tension or arouse uneasiness. A more complex image appears in CBS executive Lou Dorfsman's newspaper advertisement in the *New York Times* in 1968 for a seven-part documentary television series entitled "Of Black America" featuring a three-quarter view photograph of an African-American man's face overlaid with the stripes of the American flag that appear like the bars of a prison cell (Figure 5.37).

The Doyle Dane Bernbach creative team emphasized surprise—the unexpected freshness and shock of confronting racially and ethnically diverse addressers in striking contrast to ubiquitous ads for food products featuring white children, adults, and families. But as American historian

Roland Marchand noted more than thirty years ago in his book *Advertising the American Dream: Making Way for Modernity, 1920–1940*, advertising (even when it purports to "tell the truth" honestly as Bernbach touted) is a distorted mirror of society, reflecting foremost the interests of manufacturers and advertisers, rather than social reality, communicating values that sell products and services, including a reassuring belief in or hope for racial or ethnic equality and harmony, in other words, the belief that "things will get better" if we only stay the course (Marchand, 1985).

While there was no shortage of criticism leveled at "The Family of Man" for ignoring the fault lines in a reassuring but biased unifying narrative, the Levy's poster campaign seems to have succeeded both commercially and critically. In a photograph taken by Laurence Henry, militant African American activist Malcolm X (1925–65) appears, smiling, beside the Levy's poster featuring a young African-American boy (Figure 5.38); according to Henry, Malcolm X saw the poster and asked Henry to take the picture, and it was published in the magazine *Now!* in its March–April issue (1966). While "The Family of Man" provoked a wide range of responses and interpretations, the Levy's advertising posters successfully limited such semiotic "noise." Keep in mind of course that the exhibition featured more than 500 photographs while the rye bread campaign consisted of fewer than a dozen closely related images, but Doyle Dane Bernbach was adept at controlling meaning through a most carefully considered process of selection of photographs that created empathy with viewers while avoiding controversy, and respecting continuity with the selling points the agency had been working to develop for over a decade.

FIGURE 5.37 *Lou Dorfsman, newspaper advertisement for "Of Black America" television series for CBS*, New York Times, *1968, CBS*

FIGURE 5.38 *Laurence Henry, photograph of Malcolm X with Levy's real Jewish rye bread poster, published in* Now!, *March, 1966*

Conclusion

In August 1960, *Printers Ink* reported on a German documentary film devoted to the subject of advertising in the United States directed by German filmmaker Peter von Zahn (1913–2001) and aired on West German television earlier that year. Titled "The Race for the Consumer" (possibly a play on the contemporary Cold War "space race" between the USSR and the United States), the documentary explored for its German audience the mind-boggling expenditures on advertising by US businesses, quoting astonishing figures (93 million dollars annually for Proctor & Gamble products alone in 1959), and articulating the American advertising industry's belief that the "consumer is king, ... pushing frontiers into the fascination of abundance." In today's world there's very little that appears shocking or misguided about a consumer-led economy or the role that design, manufacturing, and advertising play in stimulating consumer spending and its relationship to technology, trade, employment, and the standard of living. In Europe, the advertising industry was regulated under the auspices of joint trade organizations such as the Organisation for European Economic Cooperation (OEEC, founded 1948 and precursor to the foundation in 1993 of the European Union) that sought to prohibit misleading claims in advertising through regulation (see chapter 1 on advertising and Swiss Style, pp. 16–18). Yet for its European audience at the time, the connection between American prosperity and the untrammeled growth of American *advertising* was both striking and unsettling. A similar ambivalence toward advertising appears in books by American authors such as David Potter cited above (p. 131).

Despite the contribution of interwar European design to the visual and verbal means that helped to shape the "New Advertising" in the United States, contemporary advertising in Europe was tame in comparison with the sheer volume, expenditures, public and industry discourse, and relentless appeals to consumer desire that characterized advertising in America. The shift from a production to a consumption economy, initiated between World Wars I and II, was moving full steam ahead, advertising was steering the ship, and graphic design was supplying the creative and pragmatic fuel not simply to maintain but to accelerate the pace.

The so-called "creative revolution" in advertising might be seen as a "rebellion" against the conservatism of industry practice and the challenge it posed to the existence of "immutable principles" of advertising, including the overriding importance of research-based information in determining selling points, the appeals to insecurities, and a hierarchical organization of agencies that favored copy-writing over art direction. But in opting for a lower-key, clever, conversational advertising strategy and an "active" relationship with viewers and readers, the purpose of advertising remained unchanged: to promote products—*not* to question the ethics of consumption. As noted above, the "New Advertising" may have indeed been novel, but it was still advertising—and its goal was persuasion. Moreover, the blurring of entertainment and persuasion, which the "New Advertising" encouraged (and which Super Bowl advertisers and audiences celebrate), deflected governmental and consumerist pressure on the advertising industry and contributed to the continued growth of that industry and of the graphic design profession, responsive to the growing medium of television and to a renewed focus upon and attention toward changes in the consumer market, from the emergence of a youth market, to diversity, to an awareness of consumer health, safety, the environment, an embrace of humor, and a healthy skepticism towards authority.

Just as the Levy's rye bread campaign engages race but steers clear of controversy, so do food advertisements today generally paint a healthy picture of race relationships, with more diverse but friendly gatherings of families or millennials enjoying one another's company while eating snacks, pizza, drinking beer, or visiting fast food and nationally franchised chain restaurants. Food remains a great leveler, offering appealing, equal-opportunity products for mass consumption to middle-class consumers, the tangible result of social progress afforded by integrated schools, minority opportunities in employment, and more diversity in the office, in higher education, in factories. Rather than a series of individuals from racially diverse backgrounds, today's food commercials tend to feature the conviviality of social gatherings in the home or in bars or restaurants. Such ads reaffirm mainstream beliefs in racial harmony and opportunity, and African American endorsers (e.g. Tiger Woods for Tag Heuer, Michael Jordan for Coca Cola, Kanye West for Adidas) encourage us to accept or to believe that race is no barrier to achievement, financial success, and celebrity. They also mask persistent racial tension and power relations in American society that have emerged most recently in the "Black Lives Matter" and "I Can't Breathe" movements.

So what makes the 1960s Levy's real Jewish rye bread poster campaign so significant in the history of graphic design? In its time it was one of numerous ad campaigns to validate the effectiveness of reduced copy, photography, and the importance of surprise, humor, and viewers' enjoyment of having their expectations challenged—more importantly the campaign engaged the contemporary social and political reality of racial and ethnic identity in America, and demonstrates that representations of racial and ethnic diversity could be effectively "managed" and commercially exploited by emphasizing aspects of human nature that were comforting or reassuring rather than disturbing, that used generalization but avoided troubling stereotypes, and that didn't blindly *assume* a homogenous white audience. One would have to expand the definition of the "New Advertising" well beyond the narrow limits of a "creative revolution" or "European influence" to grasp the story of Doyle Dane Bernbach's graphic design achievement.

---

*The posters of the Asian man and Asian child were reproduced in the *Art Directors Club Annual* in 1964; they may be first in the series, probably dating to the previous year. A *Life* magazine article from 1964 indicates that Buster Keaton was filming in New York in that year; Kent Wakeford's photograph of a Native American (Figure 5.11) for Levys appears in the 1965 *ADCA*, suggesting 1964 for the date of the poster of the same subject photographed by Howard Zieff, while the African American child is found in the *ADCA* for 1966, the same year that Laurence Henry's photograph of Malcolm X smiling next to the poster was published in *Now!*. The website "Washington Spark" dates the photo to 1964 (see www.flickr.com/photos/washington_area_spark/18737056258; accessed 9-20-19) Godfrey Cambridge appeared on Broadway in 1967. There's no information upon which to date the choir boy, while the notes in the Library of Congress record provide a date of 1970–1 for the Italian Woman but with no additional information:

1963: Asian Man; Asian Child

1963–4: Irish Policeman—there's no date on the Court Street Station photograph from the NY Transit Museum of this poster, but the theme of working-class white men was used in the Levy's campaign in the early 1950s, suggesting perhaps that it was among the earlier subjects in the series

1964: Native American

1965: African American Child

1965-66: Buster Keaton – according to Jack Rennert (Rennerts Gallery), the Keaton poster was not widely circulated owing to Mr. Keaton's death in February 1966; one might conclude it was printed in the later part of 1965

1967: Godfrey Cambridge

1970–1: Italian Woman

Chapter 6

Graphic Design and Politics: Thomas Nast and the "TAMMANY TIGER LOOSE"

Introduction

The 2015 Academy Award for "Best Picture" and "Best Screenplay" went to the film "Spotlight," directed by Tom McCarthy. "Spotlight" was the name of the investigative journalism unit at the *Boston Globe* that pursued leads and published records and testimonies revealing a pattern of sexual abuse by Catholic priests in the city of Boston over a period of several decades, abuses that were suppressed through a combination of indifference, negligence, and institutional intimidation that effectively concealed them from the public, and protected offenders from prosecution for criminal acts (Figure 6.1).

The critical and popular success of "Spotlight" (it grossed more than ninety million dollars) provides ample evidence that the public rallies behind campaigns that expose crime and corruption, revealed through the dogged efforts of journalists, efforts that result not only from investigative reporting amid hostile circumstances, but also that demonstrate the importance of first amendment freedoms, the power of a free press, and that remind us of the watchdog role of print journalism.

The story of illustrator and political cartoonist Thomas Nast, *Harper's Weekly* manager Fletcher Harper, the *New York Times* owner George Jones and editor Louis J. Jennings, and a cover-up by New York's powerful political organization known as Tammany Hall (named for the seventeenth-century native American chief also known as Tamanend) that controlled the city's democratic party in the late 1860s and early 1870s, is an earlier example of the battle against local corruption instigated by a group of determined, high-minded and principled print journalists. For the history of graphic design, the episode is of interest because it was aided, if not led, in no small measure, by an unrelenting series of powerful political cartoons by Thomas Nast (1840–1902) and other artists who marshaled text, caricature, a popular understanding of ancient history, and the bold use of the pictorial conventions of Western narrative painting to gain and maintain public attention, resulting in a surprising electoral outcome followed by direct legal and judicial action against local government officials, along with at least a partial restoration of public trust and political accountability in New York City politics.

FIGURE 6.1 *Edgar Acensão, "Spotlight," poster, offset lithograph, 60 × 40 cm, film directed by Tom McCarthy, 2015, courtesy of the artist*

The political cartoon is certainly part of the history of graphic design in the nineteenth century, though it tends to receive less critical attention in the twentieth and twenty-first centuries than it may deserve. Among graphic design surveys to include material on the nineteenth century, only Meggs/Purvis's *History of Graphic Design* devotes attention to Thomas Nast. There the authors make Nast's cartoons responsible for increasing the circulation of *Harper's Weekly*, and link the artist's popularization of symbols such as the Republican Party Elephant (Nast was a Republican, a supporter of Abraham Lincoln and opposed to slavery) and Santa Claus to an "increased communicative effectiveness" that contributes to "progress" in the development of the graphic design profession. I'd like to think that Nast's cartoons merit further investigation and that a case study may increase general awareness of his work and promote a better understanding of the particular relationship between graphic design and politics during Nast's time at *Harper's Weekly*.

While Nast's cartoons have only infrequently been the subject of study by art or graphic design historians, his cartoons have received considerable attention by scholars in other disciplines. The illustrator was something of a celebrity during his own lifetime, whose fame, talent, and rise from humble immigrant origins were chronicled in a well-documented feature in *Harper's Weekly* (1871; Figure 6.2). Recent scholarship reconsiders Nast's increasingly contentious relationship with *Harper's* editors amid growing concerns about editorial license and the nature of political discourse in print beginning in the later 1870s; the artist left the magazine in 1886. A lengthy illustrated biography of Nast was published by author Albert Bigelow Paine in 1904, just two years after Nast's death. By that time Nast's fame had dimmed, but Paine's book still seems remarkable in its attention to the career of a graphic designer.

It is not surprising that political (and popular) historians rather than art historians have been most attentive to Nast's achievements. Morton Keller wrote the introduction to the reprinting of Paine's biography, and kept Nast's legacy alive with his own monograph on the artist (1968). Nast even makes a cameo appearance in a scene from Martin Scorsese's 2002 film *Gangs of*

FIGURE 6.3 *Thomas Nast sketching, film still from* Gangs of New York, *directed by Martin Scorsese, 2002, Miramax Films*

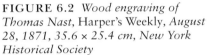

FIGURE 6.2 *Wood engraving of Thomas Nast*, Harper's Weekly, *August 28, 1871, 35.6 × 25.4 cm, New York Historical Society*

New York (Figure 6.3), whose fictional plot takes place in the streets of mid-nineteenth century Manhattan and includes several historical characters and events of the time, including William Tweed (played by Jim Broadbent), Nast's chief nemesis in the pages of *Harper's Weekly* in the later 1860s and early 1870s.

More recently, Kenneth Ackerman published a lively narrative account of William Magear (aka "Boss") Tweed (2005), while John Adler (2008) chronicled Nast's role in bringing down the infamous "Boss" of Tammany Hall and his "Ring" of corrupt political cronies who controlled the purse strings of New York City's treasury.

The present chapter focuses upon a single but particularly powerful example of Nast's political cartoons, published in *Harper's Weekly* dated November 11, 1871, but available on the city's newsstands a week earlier, on November 4th, just days before the November 7th election whose results heralded the end of the Tammany Democrat's stranglehold on New York City politics (Figure 6.5). An examination of the double-page cartoon illuminates Nast's approach to visual propaganda, and reveals the particular design strategies and historical circumstances that propelled the cartoons beyond awareness, opinion, and satire toward activism, confrontation, and direct political action.

Harper's Weekly and the Illustrated Newspaper

Nast's career coincides with the popularity of the weekly illustrated press both in the United States and in Europe. Featuring cover illustrations and combining reporting on current domestic and foreign events with self-help, appeals for charity during the holidays, occasional satire and political commentary, contemporary fiction and biographical sketches, advertisements, and humor (in a regular "Humors of the Day" section), the illustrated weekly differed from daily newspapers as well as from illustrated magazines by its mass circulation, expert use of the process of wood-engraving, and high-speed printing by electrotype. *Harper's Weekly* began publication in 1857, joining an earlier journal initiated by the Harper Brothers in New York titled *Harper's New Monthly Magazine* (1850). Subtitled "Journal of Civilization," *Harper's Weekly* was managed by the youngest of the Harper brothers, Fletcher (1806–77). From 1863 the weekly's editor was author George W. Curtis (1824–92). The magazine was one of numerous print news outlets in New York City in the mid-nineteenth century, at a time when print was the major source of daily and weekly information and opinion, when increasing numbers of children were attending public schools, and when literacy was rising, reaching close to 90 percent by 1900. Inspired by the success of high-quality illustrations in the *London Illustrated News* (first printed in 1842), the Harper Brothers invested in the recent technology of wood engraving to combine print journalism with high-quality illustrations. Cutting against the grain and piecing together blocks of wood that could be distributed among teams of skilled engravers, the technique produced high-quality illustrations for high-speed and high-volume printing on inexpensive paper. Illustrators such as Nast or his contemporary Winslow Homer (1836–1910) submitted their drawings to the journal where they were traced and then cut on blocks and reproduced for printing. Fidelity was remarkable and the size large (15 7/8 × 11"). Each issue numbered sixteen pages in addition to occasional "supplemental" issues, and illustrations increased sales while advertising helped to compensate for production costs and eventually reduced the newsstand and subscription cost to readers (each issue was sold separately for 10 cents or 4 dollars per annual subscription including supplements). In addition to *Harper's Weekly*, *Frank Leslie's Illustrated Newspaper* (beginning 1855) offered competition in its wide-ranging content and inclusion of wood-engraved illustrations.

Harper's Weekly's circulation had reached 100,000 copies per week by 1865, but increased to 275,000 in the later part of 1871 (New York City's population in 1870 was 942,000). Nast's

FIGURE 6.4 *Illustration of Chicago Fire in* Frank Leslie's Illustrated Newspaper, *wood engraving, 41 × 30.5 cm (page), October 28, 1871, Library of Congress*

cartoons criticizing William Tweed and the "Tweed Ring" may have played a part in the rise in circulation during that year, and especially during the time of the early November election, but they were hardly the only items that attracted and sustained editorial and reader attention at the time, and criticism of Tweed in the journal had begun as early as 1869; *Harper's Weekly* devoted considerable text and illustrations to the more dramatic news of the time, such as the Chicago Fire that was also covered in Frank Leslie's more sensationalist *Illustrated Newspaper* (October 28, 1871; Figure 6.4); the Chicago fire was a natural disaster attracting the same degree of media attention given floods or hurricanes in our own time, garnering intense public interest and sympathy. Internationally the newspaper closely followed military conflicts including the Franco-Prussian War (1870) and the riots between the French army and protestors caused by the Paris Commune (May, 1871) and the unification of Germany (1870), all accompanied by illustrations, whether by Nast or by other contemporary illustrators. As art historian Baird Jarman explains, *Harper's Weekly* and other new weekly or monthly publications of the time occupied a middle ground between the sensationalism and biased opinion of many daily newspapers and higher-minded "civilizing" literature associated with books: "At midcentury magazines existed as a somewhat nebulous cultural formation, caught between two markedly different productions of the publishing world, the newspaper and the book. Newspapers operated within the unruly public sphere with its raw market forces and partisan politics, whereas books accessed more polite realms of history and literature" (Jarman, 2010).

Description

"THE TAMMANY TIGER LOOSE—What Are You Going To Do About It?" was the title of Nast's double page illustration in *Harper's Weekly* for November 11, 1871 (Figure 6.5). As noted above, the issue appeared on newsstands and was delivered to subscribers *before* the election on November 7, when several members of New York's Democratic Party were defeated, a victory for the Republican party that Nast and his editors at *Harper's Weekly* endorsed. The illustration is set in a Roman amphitheater, the scene of staged, unevenly matched contests in Roman imperial times pitting animals against enemies of the state as a very public display of imperial power. A fierce tiger with gaping mouth and four sharp teeth dominates the composition at its center, turning its body, rendered in a three-quarter view, to stare the viewer directly in the eye. The tiger is also the most detailed rendering in the scene, creating a sense of clear hierarchy for the viewer not only in terms of its size and center placement but also in sheer amount of visual information and contrast this section of the illustration contains. It wears a collar inscribed with the word "Americus," a reference to the name of the neighborhood volunteer Fire Company and Social Club of which William Tweed was a founding member and where he earned his early reputation as an affable and community-minded New York resident. The tiger stands astride a prone female figure wearing a tunic fastened at the right shoulder. She is faceless, but a crown lying nearby identifies her as the "Republic." Faintly etched stars suggest she once held the American flag, now in tatters, the attribute of "Columbia," a popular literary and pictorial personification in the nineteenth century and also depicted by Nast and other artists of the time as a symbol of the United States and its citizenry, the female counterpart to the now more familiar "Uncle Sam." In the lower right corner the blade of a broken sword is labeled "Power" and to the left of the Tiger's massive head is a broken sphere labeled "Ballot," a reference to the abuses of the voting process. Two other bodies, one lying face up the other face down, also appear to the tiger's left. One is a male figure, who once wore a helmet and carried a caduceus signifying trade (the word is written on the nearby helmet), symbolized by the Roman god Mercury, while the other figure, this time female, also lies next to a broken sword and scales, both attributes of the personification

FIGURE 6.5 Thomas Nast, "THE TAMMANY TIGER LOOSE—*What Are You Going To Do About it?*," Harper's Weekly, November 11 (issued November 4), 1871, wood engraving, 50.8 × 68.6 cm, New York Historical Society

FIGURE 6.6 *The Imperial Box, detail from Thomas Nast, "THE TAMMANY TIGER LOOSE—What are you going to do about it?," Harpers Weekly, November 11 (issued November 4), 1871, wood engraving, New York Historical Society*

of Justice. Above and to the left of the tiger is the imperial box (Figure 6.6), where the corpulent figure of William "Boss" Tweed sits, wearing a cape, pendant, and belt from which hangs three straps, in the manner of sculptures of Roman emperors in military dress. He holds a staff labeled "Iron Rod," and is surrounded by a group of soldiers and attendants.

These include the members of his "Ring," the mop-haired former District Attorney Peter Sweeny to Tweed's right, the spectacled mayor Oakey Hall to the Boss's left, and city comptroller Richard Connolly partially hidden behind Tweed's left shoulder. The mustachioed New York governor John Hoffman holds one of the standards toward the back of the imperial box. Similar depictions of all four major characters in the drama appeared in earlier Nast cartoons, including one on August 19, 1871 with the tagline "Who stole the people's Money?" (August 9, 1871). John Adler identified several others in the box, all connected with the Ring as Tammany-backed candidates for public office as well as recipients of kickbacks for city contracts that had been published in July 1871 by the *New York Times*.

Next to the governor is a tiger emblem and pendant etched with the number "6," along with two standing guards holding standards labeled "Spoils." A fireman's hat sits atop one of the standards. The tiger appears on another round emblem on the wall below the seated figure, repeating the word "Americus" that appears on the tiger's collar (the Americus Club was named for the Italian explorer "Americus [Amerigo] Vespucci" and also known as "Big Six"). To the right of the imperial box are scores of smaller onlookers, sketchily rendered in two tiers, in front of arched openings. Above them are a series of struts, presumably supporting a stretch of canvas to shield them from the sun. The various symbols not only portray the Ring's accretion of political power, but also serve as a visual summation of Tweed's political career, including his association with the familiar civic-minded fire companies and social organizations in New York, branded by their emblems, buildings, engines, and liveries.

The illustration is carefully constructed. Viewers' attention is drawn to the tiger at the center, then diagonally below to the sword and figure of the "Republic" and diagonally again, upward to the imperial box, followed by the vast throng and accompanying dead victims in the arena. The three focal points of the composition (tiger—victim—emperor) may be circumscribed within the triangle that unites them, creating a clear sense of unity, order, and hierarchy: William Tweed and the "Spoils" standard sit at the apex of the triangle, normally the culmination of a complex scene's visual drama, but here the attention is diverted to the Tammany Tiger and its victim, occupying stage center and attracting visual interest by the tiger's size, detail, and degree of contrast, and standing also at the juncture of two crossing diagonals, first from lower right to upper left and second from upper right to lower left. The three victims on the floor of the arena are also linked: a line from the broken sword near Columbia's body and ballot box leads to the foot of "Justice" and then from her body to that of Mercury, forming a zigzag pattern leading the eye in a step-wise movement to explore the receding space to the right of the tiger.

By 1870 Nast was using a soft pencil to draw his illustrations on the wood block (rather than pen and ink wash), subsequently carved by craftsmen to create an engraved relief for printing. A pencil drawing from 1870 entitled "Editor's Easy Chair" depicts Nast seated on the floor of his editor's (George W. Curtis) office, sharpening a pencil as he prepares to draw on a block of wood (Figure 6.7). The drawing also demonstrates Nast's use of closely placed parallel lines and occasional cross-hatching to model the figures three-dimensionally, in this case with the light falling on the scene from the right, creating consistent highlights and shadows. Nast's signature, located on another block of wood in the wicker trash basket at the right, is written backwards, so

FIGURE 6.7 *Thomas Nast, Drawing, Study for Cartoon, "Editor's Easy Chair," 1870. Graphite on paper, 28.9 × 21.3 cm Gift of Cooper Union Library, 1953-10-47. Photo: Matt Flynn © Smithsonian Institution. Cooper Hewitt, Smithsonian Design Museum, New York, NY, USA. Photo Credit: Cooper Hewitt, Smithsonian Design Museum/Art Resource, NY*

that it would read left to write when printed through the letterpress. To judge from this example of an original drawing, the wood-engraving process, with engravers using more sharply pointed tools, tended to create strong contrasts and sharp contours, as with the central figures in "THE TAMMNY TIGER LOOSE." While Nast's later departure from the staff of *Harper's Weekly* has been blamed by historians on growing tensions between the artist and his editor, the two men embraced the same moral principles and Republican party platform, disagreeing only on the means rather than the substance of political debate, with Curtis concerned that the increasingly violent and combative tone of Nast's cartoons might alienate rather than persuade its broad readership (Jarman, 2010).

The captions for Nast's illustrations appear below the wood-engraved images. The use of upper-case letters ("THE TAMMANY TIGER LOOSE") is the same size and transitional Scotch Roman font often used for body type in *Harper's Weekly*. Nast also frequently used hand-drawn lettering in his illustrations, sometimes more extensively than in "The Tammany Tiger Loose," where he only identifies objects and figures (e.g. "SPOILS," "THE BALLOT," "REPUBLIC," "POWER"); in other illustrations the sub-scripted captions are hand drawn (September 30, 1871 "WE KNOW NOTHING ABOUT THE STOLEN VOUCHERS; TOO THIN; WE ARE INNOCENT"), have longer accompanying texts ("The Only Thing They Respect or Fear"—October 21, 1871), or have hand-drawn captions directly in the illustrations, as if they are headlines from newspapers or poster announcements affixed to buildings (December 2, 1871—"To Whom it May Concern," where the caption is actually being pasted to the wall behind the figures). In all cases texts are visually subordinate to the illustrations and yet essential to supply information and clarify meaning, reinforcing the editorial moral high ground.

Certainly there was an element of humor in Nast's narratives and caricatures of public figures: while the texts tend to reinforce their serious nature and strengthen the persuasive political message of Nast's pen, they also feature plays on words ("prey" for "pray;" "haul" for mayor Oakey "Hall"), double-entendres that signified the meaning "behind" the words. In the case of "TAMMANY HALL TIGER" the question Nast poses ("What are you going to do about it?") adds urgency to the tiger's confrontational pose and ferocious teeth. In partnership with the *New York Times*' critical editorials and that newspaper's publication of evidence of kickbacks and padding of public expenditures, Nast's illustrations and their texts aroused interest and maintained political pressure to investigate corruption in New York City's and the state's government, targeting "Boss" William Tweed and his circle of friends known as the "Ring." The artist's choice of Tweed as a focus was astute: he was a conspicuous public figure, well-known to New Yorkers, active in state politics as a senator in the state capital at Albany, and was "Sachem" or chief of Tammany Hall, the headquarters of the city's Democratic party, located in an impressive new building completed in the fall of 1868 on Union Square. As a result of political maneuvering in the pursuit of fiscal independence or "home rule" for the city of New York, Tweed was able, with the help of the mayor, comptroller, and city solicitor, to appropriate taxpayer dollars from the city's treasury for a massive campaign of building and construction while at the same time siphoning vast sums of money into his own and other friends' pockets, amassing a fortune which he often conspicuously displayed in lavish spectacles of wealth, including the purchase of homes and yachts, generous charitable donations, and with hosting or attending well-publicized social events such as the Americus Ball in Greenwich, Connecticut (see p. 210) and celebrating the wedding of one of his daughters in 1871. On the eve of the November 7th election, Nast penned "The Brains," with a bag of money substituting for Tweed's head and a shining diamond pin on his shirt (Figure 6.8).

FIGURE 6.8 *Thomas Nast, "The Brains," October 21, 1871, wood engraving, 4 ½ × 4 ½," New York Historical Society*

Iconography: The Academic Tradition

The pictorial devices Nast marshaled for use in illustrated print journalism have a long history. In 1972 art historian Albert Boime published an article with the title "Nast and French Art" in the *American Art Journal*. The article brought Nast's oeuvre to the attention of art historians (rather than to a readership more interested in American history and politics); Boime identified specific connections between French academic painting (rather than with contemporary avant-garde painters and movements such as Realism and Impressionism) and several of Nast's cartoons and illustrations for *Harper's Weekly*, citing examples that demonstrated Nast's awareness of French academic art, and reminding readers that Nast had received training and exhibited oil paintings at New York's National Academy of Design. One instance is a painting by French artist Jean-Léon Gérôme (1824–1904) entitled "Ave Caesar Imperator, morituri ad salutant" ("Hail Caesar, Those who are about to die salute you") dating to 1859 and exhibited in the Paris Salon of that year (Figure 6.9 and color plate). The painting is set in a Roman amphitheater, with soldiers saluting the emperor as they are about to begin combat, and the bodies of dead gladiators from the previous contest sprawled on the ground.

Boime pointed out that Nast visited Paris as a young child en route from his native Bavaria to the United States (he later recalled Notre Dame Cathedral but didn't mention seeing any paintings!—he was but six years old), that Gérôme's paintings were avidly collected in the United States, and that the academic tradition of which Gérôme was a part was assiduously followed at institutions including the National Academy of Design in New York and the Pennsylvania Academy of FineArt in Philadelphia. Later in his career Nast visited Paris again to attend the 1878 World's Fair. Moreover, works of fine art were frequently reproduced as prints for purchase and circulated more widely. Gérôme's "Ave Caesar" was exhibited at the Paris World's Fair of 1867, and that event was covered in the popular press that included illustrations of artworks on display. Gérôme's father-in-law, Adolphe Goupil, owned a company that produced and sold

FIGURE 6.9 (and color plate) *Jean-Léon Gérôme, "Ave Caesar Imperator, morituri ad salutant", oil on canvas, 92.6 × 145.3 cm, 1859, courtesy Yale University Art Museum*

prints and print reproductions of paintings, and had opened a storefront in New York City in 1847. It's likely that Gérôme's "Ave Ceasar" was available as a print at the time, and a colored print of another Roman-inspired 1872 painting by Gérôme, also set in a Roman amphitheater and titled "Pollice Verso" ("Turned Thumb"), is in the collection at Lyndhurst, a Gothic Revival home and estate in Tarrytown, New York built in 1838 by architect Alexander Jackson Davis for New York city mayor William Paulding but purchased from him in the later nineteenth century (1893) by railroad magnate Jay Gould (Figure 6.10).

Boime argued that Nast's art deserved more art historical attention than it had received, that "the borderline between political cartooning and nineteenth-century Neoclassicism is a fluid one." He also noted that the tradition of academic or "salon" painting reached a diverse audience through the publication of engravings and chromolithographs, broad public attendance at world's fairs, as well as through wood-engravings in popular weekly newspapers such as the *London Illustrated News, Frank Leslie's Illustrated Newspaper,* along with *Harper's Weekly.* The reproduction of works of art constituted part of the mission of these nineteenth-century illustrated weeklies; after all *Harper's Weekly* was subtitled "Journal of Civilization," and the earlier English illustrated *Penny Magazine* (1832 and 1845), that also reproduced well-known works of art in wood engravings, was published under the auspices of an organization titled the "Society for the Diffusion of Useful Knowledge." The practice extended from well-known masterpieces of Western art to contemporary works of art as well, including a wood-engraved double-page reproduction of Winslow Homer's "Snap the Whip" painting in *Harper's Weekly* for September 20, 1873, or, earlier, French academic painter William-Adolphe Bougereau's

FIGURE 6.10 *Jean-Léon Gérôme, "Pollice Verso," 1872, oil on canvas, 96.5 × 148.9 cm, courtesy Museum of Art Phoenix*

FIGURE 6.11 *William-Adolphe Bougereau, reproduction of "Infantine Caresses,"* Harper's Weekly, *April 15, 1871, wood engraving, 34.3 × 25.4 cm (coincidentally, the original painting is also at Lyndhurst, Tarrytown, NY, 195.6 × 128.3 cm, titled "Premières Caresses," purchased by Jay Gould, 1880)*

"Infantine Caresses" (1866) that was shown in the Paris Salon of that year and was reproduced in *Harper's Weekly* in April 1871 (Figure 6.11).

Boime's research on Nast predates the emergence of graphic design history as a field of study in the early 1980s; his article concentrates upon identifying quite convincing pictorial sources for several of Nast's illustrations, but does not explore the relationship of his illustrations to the content or political context of *Harper's Weekly*, nor Nast's role as a political reformer (or radical!) and propagandist, nor why, for instance, Nast turned to the imperial Roman past as a visual metaphor to expose in visual form the unchecked political power of William Tweed and the Tweed Ring in New York City.

A Common Ground: Ancient Rome and Elizabethan England

Boime noted that the use of the past as a metaphor for the representation of current events was employed frequently in academic painting as well as more popularly in illustration and later in film. Such references, whether to ancient Greece, ancient Rome, or in the case of other political cartoons in Nast's oeuvre, Elizabethan England, served the purpose of demonstrating not just the relevance of the past for an understanding of the present, but the persistence of common, stable moralizing themes pitting good against evil, virtue against vice, public against private interest and greed.

Nast's first reference to ancient Rome occurred in July 1867 in a double-page illustration aimed at Andrew Johnson (1808–75), who had become US president following the assassination of Abraham Lincoln in April, 1865. Captioned "Amphitheatrum Johnsonianum—Massacre of the Innocents," the illustration was set in a Roman arena with President Johnson and his cabinet dressed as counselors and soldiers overlooking the slaughter of defenseless blacks by groups of armed Roman soldiers. Above the imperial box are wreaths inscribed with the words "New Orleans" and "Memphis," references to racial violence and recent repressive measures taken in those cities to deny equal rights for African Americans whose newly gained freedom was violated. Here again the text clarifies Nast's invocation of the past: the incidents in Memphis and in New Orleans are compared to the New Testament Massacre of the Innocents at the order of King Herod (Matthew 2; 16–18; Figure 6.12). The scene takes place not in an open field as in the typical biblical rendering of the subject but in an amphitheater, portraying the event from the point of view of the emperor himself as a sordid form of spectator sport. Nast and his staunch Republican editors viewed Johnson's administration as a betrayal of equal rights of citizenship granted to blacks in the Constitution by the thirteenth amendment (ratified in 1865).

The association between the Roman amphitheater and the public display of power with violence as punishment draws upon ancient Roman authors who recorded the imperial sanction of the execution of Christians as an assertion of imperial authority, a reminder of the "price" paid for resistance, and of the very public means taken to ensure order. Historians who have written about the function of human sacrifice in the Roman Empire have noted that the victims of violence were condemned as being dangerous to the city or state, and that the so-called contests or spectacles (known as *munera*) served to appease the populace, catering to the crowd's baser instincts.

The amphitheater, imperial box, and military garb found in "Amphiteatrum Johnsonianum" appear as well in "TAMMANY TIGER LET LOOSE." Again, the connection to the ostentation and power politics of William Tweed and his "Ring" could hardly be more direct: despite the kickbacks to Tweed and his friends and Tweed's lavish displays of personal wealth, the local government brought about visible improvements to the city, including the Brooklyn Bridge project (begun in 1869, completed in 1884),

FIGURE 6.12 *Thomas Nast, "Amphitheatrum Johnsonianum," Harper's Weekly, March 30, 1867, 50.8 × 68.6 cm, Paley Library, Temple University*

the construction of a new courthouse in lower Manhattan (see p. 207), and the widening of streets and avenues to accommodate increased vehicular and pedestrian traffic. But in Nast's view the price paid for such progress was too dear—despite claims of modernization (Tweed was referred to as the "Baron Haussmann" of New York, a reference to the latter's massive restructuring of the city of Paris in the 1860s), Tweed's efforts betrayed rather than furthered the public interest, resulting in staggering debt that crippled the city treasury while lining the pockets of the "Boss" and his friends in city government. In "Amphiteatrum Johnsonianum" Nast also made use of idealized human figures to represent ideas such as "Justice" and "Columbia" (the United States), often identified with captions to reinforce easy recognition.

References to ancient Rome were ubiquitous in the nineteenth century. Educated Americans were required to study Latin (although translating "Amphitheatrum Johnsonianum" wouldn't require a Latin education) and ancient history, and references to knowledge of the Latin language and Roman history occur in a variety of ways, from the names of organizations and societies to the use of neoclassical architecture for public buildings and furnishings for private homes. During the American Revolution, the "image" of Rome referred to the Roman Republic, a model of democracy and public debate given form in the Declaration of Independence (1776) along with the balance of powers enshrined in the Constitution.

But ancient Rome also appeared on a more popular level, for instance through the everyday encounter with stately architecture in public buildings, banks, and the recently completed cast-iron dome of the United States Capitol Building in Washington, DC (1855–66). Another source of popular exposure was the theater, where plays set in ancient Roman times were regularly performed in New York and in other American cities. Examples include the plays of William Shakespeare such as *Julius Caesar*, as well as productions of contemporary works such as "Gladiator," written by playwright Robert Montgomery Bird (1806–54), starring one of the period's most acclaimed star actors (Edwin Forrest, 1806–72) and performed regularly in New York and elsewhere beginning in 1831, recounting the slave rebellion instigated by Spartacus in the third century BCE, retold in the twentieth century by author Howard Fast in the novel *Spartacus* (1951) and reenacted in a film version starring Kirk Douglas in 1961. Another source for the popular appropriation of ancient Rome was religion: the Roman Empire served as the setting for the New Testament biblical narrative of Jesus's life in Roman-occupied Judaea and in the lives (and martyrdoms) of saints throughout the later Empire. In both the bible and in the theater, this popular "image" of imperial Rome centered on the attitude toward unchecked authority and the struggles of the persecuted who suffered for their beliefs. Historical and yet also timeless, Nast's "TAMMANY TIGER LOOSE" contains the elements of the battle for moral justice on behalf of the oppressed—a powerful and bloodthirsty beast representing the iron-fisted authority of New York's political bosses and witnessed by scores of spectators dares the viewer to intervene and to take up the sword (or in this case the ballot) in defense of justice, fair trade, and the Republic. While Nast was not educated in the manner of his manager Fletcher Harper or editor George W. Curtis at *Harper's Weekly* or the editors at the *New York Times*, at some level they shared a common language (rhetorical for the editors, visual for the artist) of historical reference; referring to the past powerfully demonstrated its relevance to the present and the persistence of common themes of authority and corruption, power and persecution. Nast was gifted at providing these themes not only with visible form but also with dramatic urgency. The artist's training at the National Academy of Design in New York and familiarity with the work of painters such as Jean-Léon Gérôme or the illustrator Gustave Doré provided the background for Nast's political appropriation of the imperial Roman past.

Rome was not the only reference Nast made to history. He lampooned Horatio Seymour, governor of New York and Ulysses Grant's Democratic opponent for president in the 1868 election by portraying him as Lady Macbeth in a cartoon, a reference to Shakespeare and Elizabethan England that also occurs in cartoons devoted to William Tweed, including Nast's identification of Tweed with the dissolute Falstaff, a Shakespearean character (who appears in *Henry IV*), prone to surrender to worldly pleasures, in "A Modern Falstaff, Reviewing His Troops" (Figure 6.13). The artist's knowledge of Shakespeare appears yet again in the 1870 drawing (Figure 6.7: "Editor's Easy Chair") which contains a quotation from *Hamlet*. Act 3, Scene 4: "I must be cruel, only to be kind"). Another familiar if more recent historical reference or metaphor was Nast's depiction of Tweed as Napoleon in a cartoon with the caption "Baptism by Fire" from April 22, 1871, with "Boss" Tweed cast as a rotund Napoleon standing above a cowering and kneeling New York governor John T. Hoffman. Whether looking to ancient Rome, Elizabethan England, imperial France, popular history, and even nursery rhymes, Nast communicated his political sympathies with a wide variety of literary and visual references familiar to a highly literate as well as a more diverse general readership.

FIGURE 6.13 *Thomas Nast, "A Modern Falstaff Reviewing his Troops,"* Harper's Weekly, *November 5, 1870, 25.4 × 36 cm, New York Historical Society*

Comparison

Nast drew illustrations both for *Harper's Weekly* and for *Frank Leslie's Illustrated Weekly*, and political cartoons similar to those Nast supplied to *Harper's Weekly* also appeared beginning in 1871 in the German and English language periodical *Puck*, using the technology of chromolithography. One of *Puck's* early cartoons bears a remarkable similarity to Nast's "TAMMANY TIGER LOOSE." Drawn by German-born illustrator Joseph Keppler (1838–94), the cartoon shows a tiger with a collar labeled "Corruption" in combat with a female figure wearing a headband with the text "Reform," set in an amphitheater, with banners naming four states (Louisiana, Missouri, Arkansas, New York) flying above (Figure 6.14). Locked in a struggle similar to Gustave Doré's 1866 illustration for the biblical story of Jacob Wrestling with the Angel (Genesis 32: 22–32; Figure 6.15), the text at top and bottom reads "Who will conquer?".

Comparing Nast's "TAMMANY TIGER LOOSE" with Keppler's slightly earlier "Who will conquer?" reveals significant differences beneath similarities of setting, the use of an allegorical figure, and the tiger. Keppler's cartoon pits reform against corruption in a national context, without targeting particular individuals in the city of New York; by contrast, Nast's tiger is linked directly to Tammany and to Tweed, threatening Justice and the Republic on the *local* scene, along with commerce and the economy. By turning the tiger's head outward attention shifts to

FIGURE 6.14 *Joseph Keppler, "Who will conquer," wood engraving*, Puck, *October 22, 1871, 29.8 × 45.7 cm, New York Public Library*

FIGURE 6.15 *Gustave Doré, Jacob Wrestling with the Angel," wood engraving, 24 × 19.4 cm*, The Holy Bible with Illustrations by Gustave Dore, *London, Cassell, Peller and Galpin, 1886, no. 22 (first published 1866), Courtesy Kislak Center for Special Collections, Rare Books and Manuscripts, University of Pennsylvania*

the viewer with a heightened sense of engagement as well as urgency. Also, Keppler's cartoon is portrayed as a battle of equals—both protagonists are of the same height and "Reform" holds her own in the struggle, fending off the tiger with a stiff left arm, while for Nast the *viewer* is tiger's next victim.

Nast: From Illustration to Cartoon

Thomas Nast's "THE TAMMANY TIGER LOOSE: What Are You Going To Do About It?" and other cartoons he supplied for *Harper's Weekly* were a departure from the more journalistic illustrations that he and other artists provided as visual "reporters" for *Harper's* and other contemporary illustrated magazines. It was in his role as an on-the-spot reporter that Nast appears briefly in the film *Gangs of New York*, sketching on site during a boxing match in lower Manhattan (see Figure 6.3, earlier in his career Nast was sent by *Harper's Weekly* to cover a bare-knuckle heavyweight boxing match in England); at times it seems Martin Scorsese based his direction of the scenes of bloody massacre upon nineteenth-century illustrations by Nast and other contemporary print artists, often viewed from a distance at street level with clashing clubs and swords. Other examples of this type of illustrated journalism that Nast witnessed and recorded included scenes depicting Giuseppe Garibaldi's role in bringing about Italian liberation and independence in 1860, supplied on assignment to *Harper's Weekly*; it's also possible that

Nast sketched first-hand from the battlefield as a correspondent during the American Civil War. Whether first-hand or not, his wartime illustrations included battle scenes (Figure 6.16) along with more sentimental illustrations around holiday time, such as "Christmas 1863," a double-page illustration of a Union officer on furlough enjoying the comforts of home and family in a series of vignettes, one of which includes a small image depicting Santa Claus ("furry Nicholas"), whose very image was popularized by Nast (Figure 6.17).

Like the later "TAMMANY TIGER LOOSE: What Are You Going To Do About It," Nast's illustrations drew upon an arsenal of visual devices gleaned from his academic training at the National Academy of Design in New York from 1853 to 1856. Even his Civil War battle scenes, submitted as "on the scene reporting," used compositional conventions that present a well-rehearsed heroic visual organization. For instance, "On to Richmond" (see Figure 6.16) depicts officers and soldiers leading a charge toward the right. The pyramidal composition has the tattered Union flag at its apex, with General William Smith at the front of the charge and General Grant on horseback as a secondary focus. Despite the presence of fallen soldiers in the foreground, the narrative is monumental, intended to demonstrate the resolve and bravery of the Union army. And while the scene represents particular individuals who took part in the battle, it seems to have more in common with the conventions of monumental painting than with the factual record of a moment in the battle itself, recalling elements of Delacroix's "Liberty Leading the People" (1830) in the poses of fallen soldiers and the position of the flag. Moreover, the imagined scene for Nast's "On to Richmond" was at odds with General Grant's own recollections of the battle, in which Confederate forces halted the Union assault, resulting in 13,000 Union casualties and one of Grant's major regrets of the Civil War. And so, Nast was not an objective observer of the events he witnessed. An anti-slavery advocate, ardent admirer of President Lincoln, supportive of

FIGURE 6.16 *Thomas Nast, "On to Richmond,"* Harper's Weekly, *wood engraving, June 18, 1864, 50.8 × 68.6 cm, courtesy Paley Library, Temple University*

FIGURE 6.17 *Thomas Nast, "Christmas, 1863" (furlough), wood engraving,* Harper's Weekly, *December 22, 1863, 50.8 × 68.6 cm, courtesy Paley Library, Temple University*

the president's bid for reelection in 1864 and a defender of his unpopular prosecution of the war (ordering a draft that resulted in riots in New York City), Nast's Civil War illustrations were often sweeping in scope, heroic in conception, rendering sacrifice in the face of danger as the price paid for victory and the ideal of liberty it promised. In addition to interpreting particular battles and events during the Civil War, Nast also contributed generic or "typical" scenes, often at the time of holidays such as Thanksgiving or Christmas (see Figure 6.17), or to remind readers of war's higher moral purpose to end slavery. Lincoln's assassination on April 14, 1865 was illustrated not with a scene from Ford's Theatre or the actual funeral, but rather with an illustration of the nation, personified by the female figure of Columbia, bowed by grief and touching the casket of the president in a darkened space. In one sense the scene was not entirely an imaginative one, for Lincoln's casket not only lay in state in Washington, DC, but traveled by train to several locations where additional viewings were held and ceremonies performed and repeated.

Cartoon, Caricature, and Stereotype

When the Civil War ended Nast's editorial interests turned to political commentary via cartoon along with more detailed illustration. One of the contemporary issues he targeted was postwar reconstruction and criticism of Andrew Johnson for not living up to the government's commitment to emancipation and racial equality. An illustration of a festive gathering in New York depicting Johnson appeared in *Harper's Weekly* on April 14, 1866 (Figure 6.18), along with well-known figures in the life of the city and the nation, including Nast himself! Nast's illustrations of Johnson often took the form of caricature, that is, a combination of humor and sarcasm achieved by a combination of simplification and exaggeration of the president's face that presented an easily recognizable image, focusing upon a particular, essential characteristic such as hair, a moustache, or a nose.

Nast's use of caricature was contemporary with a similar form of political criticism in France and even earlier in England, depicting monarchs or other powerful political figures in unflattering ways. Subjected to official monitoring and censorship at times, caricature was a vehicle for unofficial, popular political expression, based upon exaggeration and distortion. Caricature is often associated with sensational subjects appealing to the commercial interest of print publishers, and in terms of graphic design the summary nature of its form in the nineteenth century might be explained not only in light of being designed for reproduction by wood engraving or lithography to be issued in a timely fashion for printing, but also because by eliminating detail and concentrating upon exaggerating a physiognomic or bodily feature (a nose, corpulence), a caricature rendered that feature immediately recognizable to a casual reader/viewer, not unlike a brand. Used as an element in "THE TAMMANY TIGER LOOSE," the figures of Tweed and his "Ring" assumed less prominent features and exaggerated proportions in deference to the snarling tiger, but elsewhere, when placed singly or as a focused group rather than a secondary element within a narrative tableau, there was a tendency to enlarge the size of heads, a common characteristic of the caricature generally, found as well in French examples in the work of Honoré Daumier (1808–79) or Jean-Jacques Grandville (1803–47) and printed in journals such as *Charivari*. An example

FIGURE 6.18 *Thomas Nast, "Grand Masquerade Ball Given by Mr. Maretzek at the Academy of Music" (New York), wood engraving,* Harper's Weekly, *April 14, 1866, 50.8 × 68.6 cm, courtesy Paley Library, Temple University*

FIGURE 6.19 *Thomas Nast, "That's What's the Matter," wood engraving,* Harper's Weekly, *October 7, 1871, wood engraving, 11.4 × 11.4 cm, New York Historical Society*

is found in a Nast cartoon in *Harper's Weekly* for October 7, 1871 a month before the November election, titled "That's What's the Matter," showing an imposing and rotund Tweed leaning against a ballot box with the words "In counting there is STRENGTH," and with Tweed uttering "As long as I count the votes, what are you going to do about it, say!" (Figure 6.19).

On July 12, 1871 Nast was mobilized as a reserve member of the Seventh Regiment Guards to help control the outbreak of violence during the "Orange Day Riot," an annual gathering of Irish Protestants in New York commemorating the Battle of the Boyne (1690) when William of Orange defeated the Catholic king of Britain, James II. The gathering angered the large immigrant community of Irish Catholics in the city, whose political allegiance was to the Tammany-controlled Democratic Party. Nast's double-page cartoon offers a glimpse of the artist's increasingly polemic views and an approach to his cartoons that marshaled caricature and symbol in the service of propaganda (Figure 6.20).

Here the Irish Catholics are represented as sword and club-wielding ape-like thugs, the politicians as seated and kneeling do-nothings, with allegorical figures of Columbia and Uncle Sam defending the marchers, peacekeepers, women, and minorities. Captions identify each vignette in the composite symmetrical arrangement of major and minor scenes, with a poem below to either side, at the left assuming the voice of Columbia and to the right the views of an Irish Catholic observer. At the bottom the text "SOMETHING THAT WILL NOT BLOW OVER" appears: here, in addition to Nast's representation of the Tweed Ring three times in the cartoon, the artist called attention to Tweed's alleged response when evidence of corruption was published on the front page of the *New York Times* on July 22, 1871, detailing exorbitant expenditures and overpayments which ended up in the pockets of William Tweed and his Ring.

FIGURE 6.20 *Thomas Nast, "Something that will not blow over," wood engraving,* Harper's Weekly, *July 29, 1871, 50.8 × 68.6 cm, New York Historical Society*

Tiger

In "THE TAMMANY TIGER LOOSE," caricature and its entertaining combination of humor and ridicule take a back seat to Nast's bloodthirsty tiger. Author John Adler noted that Nast based his tiger upon illustrations in a natural history book that he owned, but the shift of viewpoint from behind the imperial box in the 1866 "Amphitheatrum Johnsonianum" cartoon to the viewer's frontal confrontation of the snarling tiger amounts to a leap, not only subordinating the caricatures of Tweed and his comical Tammany buddies, but in foregrounding the open hostility of the tiger toward the viewer, his next prey (see Figure 6.5)

And the resulting note of danger here is significant; it transforms political commentary and satire into an immediate call to arms, that is, the tiger poses an imminent threat that requires action, reinforced with Boss Tweed boasting "What are you going to do about it?," an added element of urgency on the eve of an election; Nast employed the same phrase in a cartoon of October 7, 1871, with a cigar-smoking Tweed standing next to a ballot box above the legend "As long as I count the Votes, what are you going to do about it?" with voters lining up to submit their ballots (as it turns out, Tweed didn't smoke). A half-century later during World

War I (1914–18), viewer confrontation was employed in posters to urge the public to enlist (Figure 5.17), to invest (e.g. in war bonds), or to be productive, sometimes in the name of patriotic duty, at other times in response to threats of violence from a brutal enemy, and all in reaction to an impending crisis. In Nast's case the immediate threat was to the ideals of justice, (fair) commerce, and democratic government, with these abstract concepts given both a historic (ancient Rome) *and* local context in New York. While Nast's reputation may have waned in his later years and his hard-hitting approach to his subjects led to conflict with his editors later in his career, his "TAMMANY TIGER LOOSE" helped to cement his reputation not only as an artist who was able to mold public opinion, but who was able to convert and to mobilize that opinion into direct political action, all the while honing and inventing some of the elements of the graphic design toolbox that would be put to powerful use during World War I (and afterwards in advertising). Indeed, even during his lifetime Nast's combative nature and exaggerated pictorial strategies were described by writers in military terms. Nast's friend James Parton wrote in 1875 that the artist "waged brilliant and effective warfare" with his illustrations And an author for the *North American Review* wrote that Nast's cartoons "proved so formidable a weapon in the final struggle against the Ring" when the *Weekly* "took up the cudgels" against the Tweed machine (Jarman, 2010).

Who Was Boss Tweed?

William Magear Tweed (1823–78) became Nast's main target of derision in the artist's political cartoons directed against New York City government. It's probably fair to say that Tweed was a ring leader, but he needed a ring to lead. Tweed's career, and his charisma, were the subject of countless newspaper stories during his lifetime. His public "image" was forged early on, as a member of a very visible local volunteer fire company and social club, the "Big Six" which he helped to found in 1848. References to "Americus" and the "Big Six" crop up in Nast's "THE TAMMANY TIGER LOOSE" as a reminder of Tweed's local ties and reputation. Tweed was active in New York City politics, first as a young city alderman elected in 1851, a member of the city's Board of Supervisors and chairman of the Democratic Party General Committee from 1863, whose headquarters were located in Tammany Hall ("Sachem" in the parlance of Tammany Hall). In these roles and as a state senator in the upstate capital of Albany from 1868 to 1873, he helped to secure "home rule" that established financial autonomy for New York City, and as the sponsor of highly visible charitable and capital projects he cemented a reputation for getting things done and serving the city's and his constituents' interests. Tammany Hall was also known for its support of the city's growing Irish Catholic immigrant community. In his role as Sachem he was able to organize support for elections to help ensure Democratic control of city offices. His reputation was also bolstered during the Civil War when riots protesting President Lincoln's draft law of 1863 broke out in the city. While New York's mayor George Opdyke and Governor Horatio Seymour waffled in their defense of federal law and did little to end to violent protests, order was restored with the help of the police and Tammany Hall, for which Tweed received credit.

At no time was Tweed's notoriety greater than in 1871, the year of Nast's "THE TAMMANY TIGER LOOSE" (November 11, 1871). The cartoon was the culmination of editorial commentary and illustration that had begun as early as January 22, 1870 with Nast's double-page vignettes titled "Shadows of Coming Events." These cartoons highlighted particular areas of local political corruption that included election irregularities, insufficient funding for public schools, the increasing role of the Catholic Church in education and charitable appropriations, and expenditures on public works such as the courthouse on Chambers Street (known today as the Tweed Courthouse and housing the headquarters of the New York City Department of Education). These issues reappeared in cartoons by Nast and other artists throughout the next two years, not only through the repetition of caricatures of well-known public figures such as Tweed, Mayor Hall, and Treasurer Connolly, but also the repeated use of phrases such as "What are you going to do about it" or "Something will Blow Over" that suggested the confident and arrogant authority of those in power in city government. A more allegorical anonymous cartoon that appeared in the same January 22nd issue features a winged devil identified in the caption as the "Modern Archimedes," moving the earth with a lever on which he places his raised left leg. "The Lever that Moves the World" is "GREED," written in large letters beneath the earth (Figure 6.21). The image of "earth" only identifies the southern hemisphere (South America)—with the word "GOLD" written on the devil's lever; the target here is European economic interests in the sovereign nations of the Carribbean. As an example, the newspaper reported throughout 1871 on a proposal by President Grant and his supporters in Congress to annex the nation of Santo Domingo (the Dominican Republic). Maps and illustrations drew attention to the island, while texts weighed the benefits and perils of annexation, in particular the fear of European meddling on one hand and concerns about the United States' own commercial and military intervention on the other. The proposal ultimately failed, but the Republican *Harper's Weekly*, which had backed President Grant, remained generally supportive.

Such examples provide the broader editorial context for the attacks on Boss Tweed by Nast in the pages of *Harper's Weekly*. The journal's larger concern and moral compass centered upon

FIGURE 6.21 *Anon., "The Modern Archimedes—the Lever that Moves the World," wood engraving,* Harper's Weekly, *January 22, 1870, 24.5 × 35.6 cm, courtesy Paley Library, Temple University*

the conflict between private and public interest and the abuses of power that issue from that conflict. Its *tools* were an adept combination of word and image, and a belief in the political role of print journalism to influence popular opinion that rested upon the freedom, and the power, of the press and the role it plays in a modern democracy. In "The Power of the Press" (November 25; Figure 6.22), Nast himself sits atop the press with pen and drawing paper in

FIGURE 6.22 *Anon., "The Power of the Press," wood engraving,* Harper's Weekly, *November 25 (Supplement), 25.4 × 35.6 cm New York Historical Society*

FIGURE 6.23 *Brackmere, "Modern Laocöon,"* Harper's Weekly, *wood engraving, October 7, 1871, 27.9 × 23.2 cm, New York Historical Society*

hand. The same theme appears earlier in 1871 in a cartoon by an illustrator named Brackmere (October 7; Figure 6.23) depicting Tweed as Laocöon, being strangled by two snakes labeled "THE PRESS."

Tammany and Tweed in Context

The effect of the "Tammany Tiger Loose" upon *Harper's Weekly* readers might be better gauged through an awareness of the newspaper's anti-Tammany cartoons and editorial campaign that began in 1869, and its impact appreciated in reference to Tweed's popularity at the time and the general support he received in the press. Aside from the *New York Times* and *Harper's Weekly*, most newspapers chronicled Tweed's activities as a member of New York City's Board of Supervisors, his rise in Tammany-controlled Democratic Party politics in the city, and his appointment as deputy street commissioner (1863) that included taxpayer-funded projects to widen and pave Broadway and other city thoroughfares, and in 1869 to initiate the construction of the Brooklyn Bridge. Tweed also supported charities both personally and with city funds, and sponsored a bill to charter the Metropolitan Museum of Art as well as the city's Mt. Sinai Hospital. Such initiatives served as expressions of his civic-mindedness and helped to maintain a positive image against charges of graft and election tampering that were alleged in Nast's cartoons and in the *New York Times*. Even *Harper's Weekly* devoted several pages to Tweed along with a flattering wood-engraved portrait in January, 1871, when he presided over a

FIGURE 6.24 *Anon., "Americus Ball," wood engraving,* Harper's Weekly, *January 21, 1871, 25.4 × 35.6 cm, New York Historical Society*

lavish ball in Greenwich, Connecticut sponsored by the Americus Club with 6,000 people in attendance, including illustrations of the well-dressed attendees on the dance floor (Figure 6.24).

As charges of corruption mounted in the *Times* and in *Harper's Weekly*, Mayor Hall convened a commission to review city financial records to head off criticism of spending and accounting irregularities. The commission was composed of well-known businessmen and financiers, who concluded that the records were sound and revealed no proof of malfeasance.

But when the *New York Times* received transcribed evidence from city financial records demonstrating the gross misuse of city funds on building and other projects, along with irresponsible borrowing and rising city debt on July 22, 1871, its publication (disputed by Tammany's defenders but corroborated later in court) strengthened allegations that both the *Times* editorials and Nast's *Harper's Weekly* cartoons had been suggesting since 1869. In this context, the Orange Day Riot in July 1871 appeared as a demonstration of city government's inability to control mob violence and keep the peace (as they had done successfully during the Draft Riot of 1863), a long-standing concern of the Republican Party.

The downfall that ensued began with the November 7, 1871 election that was the target of "THE TAMMANY TIGER LOOSE: What are you going to do about it?" bolstered by the *New York Times'* editorials and detailed exposure of the city financial records. Several Democratic Party candidates failed to win, although Tweed himself was reelected to the New York State Senate. In 1873 Tweed was arrested on charges of larceny and forgery, escaping in 1875 to Spain, where he was re-arrested and returned to New York. While serving jail time on Blackwell's Island (now Roosevelt Island), Tweed became ill. Despite his efforts to offer testimony in exchange for his release, the former "Boss" remained incarcerated and died in prison on April 12, 1878. Other members of the Ring survived but were marginalized within a more reform-minded but still Tammany-controlled Democratic party in New York.

The power of Nast's cartoons derives at least in part from his efforts to demonize Tweed and to paint the members of the Irish Catholic immigrant community in New York that the Democratic Party mobilized as lawless thugs prone to drinking and violence, perpetuating ethnic stereotypes that reinforced a narrative of corruption, collusion, and threats to the public welfare. Propaganda often involves simplification, and simplification leads to stereotypes, characterizing groups of people not as individuals but as "types" associated with particular behaviors. Stereotyping served Nast's objectives and also revealed his own biases. He lumped Irish Catholics together as second-class, prone to mob violence, easily manipulated with appeals to base instincts, bribes, and favors, with a penchant to drunkenness; as to Tweed, his own display of wealth, symbolized by his heft and prominent display of a large round diamond pin prominently depicted on the front of his shirt and reported to be worth fifteen thousand dollars, were the most obvious targets of criticism, not only because his affluence was earned dishonestly, but also because he represented "new money" that encroached upon the traditional exclusivity of New York's older social elite.

Conclusion

It can be reasonably argued that Thomas Nast was the most recognized graphic artist of the nineteenth century and possibly the most influential graphic artist in the history of the profession. This may come as a surprise to some readers. After all, James Montgomery Flagg's "I [Uncle Sam] Want You" is more often cited as an example of propaganda, along with the technically demanding and politically charged photomontage covers of John Heartfield and their hard-hitting criticism of national socialism in interwar Germany. While graphic designers such as Milton Glaser or Paul Rand have become household names whose work is easily recognized and popularly appreciated, Nast matches them for general recognition and a living legacy: after all he popularized the image of Santa Claus and other familiar symbols as ubiquitous as Glaser's "I ♥ New York" or Rand's "abc" and "IBM" logos. But what distinguishes Nast is that his "TAMMANY TIGER LOOSE" was not simply "political" in the sense of raising awareness, expressing an opinion or mustering sympathy toward a particular political cause; rather, his work was demonstrably "activist;" it was not simply a poignant commentary on a troubling situation. It possessed the urgency not just to mold opinion but to affect direct action and demonstrate the consequences of "inaction." His pen was a real threat to the status quo in New York politics: at one point during the summer 1871 Nast was offered $100,000 to simply leave New York for Europe, but refused the bribe; in the feature on Nast that ran in *Harper's Weekly*, the newspaper stated:

> It is said that the Boss and Head-Centre of the Tammany Ring himself [i.e. Tweed] has declared in his wrath that while he doesn't care a straw for what is written about him, the great majority of his constituency being unable to read, these illustrations, the meaning of which every one can take in at a glance, play the mischief with his feelings.

And how many graphic designers can boast that not one, but TWO United States presidents personally thanked them for helping to ensure their election: Abraham Lincoln and Ulysses. S. Grant? Nast's accomplishment required firm belief, commitment, and an ability to draw, literally and figuratively, sharp battle lines; and his achievement would not have been possible without the very particular context of his cartoons: the technology of wood engraving, the rise of illustrated weekly newspapers, and weekly repetition of familiar figures and motifs as well as phrases that communicated news and opinion visually to a growing audience.

As Baird Jarman has shown, increasingly throughout the 1870s, Nast's combative demeanor and often violent visual rhetoric led to conflicts with *Harper's Weekly*'s management, who began to adopt a less polemic approach to editorial opinion and illustration, hiring new illustrators whose approach was more even-handed and concerned that heavy-handed propaganda was alienating rather than persuading readers, violating standards of middle-class propriety and a belief in constructive political discourse.

Nast's achievement also benefited from the freedom of the press and free elections as bulwarks of the democratic system in the United States, that is, the complex, messy, and easily manipulated systems of national, state, and local politics that is American democracy.

Chapter 7

The Politics of Learning: Dr. John Fell and the Fell Types at Oxford University in the Later Seventeenth Century

I may hope that our Endeavors here may produce somewhat which the publick may reap advantage from, and be concerned to encourage.
—JOHN FELL

"I do not love thee Dr. Fell, …"

Among the objects on display in the small museum at the Oxford University Press is a book of type specimens, dating to 1695, opened to its title page (Figure 7.1), which reads:

A Specimen
of the
Several Sorts of Letter
Given to the University
by Dr. John Fell
Sometime Lord Bishop of Oxford

Today few students are familiar with the Fell Types or the place the early "Learned Press" at Oxford University occupies in the history of typography. Although there was a revival of the Fell Types in the later nineteenth century accompanying the rise of the Private Press Movement in England, interest has been for the most part limited to a few printers, typophiles, and collectors of rare books.

The name of Dr. Fell (1625–86), however, is reasonably familiar to many readers: he claims an amusing survival in a well-known Mother Goose nursery rhyme attributed to Thomas (Thom) Brown (1662–1704), an English essayist and a student at Christ Church College at Oxford during the time Dr. Fell served as dean of the college and vice-chancellor of the university. Fell had a reputation for enforcing a strict code of conduct at the college, which included spying on the growing number of ale houses in the town of Oxford that distracted undergraduates from their studies. When Brown violated one of the college's rules for appropriate student behavior (there's no record as to which rule Brown broke), Fell expelled him, but gave Brown an opportunity for redemption: if he could translate a verse (the 32nd epigram) of the Roman writer Martial, whose works in Latin were a standard part of a university education at the time, Brown would be re-admitted. And Brown did so, inserting Fell's name in place of the anonymous subject in Martial's original verse:

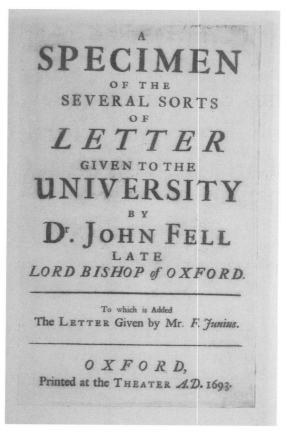

FIGURE 7.1 *Title Page,* A Specimen of the Several Sorts of Letters ..., *London, James Tregaskis & Son, 1928, 14.5 cm × 22 cm (facsimile of 1693 printing), Oxford, Oxford University Press, Courtesy Kislak Center for Special Collections, Rare Book Collection, University of Pennsylvania*

> I do not love thee Dr. Fell,
> The reason why I cannot tell;
> But this I know and know full well,
> I do not love thee, Dr. Fell.

Despite the reprieve, Brown never earned his degree from Oxford University. The verse, however, earned a place in Mother Goose's nursery rhymes, casting Dr. Fell in the role of strict teacher, the archetype of the stern disciplinarian who strikes fear into the hearts of his students.

While not connected with typography in any obvious way, the episode fairly communicates Fell's views about the serious purposes of a university education, and demonstrates both his identification with Christ Church and the college's mission to prepare young men for service to the English nation and to its Anglican church. Of relevance to *Reading Graphic Design History*, Dr. Fell's views on education were linked no less strongly to the form of the printed word, the culmination of his determined effort to merge medium and message.

What are the Fell Types?

This chapter explores the cultural meaning of letterpress typography in the context of the English Civil War (1642–51) by examining the early history of the Oxford University Press in the later seventeenth century under Dr. Fell's direction. In his publishing venture Dr. Fell went to great lengths to acquire a sizeable collection of fonts he then bequeathed to the university, known today as the "Fell Types." The Fell Types are neither the most extensive assemblage of historic type material of their time nor do the early Oxford University Press books always achieve the consistently high levels of production value found in contemporary publishing ventures in Paris at the Imprimérie Royale, in the best products of commercial type foundries in cities in Dutch cities such as Leiden and Amsterdam, or in Rome under the auspices of the Catholic Counter-Reformation Church beginning in the later sixteenth century. Among historians of type, they owe their importance today primarily to the role the types played in improving the quality of printing and the professional status of the printing trade in England, establishing a foundation for the careers of better known figures who followed such as William Caslon, whose London foundry (established in 1739) achieved international recognition, and whose types were used by John Dunlop in Philadelphia for the printing of the United States Declaration of Independence as a broadside in 1776. But Caslon was a typefounder rather than printer or publisher; investigating the combination of the Fell Types themselves, the titles selected for publication, and the political motivations surrounding Dr. Fell's printing efforts offers some insight into the meanings typography held for Fell and his broader vision for the Oxford University Press in England.

An Exemplar

One of the publications of the Oxford University Press during Fell's stewardship was an edition of writings by the early Christian third-century North African theologian St. Cyprian, published in 1682 (Figure 7.2).

FIGURE 7.2 *Title Page, St. Cyprian,* Opera, *Oxford, Oxford University Press, 1682, 38.1 × 22.9 cm, Courtesy Kislak Center for Special Collections, Lea Collection, University of Pennsylvania*

FIGURE 7.3 (and color plate) *Sir Christopher Wren, Sheldonian Theatre, Oxford, 1664–9, photo: author*

The title page lists the place of publication as Oxford, at the Sheldonian Theatre, a "U"-shaped building designed by the English architect Christopher Wren between 1664 and 1669 as a gift to the university from its chancellor Gilbert Sheldon (Figure 7.3 and color plate).

The theatre was used mainly for university ceremonies, but Fell persuaded Sheldon to allow its basement to be used as the press's first home. While carefully edited and annotated to exemplify high standards of scholarship as well as print production, the choice of Cyprian (which Fell had translated into English and also published at Oxford in 1681) is telling: the writings of this Church Father, in particular a treatise entitled "On the Unity of the Catholic Church" supported Fell's views on the primacy of the Anglican Church in England and the essential role of its bishops amid persistent conflicts with Presbyterians who renounced episcopal authority in favor a less centralized ecclesiastical organization, and whose views were championed by parliament in conflict with the monarchy during the English Civil Wars.

Fell's St. Cyprian is a large folio volume, 856 pages in length, with an engraving of the Sheldonian Theatre printed on the stately title page to proudly advertise its place of publication *in Oxford*, and several sizes of coordinated capital and lower-case letters arranged in a clear and symmetrical hierarchy of information (Figure 7.2). The body type (Figure 7.4) for the preface to the 1682 Cyprian is a large serif font, in the size known as "double-pica" (corresponding to 16-point), set in a single column with ample margins and liberal leading.

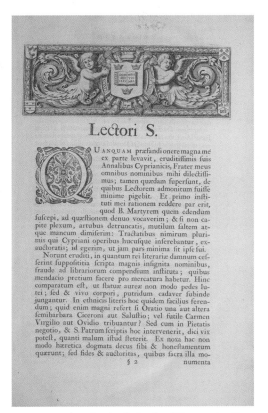

FIGURE 7.4 *Preface, St. Cyprian,* Works, *Oxford, Oxford University Press, 1682, text page with double pica roman font, 38.1 × 22.9 cm, Courtesy Kislak Center for Special Collections, Lea Collection, University of Pennsylvania*

The Cyprian marked one of the first uses of this large font at the Oxford University Press. It was most likely cut by a Dutch typefounder named Peter de Walpergen, who was brought to Oxford by Dr. Fell in 1681 to supply missing letters for fonts he had procured from Holland as well as to cut new fonts such as the double-pica to expand the range of types that were available for deluxe printing. There is a consistent weight to both the thin and thick strokes, with the contrast between them marked but not as abrupt as the "modern" or Didonic faces that began to appear later in the eighteenth century, and the serifs meet the letter stems with the slight trace of bracket rather than at a right angle, especially in the ascenders of letters.

The body type for the remainder of the book is known as "great primer" roman with a smaller size (small pica) used for the extensive annotations that accompany each page (Figures 7.5 and 7.6).

These were also cut by Walpergen and testify to Fell's desire to maintain consistency amid the variety of types and sizes that lent distinction to his publishing venture at Oxford. The impressive size of the Cyprian, the quality of its paper, the precision and overall high production value of the cast letter forms and even texture achieved in each printed page, all reach the high standards of typography and printing to which the Oxford University Press aspired, and have earned for the press a place in the history of typography, which is essentially the history of "fine printing."

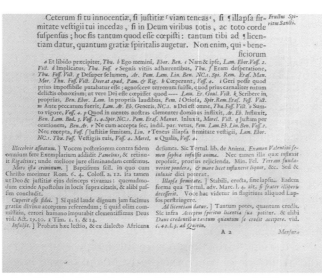

FIGURE 7.5 *St. Cyprian, Works, Oxford, Oxford University Press, 1682, Preface, with small great primer roman font designed by Peter de Walpergen in Oxford, 38.1 × 22.9 cm, Courtesy Kislak Center for Special Collections, Lea Collection, University of Pennsylvania*

FIGURE 7.6 *St. Cyprian, Works, Oxford, Oxford University Press, 1682, text page (detail), with footnotes in small pica font, cut by Peter de Walpergen, Courtesy Kislak Center for Special Collections, Lea Collection, University of Pennsylvania*

Oxford Typography and the Tradition
of "Fine Printing"

Indeed, much of the history of typography, in fact, almost *all* of this history, including its nomenclature and systems of classification, has concerned the tradition of "fine printing," that is, the scholarly editing and printing of classic religious, literary, and scientific texts intended for educated readers, establishing high standards for accuracy in editing combined with refinement in form. Stanley Morison (1889–1967), the type historian, consultant to the Monotype Corporation, and prolific author today best known for his role in overseeing the design of the ubiquitous Times New Roman typeface in 1932 for the *London Times*, defined "fine printing" as follows: "we look today for a range of types from 72-pt to 6 pt, uniform in design, reproducing some approved calligraphy, cut and justified with taste and precision in point of evenness of colour, alignment, spacing and slope, and cast with mechanical accuracy."

It's not surprising that Morison equated "taste" with "precision," for he presumed the primacy of the unquestioned taste of a privileged class, whose particular preferences were accepted as ideal, universal, as well as stable, while alternatives or deviations from these "standards" were seen simply as below the mark, rather than worthy of study in their own right, that is, in relation to their particular texts, to their audience, or to their purpose.

There were a variety of motivations behind the fine printing tradition as it emerged and developed beginning in the later fifteenth century. Competing with expert calligraphy in manuscripts certainly loomed large as a formidable benchmark and challenge to marketing printed books in the earliest years of the letterpress, while appealing to a wealthy literate readership with handsomely printed volumes for private study or display was another incentive to pursue the highest standards of craft, lending distinction to buyers assembling their own libraries, and creating respect and social standing for a new profession. During the later sixteenth century, one might add that typographic distinction asserted persuasive force in the face of an authority challenged by the expanding commercial printing industry itself and the spread of knowledge it brought: fine printing signified the exclusive top-down dissemination of knowledge to an increasingly literate but also more socially diverse public as a means of ensuring that new readers would acquire or aspire to the habits and manners of their social betters, promoting social harmony through shared beliefs, values, and a particular set of exacting aesthetic standards in the printing of texts. This "political" or "publick" meaning of knowledge figures strongly in Dr. Fell's awareness and pursuit of the art of fine printing.

Morison's description of fine printing using the Roman alphabet and seen in Dr. Fell's Cyprian is found in any number of contemporary printed books from the seventeenth century, for instance, at the Imprimérie Royale, founded in 1640 by Cardinal Richelieu for Louis XIV. As an example we can examine Jean Chartier's folio-size royal biography *Histoire de Charles VII, Roy de France* dating to 1661 (Figure 7.7).

This volume also begins with a stately title page that includes different sizes of finely cut capital letters, the engraved mark of the royal press in Paris with crown and fleur de lis, and is designed with the wide margins, ample leading, even impression, consistent stroke weight and regular base line that Morison identified as characteristics of fine printing (Figure 7.8). At their best, the books Dr. Fell supervised are firmly within this tradition.

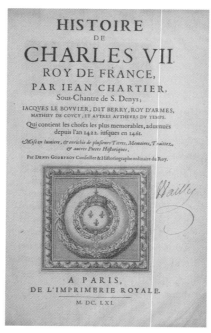

FIGURE 7.7 *Title Page, Jean Chartier,* Histoire de Charles VII Roy de France, *Paris, Imprimérie Royale, 1661, 36.8 × x 23.8 cm, Courtesy Kislak Center for Special Collections, Lea Collection, University of Pennsylvania*

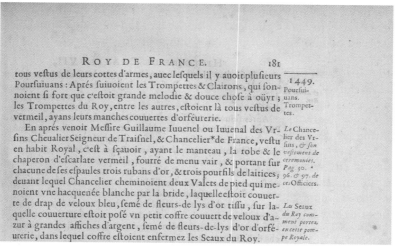

FIGURE 7.8 *Jean Chartier,* Histoire de Charles VII, Roy de France, *Paris, Imprimérie Royale, 1661, p. 181, 14 ½ × 9 3/8," Courtesy Kislak Center for Special Collections, Lea Collection, University of Pennsylvania*

Acquiring the Fell Types

The Fell Types primarily comprise a combination of punches and matrices purchased in Holland together with types acquired through earlier gifts, as well as fonts cut by typefounder Peter de Walpergen, who is documented as living in Oxford by 1681. The Fell Types include several sizes of roman letters, extensive type for musical notation, decorative letters and "printers' flowers" or fleurons, as well as type in a wide variety of languages that include Greek, Syriac, Hebrew, Armenian, Coptic, Samaritan, and Arabic.

Fell's typographical achievement at the Oxford University Press did not go unnoticed. Even during the bishop's lifetime his efforts to improve the quality of printing in England, *and* to communicate with a broader reading public, were recognized and admired. His London-based contemporary, the printer and globe maker Joseph Moxon (1627–91; there's no record that the two ever met), published the first practical guide to printing in England in 1683, titled *Mechanick Exercises: The Art of Printing*, and dedicated the book to Dr. Fell (along with the two "silent" partners who contributed funds for an annual stipend to the university to establish and maintain the Oxford University Press) with the following words:

> Your ardent affections to promote Typographie has eminently appeared in the great Charge you have been at to make it famous here in England; whereby this Royal Island stands particularly obliged to your Generous and Publick Spirits, and the whole CommonWealth of Book-men throughout the World, to your Candid Zeal for the promulgation of good Learning. Wherefore I humbly Dedicate this Piece of Typographie to your Honour[s]; –Joseph Moxon

Moxon's dedication to Dr. Fell is worth thinking about: he praises him not only for bringing fine printing to England, but also with the "public" benefit that would accrue from his efforts, that is, with the sharing of knowledge. Fell himself professed the same objectives, on the one hand academic and refined, and on the other concerned with the wider dissemination of knowledge and the means through which those institutions that were the *source* of knowledge might be strengthened. In one of his letters Fell wrote: "when I consider how much the Hollanders have added to their esteem in the World by printing well: as also that the king of France himself receives an addition from his Louvre presse [i.e. The Imprimérie Royale]: I may hope that our Endeavors here may produce somewhat which the publick may reap advantage from, and be concerned to encourage."

As mentioned above Fell aspired to the independence and control that would derive from the combination of typefounding, printing, and publishing, a combination that had been pursued in contemporary and institutionally sponsored printing houses established under the auspices of Popes Sixtus V and the Counter-Reformation Catholic Church in Rome (1587) and during the reign of Louis XIV at the Imprimérie Royale in Paris (1640). These presses combined the high standards of fine printing with institutionalized control toward which Dr. Fell's project for a learned press at Oxford aimed, that union among the selection and editing of texts with their printing under one roof, controlling both form as well as content in a single enterprise to consolidate and strengthen a centralized religious or secular authority, bolstering those authorities against competition from dissenting views that might undermine the monarchy or the established and recently restored Anglican church in England. Bishop Fell's printing venture stemmed from the assumption that the few could provide to an expanding and increasingly informed and diverse public the best sources of knowledge in an authoritative form communicated through the selection and editing of texts wedded to sophisticated standards of print design and production.

Fell might have subcontracted his texts to a local printer, as his counterparts at Cambridge University and predecessors at Oxford had done when the two universities received privileges from the king to own and operate their own presses in the 1630s, but his interests required not only permission to print the texts he approved to be published, but also ownership of the forms of the letters and their disposition on the page on which those texts would be printed. One is drawn to conclude that his efforts were the visible expression of his desire to assert influence in the face of a recently restored but still threatened institutional authority. In the case of Dr. Fell the history of fine printing becomes a *political* as well as an aesthetic history though it is the latter which generally receives the attention of historians of typography in which the comparison of typefaces with one another obscures their relationship to their own time and place. The choices made by the typefounders and designers derived from principles, from beliefs in institutions that preserved and strengthened an established political and social order during a time when that authority had been undermined by civil war, had only been restored in 1660, and remained controversial. The stated objectives were not only to share with a learned community the personal satisfaction of reading canonical texts in an appealing and suitable form, but to ensure continuity with future generations of students and leaders of society by shaping their character. In the wide context of this vision, the "what" and the "how," form and content, medium and message, were inseparable, and persuasive. What's remarkable is that Fell's scholarly and administrative interests embraced design as an integral component of the *politics* of knowledge and learning.

The political context of fine printing in the seventeenth century brings to mind a painting by the Flemish-born painter at the French court Philippe de Champaigne (1602–72). His *Moses Presenting the Tablets of the Law* in the Milwaukee Museum of Art (Figure 7.9 and color plate) is not only a statement of religious and moral doctrine but the epigraphy on the stone tablets reproduces a large, finely drawn italic that resembles the contemporary calligraphy of Pierre Moreau (d. 1648), a highly regarded writing master in Paris who cut italic types and had been named printer to the king (Louis XIV) in 1643. Here again distinctive letter forms are linked to (divine) authority in the age of absolute monarchy in France.

FIGURE 7.9 (and color plate) *Philippe de Champaigne,* Moses Presenting the Tables of the Law, *oil on canvas, 99 × 76.2 cm, Milwaukee Museum of Art*

Not surprisingly, Dr. Fell, as dean of Christ Church, vice-chancellor of Oxford University, and later as Bishop of Oxford (from 1672), was at the center of the political and religious debates of his time. He was a staunch defender of the monarchy and Oxford was a stronghold of Royalist sentiment and Anglican religious practice, where King Charles I had resided (at Christ Church) during the first Civil War between 1642 and 1646. Charles was beheaded in 1649, resulting in a period of decline and diminished influence at Oxford amid debates and commissions undertaken by parliament to reduce the hegemony of Anglican worship and episcopal administration and authority. With the monarchy restored in 1660 under Charles II, Fell supported the English crown and the authority of its church. Education at Christ Church was one means of bolstering both institutions, and an independent university press was an extension of that effort. Fell's mentor, Archbishop Laud (1573–1645), had lobbied successfully to establish the right (privilege) to publish books at Oxford, obtaining those rights in agreement with the London Stationers Company in 1633, and Laud donated the first printing equipment that later became the learned press at Oxford under Dr. Fell's direction, part of an attempt to loosen regulations on the printing of books against the tight control exercised by the London Stationers to reduce competition, an exception which required royal sanction (Laud was beheaded in 1645). With some greater degree of freedom of the press, and resulting competition from outside the small and closed group of London printers, type became a means of distinguishing the products of one press from another, a guarantee of quality, both of form as well as content, indeed, a method of branding (the early title pages bear an engraved image of the U-shaped Sheldonian Theatre). While Fell challenged the monopoly on printing defended by the London Stationers Company, he understood that competition would bring with it the need to differentiate the Oxford University Press and identify its products as authoritative: in this endeavor typography, that is, fine printing, was the means he chose to create that distinction, a pursuit that required great energy and determination.

As we will see below, Fell's effort to secure types for printing at Oxford in the later seventeenth century included extensive communication and negotiation with commercial printers in Holland, who were acknowledged at the time for high standards in the printing trade. Both Moxon and Fell shared a respect for Dutch printing, and Moxon had travelled to the Netherlands early in his career eager to benefit both as printer and globe maker by expanding his knowledge and skill there. Fell remained in England, but turned to an Oxford colleague and fellow scholar, Thomas Marshall (1621–85), to act as his agent in Holland to procure not just types, but also punches and matrices so as to be able not only to print, but also to cast letters for book printing. The directive to Marshall stemmed from dissatisfaction with the quality of English typefounding and printing in the seventeenth century: "The foundation of all successe must be layd in doing things well, and I am sure that will *not* be don with English letters."

There is no single explanation for the widespread complaint about the inferior quality of English printing in the time of Dr. Fell. Contemporaries such as Moxon attributed the situation to the monopoly granted to the London Stationers Company in the mid-sixteenth century that regulated the number of printers who were permitted to practice their trade and confined printing to the City of London, requiring privileges approved by the law court known as the Star Chamber in order for a printer to set up shop. Although the monopoly was not always strictly enforced, the limits to free enterprise provided fewer choices to publishers who were prevented from setting up their own printing facilities except by obtaining such a privilege. And while both Cambridge and Oxford universities received privileges to set up printing facilities, they had little success in doing so until Dr. Fell assumed responsibility for making the university press at Oxford a reality, and for negotiating with the London Stationers in the distribution of bibles in London.

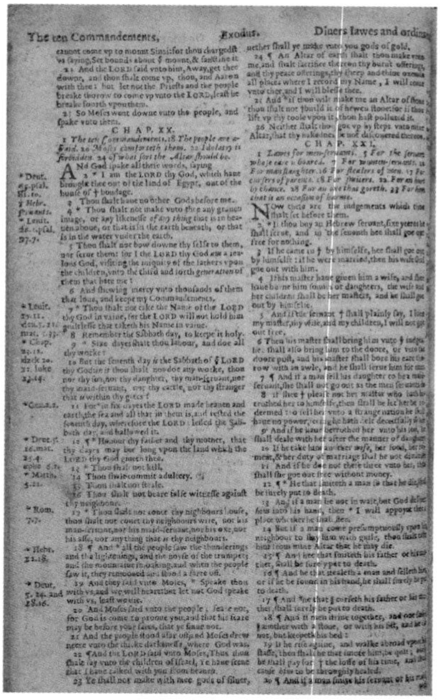

FIGURE 7.10 *Title Page, Bible, London, Robert Barker, 1631 (The "Wicked Bible"), 17.1 × 12.1 cm, Courtesy Museum of the Bible, The Signatry Collection. All rights reserved. © Museum of the Bible, 2019*

A humorous episode that provides a commentary upon the state of printing in England at the time is the so-called "wicked" bible, produced in London in 1631 by Robert Barker, printer to the king of England.

This imprint (Figure 7.10), a version of the King James Bible text (1610), hardly qualifies as fine printing: the ragged base line, irregularity and lack of contrast between thick and thin strokes in the letters, and general unevenness of texture, all confirm the general criticisms of Dr. Fell and others at the time. Moreover, in the chapter of the book of Exodus that contains the Ten Commandments (chapter 20, verses 1–17), the printer omitted the word "not" from the seventh commandment, which reads instead "Thou shalt commit adultery." The error resulted in a recall of the books (about 1,000 were printed, and six are known to exist today) and a hefty fine assessed to the printer, the proceeds of which were eventually donated to Oxford University to help contribute to the creation of the university's press.

Dr. Fell's colleague Thomas Marshall was a familiar visitor to the Netherlands, having served as "Chaplain to the English Merchants in Holland" and had acquired books that were not otherwise available in England on behalf of friends, though he was not knowledgeable in the printing trade. The exchange of letters between Fell and Marshall reveals their considerable effort, undertaken during trips in 1670 and again in 1672, to procure typographic material for the press at Oxford. The difficulties they faced ranged from deteriorating diplomatic relations and eventual war between England and Holland, to delays and frustrations in finding suitable printers with whom to deal (two of the typefounders Marshall hoped to contact in Amsterdam, Christoffel van Dyck and Bartholomeus Voskens, had died by the time he arrived, while a fire at the Blaeu foundry to the north of the city foiled another potential source for obtaining punches and matrices). In addition some foundries were understandably unwilling to offer matrices and punches for sale (rather than sorts) that would deprive them of printing orders and income. Moreover, supplies of punches and matrices might not be complete, whether lacking in particular letters or punctuation, requiring a subset of matrices that might be added through the services of a typefounder willing to relocate to Oxford to cut and cast missing letters and fonts in sizes Marshall was unable to procure, in order to have a suitable and complete range fonts at hand for fine printing.

In his will Bishop Fell bequeathed to the university the types, including punches and matrices that he had begun to acquire in 1670. These types are the material record of his effort, described by his biographers as a passion or "zeal," to place typefounding, printing, and publishing under one roof, to control both the form as *well* as the content of printed books. The collection of so-called "Fell Types" was published as a specimen book first in 1693 and have been the subject of rigorous investigation ever since, marking the beginning of a tradition of fine printing in England.

Stanley Morison provided the most complete and exhaustive study of the Fell Types in his lavish folio volume titled *John Fell, the University Press and the "Fell" Types*, published at the time of Morison's death in 1967, and printed with a wide variety of those letterpress types that remained available at that time at the Oxford University Press, located in a building on Walton Street, still the home of OUP, although not used for printing since 1989. Morison freely acknowledged his debt to previous printers and librarians associated with Oxford University including Falconer Madan, Horace Hart, and Harry Carter (the latter the father of the type designer Matthew Carter, who trained on the letterpress at the house of Enschedé in Haarlem, one of a handful of Dutch printing establishments active since the eighteenth century and still in business today). Morison concluded that the most refined types in the collection were the pica romans (*not* the double pica and other sizes used in the Fell Cyprian, cut by Walpergen), acquired by Marshall in Holland and among the best exemplars of "fine printing," closely related if not

FIGURE 7.11 *Pica Roman*, A Specimen of the Several Sorts of *Letters* ..., London, James Tregaskis & Son, *1928, 14.5 cm × 22 cm (facsimile of 1693 printing, Oxford, Oxford University Press, Courtesy Kislak Center for Special Collections, Rare Book Collection, University of Pennsylvania*

identical with the great sixteenth-century French typefounder Claude Garamond, though the punctuation, ligatures, capital letters, and small capital letters were cut in the seventeenth century to be consistent with the rest of the font. The Fell pica roman appears in the type specimens published at Oxford beginning in 1693 (Figure 7.11), and used for the body type of an octavo volume of the writings of the third-century Roman author Herodian, published at the Sheldonian Theatre in 1678. The pica roman font was also the inspiration for Walpergen's activities in Oxford.

The "Publick"

While the "learned press" served students and the scholarly community with the classic texts of venerated authors, the wider public also loomed large in Dr. Fell's vision for the OUP and, as noted above, earned the respect of Joseph Moxon. As an author, Fell edited and printed editions of the Church Fathers for clerical and scholarly study in Latin and Greek, as with the 1682 Cyprian discussed above, and the views of authors such as Cyprian coincided with established Anglican belief. But Dr. Fell also printed, and may have contributed as author, to several moralizing treatises directed to students and to the lay public, born of well meaning if paternalistic approaches to everyday living emphasizing self-discipline. One of these, entitled *The Ladies Calling*, was printed at Oxford in 1673 (Figure 7.12) and is a guide to the moral education of women, proclaiming biblical authority for the subservience of wives to their husbands and the pursuit of the "feminine" virtues of modesty, meekness, compassion, affability, piety, and virginity, including sections devoted to the proper behavior for widows (Fell did not marry).

The text expanded upon a more comprehensive manual for daily living by the same author and entitled *The Whole Duty of Man*, dating to the later 1650s and printed at the Sheldonian Theatre in 1677 as well as in many subsequent editions. Fell's authorship is disputed and both works are often attributed to Richard Allestree, an Oxford preacher who, like Fell, was a staunch royalist.

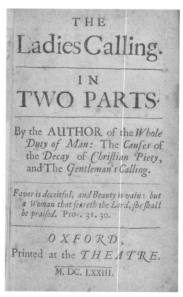

FIGURE 7.12 *Title Page, Richard Allestree,* The Ladies Calling, *17.7 × 10.5 cm, Oxford, Oxford University Press, 1673, Courtesy Kislak Center for Special Collections, Rare Book Collection, University of Pennsylvania*

That Dr. Fell's interests extended to the wider public also emerges in his printing of the English bible at Oxford in 1675. Printing the bible required a license that he applied for and obtained from the London Stationers Company. Here the motivation appears to have been twofold, not only to disseminate a corrected and standard version of sacred scripture to help ensure unity of belief, but also to print a book in small format at reasonable cost that would reach a wider audience, quite literally spreading the Word as well as turning a profit and subsidizing the more erudite but also more limited readership for editions of scholarly books that required an increasing array of foreign alphabets, including Hebrew, Syriac, Arabic, Coptic, and Persian. Fell also turned to other works of wider interest, for instance, local histories such as Robert Plot's handsome *Natural History of Oxfordshire* (1677) and *Staffordshire* (1686), with finely drawn copperplate engravings that would appeal to local gentry (though even here a biblical justification appears in the volume's preface, quoting from the book of Joshua in the Old Testament: "Ye shall describe the land, and bring the descriptions hither to me"), sermons of well-known preachers and theologians, books on regional botany, as well as recent histories, including the Earl of Clarendon's pro-royalist *History of the Rebellion and Civil War* (1702–4), printed after Fell's death and before the Press moved from its premises at the Sheldonian Theatre to the nearby Clarendon Building in 1715, purchased in part with profits from sales of that title; the *History of the Rebellion and Civil War* also included high-quality copper engravings to complement the wide range of Fell Types (Figure 7.13).

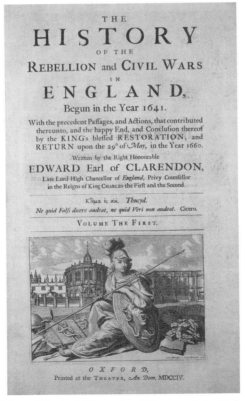

FIGURE 7.13 *Title Page, Edward Earl of Clarendon,* History of the Rebellion and Civil Wars ..., *38.5 × 23 cm, Oxford, Oxford University Press, 1704, Courtesy Kislak Center for Special Collections, Rare Book Collection, University of Pennsylvania*

The activity at the press was brisk—more than thirty titles per year were published between 1671 and 1680, almost 300 books for the decade, a pace that continued throughout the remainder of the seventeenth century. Indeed, despite a stated desire and objective to serve what Fell had called the "interest and convenience" of scholars, he was also running a business that relied upon sales and subsidies for success, leading him to print small and more affordable bibles as well as books of local interest to wealthy subscribers.

The Afterlife of Fine Printing

The eclipse of the letterpress has reduced much of the history of typography to antiquarian interest at best. Such was the view even in the early 1960s when in his history of printing author S. H. Steinberg criticized the late nineteenth-century Private Press Movement, a revival of "fine printing" (including the Fell Types), as anachronistic in an age of advancing print technology (Steinberg, 1961). While the preservation of refined types continued, Steinberg argued, it had indeed become a private and rarefied practice, far removed from the motivations that had given it broader public and political meaning in the age of Dr. Fell. To be sure, typefaces such as Garamond and other "named" types survived into the twentieth century and beyond as a result of the efforts of Stanley Morison and other typophiles and printers who studied rare books, specimens, matrices, and punches, carefully tracing their histories and accurately overseeing their redesign in the twentieth century for commercial printing on the monotype machine for letterpress, later for film setting, and more recently for Adobe as digital fonts. As such they live on, but little remains of the political and "publick" meaning they held for Fell and his contemporaries; only the books themselves and their wider history supply the context that would reveal the meaning they held for designers who cut them, the printers who commissioned or purchased them to be used to publish books, the patrons who sponsored editions, and the readers who turned the pages of those books.

One imagines that every font might have its own story to tell; my earliest exposure to type history and still among the best introductions to the careful and reasoned study of typefaces and fine printing is Alexander Lawson's *Anatomy of a Typeface* (1990), with its nineteen individual chapters devoted to not only the character of particular letter forms described with great care and respect by the author, but also the careful tracing of their extended lives in revivals and survivals amid changes in technology, revealing the efforts of a host of little-known individuals whose names and contributions, whether as founder, printer, or publisher, deserve to be remembered. While the Fell Types may not have merited an "anatomy" lesson by Lawson, the efforts of Stanley Morison and others permit an appreciation of the role that type played during a difficult but formative period in early modern English history.

Fell's interests combined erudition with the contested politics of his day along with Christian moral education. His lifelong interest in, his "zeal" for printing, stemmed from all three of these interests, and those interests are best understood as being inseparable. Indeed, without the combination of all three, the academic, the political, and the moral, it is unlikely that he would have succeeded in creating the Oxford University Press, in amassing necessary resources and in publishing a variety of works to help ensure the press's success and future. To see printing as a visual and material expression of these motivations and as a significant means to promote political and social stability under a restored monarchy and church is to recognize what we can learn from looking at and thinking about type in its particular historical context. Dr. Fell's pursuit of fine printing required much trial and error.

He was not a tradesman by training or family background, but his immersion in printing not only earned the respect of craftsmen such as Joseph Moxon, but also elevated the practice of typography in England: in 1739 William Caslon established his typefounding business in London, contributing to the tradition of fine printing in London, and in time acquiring an international reputation.

Type and Politics Reconsidered

If "knowledge is power," and if books were a primary means of communicating knowledge in the seventeenth century, then books too were a source of power, and controlling knowledge a means of asserting and consolidating power, whether in relation to taste, to religious practice, or to political belief. Dr. Fell's vision for the future of England depended upon communicating the "right" kind of knowledge, and typography was an effective means to distinguish and to distinctively and persuasively transmit the values of church and monarchy at Oxford and beyond. While we may admire the refinement of the best examples of Dr. Fell's types and the more celebrated early examples of the OUP, control and power were at the root of his project to invest considerable time and resources to fine printing. Motivated in some measure by fears engendered by political and religious turmoil during his lifetime, typography was a means of ensuring both distinction and authority to the printed word as a source of trusted knowledge sanctioned by institutional authority, especially in an age when that authority was disputed. Indeed one might hypothesize that political controversy and economic competition spurred typographic innovation in Fell's England.

Printing's "Other"

But let's conclude by returning to Thom Brown's satirical portrayal of Dr. Fell. While Fell pursued his vision for the Oxford University Press with great resolve and energy, and while those efforts secured his place in the history of fine printing thanks to the research of Hart, Carter, Morison, and others, another print history was emerging, a "popular" or bottom-up history with its own typography and design, a more inclusive history that acknowledged the economic means and varied desires of a diverse public for information, combining practical advice, humor, and a healthy skepticism of authority in prose, verse, or the occasional illustration, not unlike Thom Brown's nursery rhyme that poked fun at the staid public image of Dr. Fell. The tradition of the popular press was a staple of the printing industry, to be found less in books by acknowledged authors than in ephemeral forms of publication such as inexpensive broadsides, weekly journals, calendars, or collections of stories and colloquial sayings known as miscellanies. Their study is also rich with historical meaning; but this popular print tradition barely plays a part in the history of typography. The growth of the popular alternative press reached an early peak with the advent of mechanical presses and wood-engraved images toward the middle of the nineteenth century, but examples thrived earlier, for instance, in annual or semi-annual *Almanacks* that appeared in England in the seventeenth century and include those printed and published by Benjamin Franklin in Philadelphia beginning in 1732 under the pseudonym "Richard Saunders," better known as "Poor Richard" (Figure 7.14). For twenty-five years Franklin published his almanac; it was among his most lucrative publishing ventures, with print runs as high as ten thousand copies.

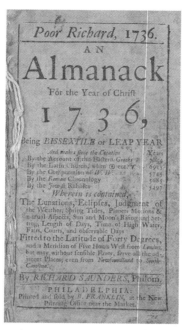

FIGURE 7.14 *Benjamin Franklin, title page,* Poor Richard's Almanack, *Philadelphia, New Market Press, 1736, 16 × 9.5 cm, Courtesy Kislak Center for Special Collections, Curtis Collection, University of Pennsylvania*

Printed on thin inexpensive (and now terribly fragile) paper in small format (6 5/16 × 3 ¾"), maximizing space with narrow margins, cramped layouts, and a busy hodge-podge of letter forms and sizes that seems at times to overwhelm a reader trying to take in the information at a glance, *Poor Richard's Almanack* is printing's "other," in content, in format, and in typography, with parodies and jokes along with proverbs that contain advice for daily living, often interspersed with tables containing a calendar, weather predictions, lunar cycles, sunrises and sunsets, religious holidays and festivals, planetary symbols *and* a wider variety of typefaces (including blackletter for the names of saints, cf. Figure 7.15—poking fun at Old Testament patriarchs who had children by hired help, Poor Richard included the following recommendation: "let thy maid-servant be faithful, strong, and homely"). In comparison to the products of Bishop Fell's Oxford University Press, *Poor Richard* was not a book at all, but an alternative print vehicle for information that satisfied a popular desire for timeliness, practicality, moral instruction, and humor, to which the standards of "fine printing," that is, the authorial book, did not apply. Like other contemporary almanacks, *Poor Richard* even included advertisements for home remedies along with cooking recipes.

In Figure 7.15, the proverb is printed in italic in the midst of the daily and weekly calendars, weather forecasts for the month of April, filling up unused space on lines, tempting the reader to find the next part of the passage. A column with numbers proceeds in order from the beginning to the end of the month, but other numbered columns report on the position of planets (identified by symbol), sun, and moon on particular days. The aphorisms are borrowed from a variety of print sources for proverbs known to Franklin. In the second column of the calendar for April,

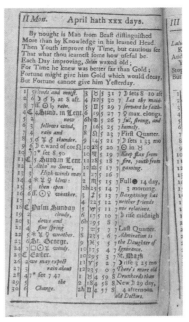

FIGURE 7.15 *Calendar Page for April,* Poor Richard's Almanack, *Philadelphia, New Market Press, 1736, 16 × 9.5 cm, Courtesy Kislak Center for Special Collections, Curtis Collection, University of Pennsylvania*

1736, in four parts, we find the following: "Relation without friendship, friendship without power, power without will, will without effect, effect without profit, & profit without ve[i]rtue, are not worth a farte" (a play on the word "farthing").

As another example of Franklin's wit, the author addressed the reader of the very first *Poor Richard's Almanack* in the guise of Poor Richard himself, an alter ego borrowed from an English almanack publisher of the same name. Franklin doesn't hide the pecuniary motive of his printing endeavor; he "levels" with the reader (not unlike the "voice" in examples of the "New Advertising," see chapter 5, p. 144 and ff.), masking the paternalistic message of frugality and hard work found in many of the almanack's aphorisms behind the foibles he shares with his readers:

I might in this place attempt to gain thy Favour, by declaring that I write Almanacks with no other View than that of the publick Good; but in this I should not be sincere; and Men are now a-days too wise to be deceiv'd by Pretences how specious soever. The plain Truth of the Matter is, I am excessive poor, and my Wife, good Woman, is, I tell her, excessive proud.

Or these tongue-in-cheek lines below a section on courts and the justice system:

For Gratitude there's none exceed 'em
(Their Clients know this when they bleed 'em).
Since they who give most for their Laws
Have most return'd, and carry th' Cause.

All know, except an arrant Tory.
That Right and Wrong's meer Ceremony.
It is enough that the Law Jargon,
Gives the best Bidder the best Bargain.

And yet is such literature simply an inferior version of fine printing governed only by a lack of taste or the overriding technical exigencies of filling up all available space on the page? Such a conclusion would deny a distinct identity to the *Almanack's* readers or an alternative intention to the genre's publishers, particularly in the creation of a means of communication that was by "design" less official, more colloquial, and more accessible and approachable to their readers. It is noteworthy as well that as a printer in Philadelphia, Franklin was also well-informed about the tradition of fine printing and communicated directly with the most respected English and European printers and typefounders of his day, producing smaller editions of classic texts as well, printed with greater care in the choice of font, in typesetting, in layout, paper quality, and at a higher cost, for instance his edition of the Roman writer Cicero's "Cato the Elder Discourse on Old Age," published in 1744 (Figure 7.16), using the English translation of wealthy Philadelphia Quaker and secretary to William Penn, James Logan (1674–1751).

For Franklin, as well as for Dr. Fell, there was a connection between politics, printing, and the public interest: it certainly appears that each desired, as printer and publisher, to inform and shape public opinion and behavior through the printed word. But Franklin's view of the public was more accepting of human nature, less restrictive, and thus more inclusive, even democratic. This view was manifest not only in the wider range of material he printed, but also in the compact and busy layouts and typographical choices found in *Poor Richard's Almanack*. Both fine and ephemeral printing have something to offer the student of graphic design.

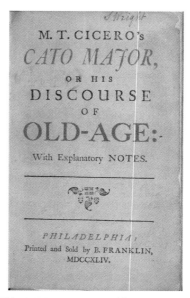

FIGURE 7.16 *Cicero, Cato the Elder's Discourse on Old-Age, 20.5 × 12 cm, Philadelphia, Benjamin Franklin, 1744, Courtesy Kislak Center for Special Collections, Curtis Collection, University of Pennsylvania*

Typography and Graphic Design

The history of modern graphic design belongs to the longer and more wide-ranging history of print communication. Essential to both histories is typography. The combination of and relationship between image and the printed word is the foundation of the graphic design profession, whether in illustrated books and magazines, political cartoons, posters, advertising, corporate identity, or information graphics and data visualization. By typography I don't mean to include *all* letter forms, but more specifically the forms of *printed* letters of the Roman alphabet, printed rather than hand drawn, invented earlier in China, but beginning in Europe in the mid-fifteenth century with the invention and rapid spread of moveable cast metal type using Roman letter forms. This tradition, the tradition of the *letterpress*, has survived to our own day, but has long been eclipsed by more modern and efficient production technologies that have drastically reduced the time, effort, and limitations of relief printing. The efficiencies afforded by modern technologies such as offset lithography and digital printing have been liberating for designers and have greatly expanded, if not entirely redefined, the professional practices of graphic designers during the past century; and yet the use of such technologies often obscures the rich combination of meticulous craft, theory, and print production that consumed the coordinated energies of generations of typefounders, letterpress printers, and publishers, whose efforts we may too easily take for granted today when we freely choose fonts from the drop-down menus of our laptop computers and word-processing programs. Type fonts such as Jenson, Garamond, Caslon, Baskerville, Bodoni, or Didot, to name but a few, each have their own histories, and the survival of these historic typefaces is in many cases the result of the painstaking study and comparison of rare books, specimen sheets, punches, matrices, and sorts preserved in museums and libraries, along with archival correspondence that have helped to establish the individual identity of the founders, printers, and publishers responsible for cutting the punches, striking the matrices, casting sorts, selecting texts, and printing books. Admiring the evenly textured pages of books on display in the cases of rare book rooms in libraries or in museum exhibitions can give way to thinking about the energy, creativity, painstaking labor, and motivation that was required to produce them.

Whether through state or church control, or a privately owned press catering to a sophisticated reading public, *fine* printing constitutes the "canon" of type history, a standard history that focuses upon "purity," that is, those books that reveal the most sophisticated, and often the most exclusive typography and book design. Of course, presses such as the Imprimérie Royale in France, underwritten by monarchs, prelates, or other wealthy individuals, did not have to contend with market pressures; but publishers such as Dr. Fell at the Oxford University Press, Christopher Plantin in Antwerp in the sixteenth century, and Benjamin Franklin in Philadelphia, also had to be level-headed businessmen, printing a wider variety of books in different sizes for a range of purses and with an eye toward meeting demand, and not all of their output was "fine"—purity may have been the goal but it was only rarely attained—the reality of the printing trade was messy rather than neat, and fine printing but a part of a rich history that included the realities of competitive business practice, ascertaining and stimulating the reading desires of an expanding market (the wives and female children of the extended Plantin family sewed and sold lace as a means of providing income and capital for the family printing business to compensate for the vagaries of the printing trade). The circumstances that produced fine printing at Oxford were very specific, and as I've tried to demonstrate, political; this may not always have been the case, but historians of typography might make such a context an object of investigation as they consider the motivations for and meaning of letter forms. It would make of that history less a search for typographic purity than a history of learning, a history of knowledge. That Dr. Fell's reputation survived in a familiar Mother Goose nursery rhyme is curious, considering that his contributions to the history of printing in England and his participation in the contentious politics of his day are now largely forgotten; perhaps he also had a softer side too—after all, he *did* give Thom Brown a second chance.

Postscript

The history of the Oxford University Press finds a local parallel in the founding of the Ashmolean Museum in Oxford in 1683, the first public museum in England. Not only are the two institutions contemporary, but they also share other similarities. Elias Ashmole (1619–72) obtained the collection of mostly botanical and scientific specimens acquired by the elder John Tradescant (1570s–1638) during visits to the Netherlands and Paris (Tradescant was a gardener responsible for planning the gardens of aristocrats such as the Earl of Salisbury as well as King Charles I), and donated the collection to the University of Oxford. The building, located near to the Sheldonian Theatre (see p. 216 and Figure 7.3) opened to the public in 1683. Dr. Fell and Elias Ashmole were both ardent supporters of the English monarchy. Ashmole studied at Oxford (not at Fell's Christ Church) and in his dedication referred to the university as his "mother." His devotion to the university strikes a chord with Dr. Fell's identification with Oxford. Ashmole also collected books and published volumes on English heraldry beginning in the 1660s, though printed in London rather than at Oxford. We do not know the degree to which Ashmole's interests extended to typography, or whether he knew Dr. Fell. But the devotion these two gentlemen shared to Oxford University, their support of the English crown, and their roles in using the press and the museum to inform and shape public opinion through the printed word and the assembly of objects and specimens, are a happy coincidence indeed.

BIBLIOGRAPHY

Introduction

Aynsley, Jeremy, and Kate Forde, eds., *Design and the Modern Magazine*, Manchester and New York, Manchester University Press, 2007

Drucker, Johanna, and Emily McVarish, *Graphic Design History: A Critical Guide*, New York, Pearson, 2013

Eitner, Lorenz, "Subjects from Common Life in the Real Language of Men: Popular Art and Modern Tradition in Nineteenth-Century French Painting," Kirk Varnedoe and Adam Gopnik, eds., *Modern Art and Popular Culture: Readings in High and Low*, New York, Abrams and the Museum of Modern Art, 1990, 52–81

Fallan, Kjetil, "De-tooling Design History: To What Purpose and for Whom Do We Write?," *Design and Culture*, vol. 5, no. 1, 2013, 13–19

Forty, Adrian, *Objects of Desire: Design and Society Since 1750*, London, Thames and Hudson, 1986

Golec, Michael, review of Heller, Steven, and Georgette Ballance, eds., *Graphic Design History*, New York, Allworth Press, 2001, in *Design Issues*, vol. 20, no. 4, 2004, 91–4

Golec, Michael, "Graphic Visualization and Visuality in Lester Beall's Rural Electrification Posters," 1937, *Journal of Design History*, vol. 26, no. 4, 2013, 401–15

Guffey, Elizabeth, *Posters: A Global History*, London, Reaktion Books, 2015

Heller, Steven, "Advertising: The Mother of Graphic Design," *Eye Magazine*, issue 17, 1995; reprinted in Heller and Balance, eds., *Graphic Design History,* New York, Allworth, 2001, 295–304

Heller, Steven, and Elaine Lustig Cohen, *Born Modern: The Life and Work of Alvin Lustig*, San Francisco, Chronicle Books, 2010

Hollis, Richard, *Graphic Design: A Concise History*, revised and expanded edition, New York, Thames & Hudson, 2001

Hollis, Richard, *Swiss Graphic Design: The Origins and Growth of an International Style*, 1920–1965, New Haven, Yale University Press, 2006

Iskin, Ruth, "Identity and Interpretation: Receptions of Toulouse-Lautrec's Reine de joie Poster in the 1890s," *Nineteenth-Century Art Worldwide*, Spring 2009 (www.19thc-artworldwide.org/index.php/component/content/article/55-spring09article/63–identity-and-interpretation-receptions-of-toulouse-lautrecs-reine-de-joie-poster-in-the-1890s)

Meggs, Philip, *History of Graphic Design*, New York, Van Nostrand Reinhold, 1983, from 1998 published by John Wiley (Hoboken, NJ); with Alston Purvis as *Meggs History of Graphic Design*, 4th ed. 2006, 5th ed. 2012, 6th ed. 2016

Ohmann, Richard, "History and Literary History: The Case of Mass Culture," James Naremore and Patrick Brantlinger, eds., *Modernity and Mass Culture*, Bloomington, Indiana University Press, 1991, 24–41.

Sontag, Susan, " Posters: Advertisement, Art, Political Artifact, Commodity," in Dugald Stermer, *The Art of Revolution: 96 Posters from Cuba*, New York, McGraw-Hill, 1970; and in Michael Bierut, Jessica Helfand, Rick Poyner, and Steven Heller, eds., *Looking Closer 3: Classic Writings in Graphic Design,* New York, Allworth Press, 1999, 196–218

Chapter 1: Joseph Müller-Brockmann: "schutzt das Kind!" and the Mythology of Swiss Design

Austin, J. L., *How to do Things With Words*, Cambridge, MA, Harvard University Press, 1962

Beegan, Gerry, "The Picturegoer: Cinema, Rotogravure, and the Reshaping of the Female Face" in Catherine Clay, Maria DiCenzo, Barbara Green, Fiona Hackney, eds., *The Edinburgh Companion to Women's Print Media in Interwar Britain (1918–1939)*, Edinburgh, Edinburgh University Press 2017 (pp. 185–203)

Beegan, Gerry, "Swiss School," *Bloomsbury Encyclopedia of Design*, ed. Clive Edwards et al., London, Bloomsbury Publishing, 2015, 294–97

Bonsiepe, Gui, "Education for Visual Design," in Michael Bierut, et al., eds., *Looking Closer 3*, New York, Allworth, 1999, 61–6

Daston, Lorraine, and Peter Galison, *Objectivity*, New York, Zone Books, 2010, first published 2007

"Dialogs on Graphic Design," *Industrial Design*, vol. 3, no. 2, 1956, unpaged

Evans, David, *John Heartfield-AIZ, 1930–1938*, New York, Kent Fine Art, Inc., 1992

Fifer, J. Valerie, *American Progress: The Growth of the Transport, Tourist, and Information Industries in the Nineteenth-Century West seen through the Life and Times of George A. Crofutt, Pioneer and Publicist of the Transcontinental Age*, Chester, CT, The Globe Pequot Press, 1988

Der Fussgänger, newsletter of the Fussgänger-Schutzverband, 1952, 1953

Garland, Ken, "First Things First," in Michael Bierut, et al., eds., *Looking Closer 3*, New York, Allworth, 1999, 54–5

Gerstner, Karl, *Die neue Graphic. The New Graphic Art. Le nouvel art graphique*, Switzerland, Arthur Niggli Ltd., 1959

Gessner, Robert, "The Graphic Designer and his Training," *Neue Grafik*, 1, September 1958, 51–2.

Herbert Matter—Foto-Grafiker—Sehformen der Zeit,. Das Werk der zwanziger und drissiger Jahre, Zurich, Lars Müller, 1995

Hölscher, Eberhard, "Eine Zürcher Polizeiaktion," *Gebrauchsgrafik*, 8, 1952, 36–9

Lizcar, Robert and Davide Fornari, eds., *Mapping Graphic Design in Switzerland*, Triest, Verlag für Architekur, Design, und Typographie, 2016

Lizcar, Robert, Roland Früh, Ueli Kaufmann, and Sara Zeller, "Swiss Graphic Design: A British Invention," unpublished paper delivered at the Design History Society Conference, New York, September 8, 2018

Lohse, Richard P., "On the Sociological Position of the Graphic Designer," *Neue Grafik*, 3, October, 1959, 59

Lupton, Ellen,"Reading Isotype," *Design Issues*, vol. III, no. 2, Spring 1986, 47–58

Müller, Lars, ed., *Josef Müller-Brockmann, Pioneer of Swiss Graphic Design*, Zurich, Lars Muller, 1995

Müller-Brockmann, Josef, *The Graphic Designer and His Design Problems—Creative Problems of the Graphic Designer: Design and Training in Commercial Art*, rev. edition, Switzerland, Arthur Niggli Ltd., 1983

Müller-Brockmann, Josef, *Grid Systems in Graphic Design—A Visual Communication Manual for Graphic Designers, Typographers and Three Dimensional Designers*, New York, Hastings House, 1981

Müller-Brockmann, Josef, *History of Visual Communication: From the Dawn of Barter in the Ancient World to the Visualized Conception of Today*, London, Tiranti, 1971

Müller-Brockmann, Josef., *Mein Leben: Spielerischer Ernst und ernsthaftes Spiel*, Regensdorf, Weser Druck, 1994

Neue Zürcher Zeitung (1951–1953)

Neurath, Marie and Robin Kinross, *The Transformer: Principles of Making Isotype Charts*, London, Hypen Press, 2009

Official Handbook of the Automobile Club of Switzerland (Baedeker's Autoguides), Stuttgart, London and New York. The Macmillan Company, 1957

Packard, V. *The Hidden Persuaders*, New York, David McKay, 1957

Poulin, Richard, *Graphic Design and Architecture, A 20th Century History: A Guide to Type, Image, Symbol, and Visual Storytelling in the Modern World*, Beverly, MA, Rockford Publishers, 2012, 137

Purcell, Kerry William, *Alexey Brodovitch*, New York and London, Phaidon, 2002

Purcell, Kerry William, *Josef Müller-Brockmann*, New York and London, Phaidon, 2006

Rand, Paul, "Good Design is Good Will" (1987), reprinted in Paul Rand, *Design Form and Chaos*, New Haven, Yale University Press, 1993

Remington, Roger and Barbara J. Hodik, *Nine Pioneers in American Graphic Design*, Cambridge, MA, MIT Press, 1989

Richter, Bettina, ed., *Poster Collection Help!: Soziale Appelle—Appeals to Social Conscience*, Zurich, Lars Muller, 2009

Rotzler, Willy and Karl Wobmann, *Political and Social Posters of Switzerland*, Zurich, ABC Edition, 1985

Scheidegger, Ernst, "Photography and Advertising Design," *Neue Grafik*, 4, December, 1959, 32–44

Statistisches Jahrbuch der Schweiz. Annuaire statistique de la Suisse, Bern, Eidgenössisches Statistisches Amt, 1950 ff.

Wakeman, Frederic, *The Hucksters*, New York, Rinehart & Company, 1946

Evans, David, *John Heartfield-AIZ, 1930–1938*, New York, Kent Fine Art, Inc., 1992

Chapter 2: Koloman Moser's Thirteenth Secession Exhibition Poster (1902): Anatomy of a Work of Viennese Graphic Design

Aynsley, Jeremy, *A Century of Graphic Design*, London, Octopus Publishing Group, 2001

Aynsley, Jeremy, "Graphic and Interior Deisgn in the Viennese Coffeehouse around 1900: Experience and Identity," in Charlotte Ashby, Tag Gronberg and Simon Shaw-Miller, eds., *The Viennese Café and Fin-de-Siècle Culture*, New York, Berghahn Books, 2013, 158–77

Beller, Steven, *Vienna 1900*, New York and Oxford, Berghan Books, 2001

Bisanz-Prakken, Marian, *Heiliger Frühling: Gustav Klimt und die Anfänge der Wiener Secession 1895–1905*, Vienna and Munich, Christian Brandstätter, 1999

Bott, Gerhard, ed., *Joseph M. Olbrich 1867–1908: Das Werk des Architekten. Austellung anlässlich der 100. Widerkehr des Geburtstages*, Darmstadt, Hessischen Landesmuseum and Roetherdruck, 1967

Bourke, Thomas, *Arnold Böcklin 1827–1901*, New York, Rizzoli, 1975

Crane, Walter, *Line & Form*, London, George Bell & Sons, 1908

Fenz, Werner, *Koloman Moser: Graphic, Kunstgewerbe, Malerei*, Salzburg and Vienna, Residenz Verlag, 1984

Gerlarch, Martin, ed. *Allegorian: Wein, Tanz, Liebe, Music, Gesang*, Series 1, Vienna, Gerlarch & Schenk, 1896

Gray, Nicolette, *Lettering as Drawing: Contour and Silhouette*, London, Oxford University Press, 1970

Guffey, Elizabeth, *Posters: A Global History*, London, Reaktion, 2015

Hevesi, Ludwig, *Acht Jahre Sezession: Kritk—Polemik—Chronik*, Vienna, Carl Konegen, 1906

Hiatt, Charles, "The Collecting of Posters," *The Studio: an Illustrated Magazine of Fine and Applied Art*, vol. 2, 1893 61–4 ff.

Hölscher, Eberhard, *Rudolf Larisch und Seine Schule—Rudolf Larisch and his School*, Berlin and Leipzig, Heintz & Blankertz, 1938

Hoozee, Robert, ed., *Bruxelles: Carrefour de cultures*, Anvers, Fonds Mercator, 2000

Hurm, Otto, "Rudolf von Larisch und die Wiener Secession," *Gutenberg-Jahrbuch* (1979), 11–17

Ilg, Albert, ed., *Allegorien und Embleme: Originalentwürfe von den hervorragendsten modernen Künstlern, sowie Nachbildungen alter Zunftzeichen* und *moderne Entwürfe von Zunftwappen im Charakter der Renaissance*, volumes 1 and 2, Vienna, Gerlach & Schenk, 1882-1885.

James, Clive, *Cultural Amnesia: Necessary Memories from History and the Arts*, New York, Norton, 2007

Joseph Maria Olbrich 1867–1908: Architect and Designer of Early Modernism, Darmstadt, Hatje Cantz, 2010

Jugendstil; Art Nouveau; Liberty, Milan and Munich, Galleria del Levante, Jugendstil—Illustrationen 50 Jahre Meggendorfer Blatter, 1972

Kallir, Jane, *Viennese Design and the Wiener Werkstätte*, New York, Braziller, 1986 (forward by Carl Schorske)

Larisch, Rudolf von, *Über Zierschriften im Dienste der Kunst*, Munich, Jos. Albert, 1899

Larisch, Rudolf von, *Unterricht in Ornamentalen Schrift*, Vienna, State Printing House, 1919 (5th ed.), first published 1905

Larisch, Rudolf, *Beispiele künstlerischer Schrfit aus Vergangenen Jahrunderten*, 5, Vienna, Austrian State Printing House, 1926 (examples of handwriting 1553–1815)

Mascha, Ottokar, *Österreichische Plakatkunst*, Veinna, J. Löwy, 1915

Mataja, Viktor, *Die Reklame: Eine Untersuchung über Ankündigungswesen und Werbetätigkeit im Geschäftsleben*, Munich and Leipzig, Duncker & Humblot, 1926 (first published 1910)

Müller-Brockmann, Josef and Shizuko Müller-Brockmann, *Geschichte des Plakates-Histoire de l'affiche-History of the Poster*, Zurich, ABC Verlag, 1971 (p. 69, no. 53 for Moser Thirteenth Secession Exhibition poster)

Nebehay, Christian M., *Ver Sacrum 1898–1903*, trans. Geoffrey Watkins, New York, Rizzoli, 1975.

Novotny, Fritz, ed., *Wien um 1900: Austellung Veranstaltet vom Kulturamt der Stadt Wien*, Wien, Brüder Rosenbaum, 1964

Raizman, David, "Thirteenth Secession Exhibition, Vienna 1902," in Steven Heller, ed., *I Heart Design. Remarkable Graphic Design Selected by Designers, Illustrators, and Critics*, Beverly, MA, Rockport Press, 2011, 168–71

Schorske, Carl, *Fin de siècle Vienna: Politics and Culture*, New York, Knopf, 1979

Schweiger, Werner J., *Aufbruch und Erfüllung: Gebrauchsgrafik der Wiener Moderne 1897–1918*, Vienna and Munich, Christian Brandstatter, 1988

Simons, Anna, *Edward Johnson und die englisches Schriftkunst*, Berlin and Leipzig, Heintz & Blankertz, 1926

Springschitz, Leopldine, *Wiener Mode im Wandel der Zeit. Eine Beitrag zur Kulturgeschichte Alt-Wiens*, Vienna, Wiener Verlag, 1949

The Studio: An Illustrated Magazine of Fine and Applied Art, London, The Studio, 1893 (vol. 1), 1898 (vol. 12 and vol. 13)

Thomas, Karen Lee, "*Rudolf von Larisch: Investigating and Analyzing the Ideas and Theories of a Lettering Reformer*," Sydney, Australia, Monash University, 2015

Tretter, Sandra, ed., *Koloman Moser: 1868–1918*, Munich, Prestel, 2007 (also Leopold, Rudolf and Gerd Pichler, Leopold Museum Private Foundation, Vienna)—contains autobiographical reflections p. 14ff

Varnedoe, Kurt, ed., *Vienna 1900: Art, Architecture & Design*, New York, Museum of Modern Art and Boston, Little, Brown, 1986

Wien: Eine Auswahl von Stadtbildern (Vienne Instantanée; Vienna through the Camera), Vienna, Martin Gerlach & Co., 1908 (?), 3rd ed. (after photographs by Martin Gerlach and notes by Professor Karl Mayreder

Witt-Dörring, Christian, ed., *Koloman Moser: Designing Modern Vienna 1897–1907*, Munich, Prestel, 2013

Witt-Dörring, Christian and Janis Staggs, *Wiener Werkstätte 1903–1932: The Luxury of Beauty*, New York and London, Prestel, 2017

Zeller, Bernhard, ed., *Jugend im Wien: Literatur um 1900*, Munich and Stuttgart, Kommission Kösel Verlag and Ernst Klett, 1974

Zweig, Stefan, *The World of Yesterday*, New York, Viking, 1943

Chapter 3: Cassandre and Dubonnet: Art Posters and Publicité in Interwar Paris

Allen, Frederick Lewis, *Only Yesterday: An Informal History of the 1920s*, New York, John Wiley & Sons, 1931

A.M. Cassandre. Posters, St. Gall, Zollikofer & Co., 1948 (Maximilien Vox)

Andrin, Pierre, "Cassandre," *L'Affiche*, no. 24, December 1926, 151–6

Arts et métiers graphiques, Paris, 1933

Aynsley, Jeremy, "Art Deco Graphic Design and Typography," in Charlotte Benton, Tim Benton, and Ghislaine Wood, eds., *Art Deco 1910–1939*, London, V&A Publications, 2003, 297–303 (and notes)

Barré-Despond, Arlette, *UAM—Union des Artistes Modernes*, Paris, Editions de Regard, 1986

Brown, Robert K., and Susan Reinhold, *The Poster Art of A. M. Cassandre*, New York, Dutton, 1979—contains reference to "doubt" and dubo —, p. 17

Cassandre, "Bifur," *Art et métiers graphiques*, 9, 1929, 578

Cendrars, Blaise, *Le Spectacle dans la Rue*, Montrouge, Seine, Draeger Frères, 1936

Cheronnet, Louis, "La Publicité Moderne: Delaunay et Léger," *L'art vivant*, 1, 1925, 890

Cheronnet, Louis, "L'art dans la rue. Affiches de Cassandre," *L'art vivant*, 2, 1926, 20–5

Le Corbusier, "La tumulte dans la rue", *L'Esprit Nouveau*, no. 25, 1924, unpaged

Deedes-Vincke, Patrick, *Paris: The City and its Photographers*, Boston, Toronto, London, Bulfinch Press, 1992

Drucker, Johanna and Emily McVarish, *Graphic Design: A Critical Guide*, 2nd ed., Boston, Pearson Publishing, 2013

Eskilson, Stephen, *Graphic Design: A New History*, 2 ed., New Haven, Yale University Press, 2012

Farago, Jason, "'Icons of Modern Art': Picassos, Matisses, Monets, Oh, My," *New York Times*, October 28, 2016

Hopkins, Claude C., *My Life in Advertising*, New York and London, Harper & Brothers, 1936

Imbert, Charles, "L'art dans la Publicité," *Encyclopédie des arts décoratifs et industriels*, vol. 7 (*Les arts décoratifs modernes*) Paris, Larousse, 1925, 499ff. (reprint Garland, 1977)

Iskin, Ruth E., *The Poster: Art, Advertising, Design, and Collecting*, Hanover, New Hampshire, Dartmouth College Press, 2014

Joubert, Roxane, *Typography and Graphic Design: From Antiquity to the Present*, Paris, Flammarion, 2006

Kitson, Harry Dexter, *Scientific Advertising*, New York, Codex Book Company, 1926

Martin, Marc, *Trois siècles de publicité*, Paris, Editions Odile Jacob, 1992

Mouron, Henri, *A.M. Cassandre*, New York, Rizzoli, 1985

"Projects for Four Posters," *Fortune*, XV, no. 3, March 1937, 120ff.

Posters by Cassandre, New York, Museum of Modern Art, 1936 (exhibition catalog, forward by Ernestine Fantl)

Quénioux, Gaston, *Les Arts Décoratifs Modernes (France)*, Paris, Librairie Larousse, 1925

Reed, David, *The Popular Magazine in Britain and the United States 1880–1960*, Toronto, University of Toronto Press, 1997

Rothchild, Deborah, Ellen Lupton, and Darra Goldstein, *Graphic Design in the Mechanical Age: Selections from the Merrill C. Berman Collection*, New Haven and London, Yale University Press, in conjunction with Williams College Museum of Art, Cooper-Hewitt National Design Museum Smithsonian Institution, 1998 (Lavin, Maud, series ed. *Art and Design from the Merrill C. Berman Collection*.)

Rouchon: Un Pionnier de l'Affiche Illustrée, Paris, Editions Henri Veyrier, 1983

Rubin, James H. *Impressionist Cats and Dogs: Pets in the Painting of Modern Life*, New Haven and London, Yale University Press, 2003

Sauvage, Anne-Marie, *A. M. Cassandre: Oeuvres graphiques modernes 1923–1939*, Paris, Bibliothèque nationale de France, 2005. (essays by Anne-Marie Sauvage, Réjane Bargiel, Pierre Bernard, and Alain Weill)

Schwartz, Vanessa, *Spectacular Realities: Early Mass Culture in Fin-de-Siècle Paris*, Berkeley, CA, University of California Press, 1998

Sheldon, Roy and Egmont Arens, *Consumer Engineering: A New Technique for Prosperity*, New York and London, Harper and Brothers, 1932

Sivulka, Juliann, *Soap, Sex, and Cigarettes: A Cultural History of American Advertising*, 2nd ed., Boston, MA, Wadsworth Cengage Learning, 2012

Starch, Daniel, *Principles of Advertising*, Chicago and New York, A. W. Shaw Company, 1923

The Art of the Book. VII. Exposition international des Arts Décoratifs et Industriels Modernes. 1925, New York and London, Garland Publishing, 1977 (facsimile)

The European Poster 1888–1939, Paris, Médiathèque de l'Architecture et du Patrimoine, 2012 (essay by Anne-Marie Sauvage), exhibition catalog Museo Picasso, Malaga, June 18 to September 16 2012

Timmers, Margaret, *The Power of the Poster*, London, V&A Publications, 1998

Tolmer, Alfred, *Mise en Page: The Theory and Practice of Layout*, London, The Studio, 1931

Vallye, Anna, *Léger: Modern Art and the Metropolis*, New Haven and London, Yale University Press, 2013, in association with the Philadelphia Museum of Art (exhibition catalog)

Varnedoe, Kirk and Adam Gopnik, *High-Low: Modern Art [and] Popular Culture*, New York, Harry N. Abrams, 1990, esp. 230–368

Weill, Alain, *The Poster. A Worldwide Survey and History*, Boston, G. K. Hall & Co., 1985

Wlassikoff, Michel and Jean-Pierre Bodeux, *La fabuleuse et exemplaire histoire de bébé Cadum*, Paris, Editions Syros-Alternatives, 1990

Chapter 4: Frank Zachary at *Holiday*: Travel, Leisure, and Art Direction in Post-World War II America

18th Annual of Advertising and Editorial Art, 1939 through 1970

Bownes, David, *London Transport Posters*, London, Lund Humphries, 2011

Callahan, Michael, "A Holiday for the Jet Set," *Vanity Fair*, May, 2013

Crosland, C. A. R., *The Future of Socialism*, New York, Macmillan, 1957

Frank, Robin Jaffee, *Coney Island: Visions of an American Dreamland, 1861–2008*, Hartford, CN, Wadsworth Atheneum Museum of Art, 2015 (exhibition catalog)

Gans, Herbert, "Design and the Consumer: A View of the Sociology and Culture of 'Good Design'," in Kathryn Hiesinger and George Marcus, eds., *Design Since 1965*, Philadelphia, Philadelphia Museum of Art, 1982, 30–6

Heller, Steven, "Catalyst-in-Chief," *Print*, June 16, 2015 (adopted from an earlier 1990 article for the AIGA: www.aiga.org/medalist-frankzachary/)

Heller, Steven and Greg D'Onofrio, *The Moderns: Midcentury American Graphic Design*, New York, Abrams, 2017

Liberman, Josh, "On Holiday," *Paris Review*, November 30, 2011

Life, July 12, 1949 (Roundtable on Pursuit of Happiness)

Lynes, Russell, "Highbrow, Lowbrow, Middlebrow," *Harpers Magazine*, February, 1949, and *Life*, April 11, 1949 (with chart)

Meikle, Jeffrey L., *Design in the USA*, Oxford and New York, Oxford University Press, 2005.

Piovene, Guido, *Italy*, English edition, trans. Herman Weinberg, Rome. Carlo Bestetti, 1958

Popp, Richard K., *The Holiday Makers: Magazines, Advertising, and Mass Tourism in Postwar America*, Baton Rouge, Louisiana State University Press, 2012

Printers Ink, April 9, 1954

Sandomir, Richard, "Ninalee Allen Craig, at the Center of a Famous Photograph, Dies ata 90," *New York Times*, May 4, 2018

Seebohm, Caroline, *The Man Who Was Vogue: The Life and Times of Condé Nast*, New York, Viking, 1982

Weiss, Thomas, "Tourism in America before World War II," *The Journal of Economic History*, vol. 64, no. 2 (June 2004), 289–327

Wright, Russel and Mary, *Guide to Easier Living*, New York, Simon & Schuster, 1954 (new and revised edition), first published 1950

Chapter 5: Food, Race, and the "New Advertising": The Levy's Jewish Rye Bread Campaign 1963–1969

Abramson, Howard S., *National Geographic: Behind America's Lens on the World*, New York, Crown Publishers, 1987

Applebaum, Sylvia, "On Desegregating Advertising," *Crisis*, June/July 1962, 313–17

Back, Jean, and Viktoria Schmidt-Linsenhoff, *The Family of Man 1955–2001: Humanism and Postmodernism: A reappraisal of the Photo Exhibition by Edward Steichen*, Marburg, Jonas Verlag, 2004

Baldwin, James and Richard Avedon, *Nothing Personal*, Lucerne, Switzerland, C. J. Bucher, 1964

Barban, Arnold M., "The Dilemma of 'Integrated' Advertising," *Journal of Business*, vol. 42, no. 4, 1969, 477–96

Barthes, Roland, "Rhetoric of the Image," in Stephen Heath, ed. and trans., *Image, Music, Text*, New York, Hill and Wang, 1977, 32–51

Benson, Richard, *The Printed Picture*, New York, Museum of Modern Art, 2008

Brodkin, Karen, *How Jews Became White Folks and What That Says about Race in America*, New Brunswick, NJ, Rutgers University Press, 2000

Buhle, Paul, *From the Lower East Side to Hollywood: Jews in American Popular Culture*, London and New York, Verso, 2004

Chevlowe, Susan, *The Jewish Identity Project: New American Photography*, New York, The Jewish Museum and New Haven, CT, Yale University Press, 2005

Cummings, Bart, *The Benevolent Dictators: Interviews with Advertising Greats*, Chicago, IL, Crain Books, 1984

Dates, Jeannette L. and William Barlow, eds., *Split Image: African Americans in the Mass Media*, 2nd ed., Washington, DC, Howard University Press, 1993

Dichter, Ernest, *Handbook of Consumer Motivations: The Psychology of the World of Objects*, New York, McGraw-Hill, 1964

Diner, Hasia, *Hungering for America: Italian, Irish, and Jewish Foodways in the Age of Migration*, Cambridge, MA, Harvard University Press, 2001

Ellwood, David W., *Rebuilding Europe: Western Europe, America and Postwar Reconstruction*, London and New York, Longman, 1992

Ethnic Images in Advertising: an Exhibition Co-sponsored by the Balch Institute for Ethnic Studies and the Anti-Defamation League of B'nai B'rith, Philadelphia, The Balch Institute, 1984

Ferretti, Fred, "Levey's Jewish Rye Will Soon Be Arnold's," *New York Times*, June 6, 1970

Fox, Stephen, *The Mirror Makers: A History of American Advertising and its Creators*, New York, William Morrow and Company, 1984

Galbraith, John Kenneth, *The Affluent Society*, Boston, MA, Mariner Books, 1998 (first published 1958)

Glatzer, Robert, *The New Advertising: The Great Campaigns from Avis to Volkswagen*, New York, Citadel Press, 1970

Golden, Thelma, ed., *Black Male—Representations of Masculinity in Contemporary American Art*, New York, Whitney Museum of American Art and Harry N. Abrams, 1994

Goldstein, Eric L., *The Price of Whiteness: Jews, Race, and American Identity*, Princeton, NJ, Princeton University Press, 2006

Hall, Stuart, "The Whites of their Eyes: Racist Ideologies and the Media," in Manuel Alvarado and John O. Thompson, eds., *The Media Reader*, London, BFI, 1990, 7–23

Harrington, Michael, *The Other America: Poverty in the United States*, New York, MacMillan, 1963

Heller, Steven, *Paul Rand*, London, Phaidon, 1999 (p. 44 Rand ads for Dubonnet 1943–1944)

Hess, Dick, and Marion Muller, *Dorfsman & CBS*, New York, American Showcase Inc., 1987

Hicks, Wilson, *Words and Pictures: An Introduction to Photojournalism*, New York, Harper & Brothers, 1952

Kamekura, Yusaku, ed., *Paul Rand: His Work from 1946 to 1958*, New York, Alfred A. Knopf, 1959

Kassarjian, Harold H., "The Negro and American Advertising, 1946–1965," *Journal of Marketing Research*, vol. VI (February 1969), 29–39

Kessel, Dmitri, *On Assignment: Dmitri Kessel, Life Photographer*, New York, Harry N. Abrams, 1985

Kugelmass, Jack, ed., *Key Texts in American Jewish Culture*, New Brunswick, NJ and London, Rutgers University Press, 2003 ("'Yesterday's Woman,' Today's Moral Guide: Molly Goldberg as Jewish Mother" (129–46), by Joyce Antler)

Lasky, Julie, AIGA medalist biography of Georg Olden, www.aiga.org/medalist-georgolden

Leiss, William, Stephen Kline, Sut Jhally, *Social Communication in Advertising: Persons, Products & Images of Well-being*, 2nd revised and enlarged edition, New York and Scarborough, Ontario, Routledge and Nelson Canada, 1990

Levenson, Bob, *Bill Bernbach's Book*, New York, Villard Books, 1987

Loring, Randall, *The Doyle Dane Bernbach Advertising Agency*, Northern Illinois University, Master's Thesis, 1988

Marchand, Roland, *Advertising the American Dream: Making Way for Modernity 1920–1940*, Berkeley, University of California Press, 1985

Miller, Abbott, "White on Black and Gray," in Ellen Lupton and Abbott Miller, eds., *Design Writing Research*, Phaidon, 1999 (first published 1996), 102–19.

Morgan, Barbara, "The Theme Show: A Contemporary Exhibition Technique," in, "The Controversial Family of Man," *Aperture* vol. 3, no. 2 (1955)

Morris, John Godfrey, "People are People All Over the World," *Ladies Home Journal*, July through December, 1948

Potter, David M., *People of Plenty: Economic Abundance and the American Character*, Chicago, University of Chicago Press, 1954

Rand, Paul, *Thoughts on Design*, New York, Wittenborn, 1947

Riesman, David, et al., *The Lonely Crowd: A Study of the Changing American Character*, abridged edition, New Haven and London, Yale University Press, 1961 (first published 1950)

Rosenblum, Naomi, *A World History of Photography*, New York, Abbeville, 1989

Sandeen, Eric J. *Picturing an Exhibition: The Family of Man and 1950s America*, Albuquerque, NM, University of New Mexico Press, 1995

Sax, David, "The Search for Real Rye Bread," *Atlantic*, October 8, 2009

Schudson, Michael, *Advertising, The Uneasy Persuasion: Its Dubious Impact on American Society*, New York, Basic Books, 1984

Smith, Betty, *A Tree Grows in Brooklyn*, New York, Harper Brothers, 1943 (Harper Collins 2001 edition, with forward by Anna Quindlen)

Starch, Daniel, *Measuring Advertising Readership and Results*, New York, McGraw-Hill Book Company, 1966

Starch, Daniel, *Principles of Advertising*, Chicago and New York, A. W. Shaw, 1923

Steichen, Edward, *The Family of Man*, New York, The Museum of Modern Art, 1955 (30th anniversary edition)

Steinberg, Kerri P., *Jewish Mad Men: Advertising and the Design of the American Jewish Experience*, New Brunswick, NJ, Rutgers University Press, 2015

The Art of Writing Advertising: Conversations with William Bernbach, Leo Burnett, George Gribbin, David Ogilvy, Rosser Reeves, Lincolnwood, IL, NTC Business Books, 1987

Wainwright, Loudon, *The Great American Magazine: An Inside History of Life*, New York, Knopf, 1986

Warlaumont, Hazel G., *Advertising in the 60s: Turncoats, Traditionalists, and Waste Makers in America's Turbulent Decade*, Westport, CT and London, Praeger, 2001

Willens, Doris, *Nobody's Perfect: Bill Bernbach and the Golden Age of Advertising*, Charleston, SC, CreateSpace, 2009

Chapter 6: Graphic Design and Politics: Thomas Nast and the "TAMMANY TIGER LOOSE"

Ackerman, Gerald M., *The Life and Work of Jean-Léon Gérome with a Catalogue Raisonne*, New York, Harper & Row, and Sotheby's Publications, 1986

Ackerman, Kenneth D., *Boss Tweed: The Rise and Fall of the Corrupt Pol who conceived the Soul of Modern New York*, New York, Carroll & Graf Publishers, 2005

Adler, John, with Draper Hill, *Doomed by Cartoon: How Cartoonist Thomas Nast and the New York Times Brought Down Boss Tweed and his Ring of Thieves*, New York, Morgan James Publishing, 2008

Bigelow, Albert Paine, *Thomas Nast: His Period and His Pictures*, New York and London, Chelsea House, 1980, first published 1904

Boime, Albert, "Thomas Nast and French Art," *American Art Journal*, vol. 4, no. 1, Spring, 1972, 43–65

Danly, Susan, *Telling Tales: Nineteenth-Century Narrative Painting from the Collection of the Pennsylvania Academy of the Fine Arts*, Philadelphia, Pennsylvania Academcy of the Fine Arts, 1991

Dewey, Donald, *The Art of Ill Will: The Story of American Political Cartoons*, New York and London, New York University Press, 2007

Fresella-Lee, Nancy, *The American Paintings in the Pennsylvania Academy of the Fine Arts: An Illustrated Checklist*, Philadelphia, Pennsylvania Academy of the Fine Arts and Seattle and London, University of Washington Press, 1989

Futrell, Alison, *Blood in the Arena: The Spectacle of Roman Power*, Austin, Texas, University of Texas Press, 1997

Halloran, Fiona Deans, *Thomas Nast: The Father of Modern Political Cartoons*, Chapel Hill, NC, University of North Carolina Press, 2012

In This Academy: The Pennsylvania Academy of the Fine Arts, 1805–1976: A Special Bicentennial Exhibition, Philadelphia, Pennsylvania Academy of the Fine Arts, 1976

Jarman, Baird, "The Graphic Art of Thomas Nast: Politics and Propriety in Postbellu Publishing," *American Periodicals* (Special Issue: American Periodicals and Visual Culture), 2010, 156–89.

Joshel, Sandra R., Margaret Malamud, and Donald T. McGuire, Jr., eds., *Imperial Projections: Ancient Rome in Modern Popular Culture*, Baltimore and London, The Johns Hopkins University Press, 2001

Keller, Morton, *The Art and Politics of Thomas Nast*, New York, Oxford University Press, 1968

Keller, Morton, *Affairs of State: Public Life in Late Nineteenth Century America*, Cambridge, MA and London, The Belknap Press of Harvard University, 1977

Lynch, Denis Tilden, *"Boss" Tweed: The Story of a Grim Generation*, New York, Boni and Liveright, 1927

Richards, Jeffrey H., ed., *Early American Drama*, New York, Penguin Books, 1997

Vinson, J. Chal, *Thomas Nast Political Cartoonist*, Athens, GA, University of Georgia Press, 2014, first published 1976

West, Richard Samuel, *Satire on Stone: The Political Cartoons of Joseph Keppler*, Champaign-Urbana, The University of Illinois Press, 1988

Chapter 7: The Politics of Learning: Dr. John Fell and the Fell Types at Oxford University in the Later Seventeenth Century

Barker, Nicholas, *The Oxford University Press and the Spread of Learning 1478–1978*, Oxford, Clarendon Press, 1978

Green, James N. and Peter Stallybrass, *Benjamin Franklin, Writer and Printer*, New Castle, Delaware, Oak Knoll Press and Philadelphia, The Library Company, and London, The British Library, 2006

Hart, Horace, *Notes on a Century of Typography at the Oxford University Press 1693–1794*, Oxford, Clarendon Press, 1970, first published 1900

Johnson, John and Strickland Gibson, *Print and Privilege at Oxford to the Year 1700*, London, Oxford University Press, 1946

Lane, John A., *Early Type Specimens in the Plantin-Moretus Museum*, London and New Castle, DE, British Library and Oak Knoll Press, 2004

MacGregor, Arthur, *The Ashmolean Museum. A Brief History of the Museum and its Collections*, London, Jonthan Horne Publications, 2001

McClinton, Katherine Morrison, *The Chromolithographs of Louis Prang*, New York, Clarkson N. Potter, Inc., 1973

Moxon, Joseph, *Mechanick Exercises on the Whole Art of Printing (1683–4)*, eds. Herbert Davis and
    Harry Carter, London, Oxford University Press, 1958
Pisano, Ronald G. *Idle Hours: American at Leisure 1865–1914*, Boston, Little, Brown and Co., 1988
Raizman, David, "The Oxford University Press Museum and Archive" essay for "sites designers should
    see" section, *Design and Culture*, vol. 3, no. 3, November, 2011, 379–82
Reed, Talbot Baines, *A History of the Old English Letter Foundries*, revised and expanded by A. F.
    Johnson, London, Faber and Faber Ltd., 1952
Steinberg, S. H., *Five Hundred Years of Printing*, Harmondsworth, Penguin Books, 1961, first published
    1955
Trevor Roper, Hugh, *Archbishop Laud 1573–1645*, 3rd ed., London, Macmillan Press, 1988, first
    published 1962

INDEX